To Matthew Fox

Reliquias veterumque vides monimenta virorum.
(You see the relics and monuments of ancient men.)

Virgil, *Aeneid* 8

And thorns shall come up in her palaces, nettles and brambles in the fortresses thereof.

Isaiah 34

Contents

List of Illustrations   xi
List of Maps   xiii
A Note on Names   xv
Introduction   xvii

Chapter One: Kent and Essex   · 5
Chapter Two: Norfolk   25
Chapter Three: London   43
Chapter Four: Silchester   60
Chapter Five: Wales and the West   75
Chapter Six: Bath   93
Chapter Seven: Hadrian's Wall   III
Chapter Eight: Scotland   137
Chapter Nine: York   161
Chapter Ten: Cumbria and the Lakes   179
Chapter Eleven: The Cotswolds
    and the South-West   198
Chapter Twelve: Norfolk, again,
    and Sussex   214

Notes   231
Places to Visit   241
Bibliography   251
Acknowledgements   263
Index   265

List of Illustrations

The genii cucullati from Housesteads. (© English Heritage) xviii

The trusty VW camper van. xix

The tomb of Longinus Sdapeze. (© Colchester and Ipswich 20
Museum Service)

A photograph from the 1909 Colchester Pagaent, with 24
Boadicea in her chariot in the foreground. (© Colchester
and Ipswich Museum Service)

Thornycroft's sculpture group of Boadicea and her daughters at 38
Westminster Bridge, London. (© UIG via Getty Images)

A fragment of Roman wall uncovered by the Blitz and 48
preserved as part of London Wall car park.

The Bank of England depicted as a ruin by Joseph Michael 51
Gandy, 1830. (© Courtesy of Trustees of Sir John Soane's
Museum, London/The Bridgeman Art Gallery)

The Roman walls of Silchester. 61

Silchester's amphitheatre. When Stukelely came here, it was 66
a large pond, a watering-hole for cattle.

The Great Work at Wroxeter. 76

Tessa Verney Wheeler at Lydney. (Photograph by Lydia Carr. 87
Image © Rt Hon Lord Viscount Bledisloe; used with
permission)

The snake-haired deity who adorns the pediment of the temple 94
to Sulis-Minerva in Bath. (© Bath & North East Somerset
Council)

Roger Tomlin's drawings of the writing on the now lost lead   106
    tablet that Edward Nicholson interpreted as part of a
    correspondence between early Christians. (Courtesy of
    Roger Tomlin)

Hadrian's Wall. (© Getty Images)   117

'Roman Wall Blues'. (© Britten/Auden)   124

Arthur's O'on: an illustration from Alexander Gordon's   149
    Itinerarium Septentrionale. (Courtesy of the British Library)

Arthur's O'on reinvented as the dovecote in the stable block   152
    of Penicuik House, south of Edinburgh. (Courtesy of Sir
    Robert Clerk of Penicuik)

A mighty bronze sculpture of Constantine the Great sits outside   163
    York Minster

The Severus tondo, showing Septimius Severus, his wife Julia   165
    Domna and their children Caracalla and Geta. The face of Geta
    has been defaced since, after his death, he was subject to *damnatio*
    memoriae. (© Bildagentur für Kunst, Kultur und Geschichte)

Hardknott Castle. The Roman camp presides over a mountain   180
    pass in one of the loveliest spots in England.

The Crosby Garrett helmet after restoration. (© Christie's   189
    Images/The Bridgeman Art Library)

The Rudston Venus – now in the Hull and East Riding   205
    Museum. (© Hull and East Riding Museum: Hull Museums)

Aeneas sweeps Dido off her feet. Part of the great Dido   212
    and Aeneas mosaic found at Low Ham, and now in the
    Museum of Somerset in Taunton. (© Museum of Somerset)

The vast walls of Burgh Castle, near Great Yarmouth.   214

A detail of the exquisite decoration on the Mildenhall Dish.   222
    (© The Trustees of the British Museum)

List of Maps

Map of Colchester   2–3

Map of London   40–41

Map of Hadrian's Wall   108–109

Map of the Antonine Wall   134–135

Map of the City of York   158–159

A Note on Names

The now customary spelling Boudica is adopted except when referring to works of art that employ 'Boadicea', frequently used in the eighteenth and nineteenth centuries. Similarly, the spelling Caratacus is used except when referring to Elgar's cantata *Caractacus*, and its main character.

Introduction

When I was eleven or twelve years old, I was taken on a school trip to Hadrian's Wall. It was a long, tedious drive to Northumberland from north Staffordshire. We visited Housesteads, one of the best-preserved forts on the line of the wall (which was built in the AD 120s, spanning England's waist between the Solway Firth and the Tyne). There was a light drizzle. It was very cold. I have no sense now of having been moved by, or even particularly interested in, the low, rubbly remains. All I can remember clearly from that trip are the well-preserved toilets, precisely the detail that a twelve-year-old would pick out: a line of stone ledges above a drain, with an English Heritage signboard showing a row of Roman squaddies relieving themselves. After looking at them, we got back into the coach and drove south again.

This was emphatically not one of the formative experiences that ignited in me an unquenchable fascination with the classical world. That such a thing did happen, I put down to two, entirely different, childhood events: a family holiday to Crete and the ancient palace of Knossos, where I got caught up in the mystery of labyrinths, princesses, minotaurs and magicians; and reading a 1950s book of stories from the *Iliad* and the *Odyssey* belonging to one of my elder brothers, the beautiful pictures in which, even more than the text, conjured fantastic visions of gods and goddesses, heroes and monsters. As time went by, the tone was set by these early encounters, fuelled by an inspiring teacher who drummed into me, slowly and painfully, the rudiments of Latin and Greek. Little by little I opened a portal on to a world of poems and stories: the thrilling ambiguities of Virgil, the passions of Catullus and Sappho, the Wildean wit of Ovid. And later, the humane expanses of Herodotus; the spiked cynicism of Tacitus.

I studied classics at university, then became a journalist. In my thirties I wrote books about Latin love poetry and Greek literature, but I still wasn't very interested in Roman Britain, except by way of an abiding love of Rosemary Sutcliff's classic children's story *The Eagle of the Ninth*, in which the young centurion Marcus Aquila ventures to the badlands north of Hadrian's Wall. Roman Britain still struck me as an unglamorous outpost on the fringes of empire, lacking any really 'good' remains to compare with those of Rome, or Africa, or even France. Nor did it seem to have produced any really interesting Romans: Spain had its Martial, Syria its Lucian, Africa its Terence, but there is no record of any literary genius sprung from Roman Britain, nor any British-born emperor, nor even a single British senator.

Something happened, though, when I visited Hadrian's Wall for the second time, in 2008. Here was Housesteads again, but I began to see how it stood in its landscape, the wall marching away on the edge of a spectacular volcanic ridge. Inside the little museum attached to the fort I saw stone carvings of curious deities, not at all part of the Olympian canon: the trio of Celtic goddesses known as the Matres, 'mothers', with fruit and bread in their laps; and a sculpture of three enigmatic cloaked figures, the Genii Cucullati, the 'hooded deities'. Housesteads also had a Mithraeum – a temple devoted to the cult of Mithras, with its perfume of Persian mysticism. Roman soldiers sprung from Germany and the Low Countries had worshipped these strange gods. This was not the Rome I thought I knew.

There were other things that caught my attention: in the guidebook was a reproduction of a drawing of the fort by the antiquary William Stukeley, dating from 1725. He showed the fields below the fort strewn with Roman gravestones and altars – not tidied away into a museum collection, just lying exposed to the weather. There was material about John Clayton, the wealthy antiquary and Newcastle upon Tyne town clerk who had bought the fort in the mid nineteenth century; and there were photographs of it being restored – or rather, from the look of it, rebuilt. It seemed to me that there were some interesting questions about how these remains had been thought about in the past, before they ended up as a neat English Heritage site.

And so I set out to discover Roman Britain in earnest, a copy of Roger Wilson's superb *A Guide to the Roman Remains in Britain* in my hand – a work, inexplicably out of print, that is the nearest equivalent, for enthusiasts of Roman Britain, to Pevsner's architectural guides. In 2009 I went to Hadrian's Wall again, walking along it from Carlisle to Newcastle. Over the next two summers, my boyfriend Matthew and I travelled in search of Roman remains in his delightful, though not particularly trusty, 1974 VW camper van, taking two journeys – a western route, from London to the Cotswolds to Wales and north to Cumbria; and an eastern one, from Edinburgh through Yorkshire and Lincolnshire to Norfolk. On the second trip, the van lasted only until York before collapsing from one of its many and varied complaints.

One July I walked along the Antonine Wall – the barrier built in the AD 140s from the Firth of Forth to the Firth of Clyde, which, briefly, marked the northernmost frontier of the empire. There were also many short forays, day trips and detours to see Roman remains, in which I would entice patient friends and members of my family to visit forts, or bath houses, or museums. One May morning I even dragged a bewildered string quintet to inspect a battered, illegible Roman inscription in a Cornish church.

This book is very far from a comprehensive account of Britain's Roman remains. Instead, I wanted to see what I could learn from an encounter with them. Not to discover what being in Roman Britain was like – for I was convinced of the irrecoverability of the lives of people from the deep past, except as manifestations of the historical imaginations of those who described them. Rather, I wanted to think about what this period means, and has meant, to a British sense of history and identity. I wanted to discover the ways in which the idea of Roman Britain has resonated in British culture and still forms part of the texture of its landscape – not just through the sublime contours of the Northumberland hills, but in humbler urban and suburban tracts of territory.

My search brought me into the company of many fascinating minds from the past, from the great sixteenth-century humanist William Camden, author of *Britannia*, a masterly topographical and antiquarian survey of Britain, to the shadowy figure of Charles Bertram, who fooled luminaries such as Stukeley with one of British historiography's most successful hoaxes. Through all this, it became clear how richly generative Roman Britain had been, how productive artistically and intellectually for those who had encountered it. There were stories by Thomas Hardy, poems by W. H. Auden and Wilfred Owen, music by Britten and Elgar, Joseph Conrad's black musings on the Romans in Britain in *Heart of Darkness*, Howard Brenton's even blacker play *The Romans in Britain*. Ideas about Roman Britain had been manipulated and metamorphosed into architecture, into song. It had changed people.

Troubling questions crowded in. How do we relate to Roman Britain now? How did this great span of time – the equivalent of the interval between Shakespeare's lifetime and our own – affect Britain's later history? Did the Romans in Britain mark the arrival of civilisation and a sophisticated culture, or was it rather about violence visited on a host population by an exploitative imperial power? Is 'Roman Britain' essentially a kind of historical throat-clearing, before the real substance of 'our island story' sets in with the arrival of the Anglo-Saxons? Different eras and different people adumbrated, I discovered, very different answers to these questions; and there is an urgency in the way people are tackling them now. The study of Roman Britain is today intensely political, coloured by contemporary concerns about modern imperialism and warfare. On the other hand, with its cosmopolitan, Mediterranean-facing outlook, Roman Britain is also being claimed in some quarters as a kind of foundation myth for modern multiculturalism.

What makes Roman Britain, to me, such a rich place is that it was literate. People in Britain – certainly not a vast proportion of the population, but clearly plenty of them – read poems, and wrote letters, and recorded on stone their devotion to their gods, and their loved ones' deaths. Because of the splendid preservative powers of the damp British sod, hundreds of letters, documents and memoranda written by perfectly ordinary Romans survive. We are lucky in our literary sources on Roman Britain: we have a first-hand account of two military expeditions by its would-be conqueror, Julius Caesar; and a biography of one of its most significant governors, Gnaeus Julius Agricola, written by his son-in-law Tacitus, perhaps the greatest of Roman historians. The writers of the classical world were the first to give Britain a literary existence. After the end of the empire in Britain, it would have no significant life in writing again until Bede wrote his *Ecclesiastical History of the English People*, over 300 years later. The Romans – for whom Britain was frequently a poetic metaphor for insular isolation and exciting, dangerous primitivism – transformed Britain into an idea: an idea that may not have reflected the reality of life there, but that was remarkably pervasive.

Some make the argument that the classical texts about Britain are severely limited in value, giving us only the conquerors' view. That, of course, is true: no words written by Britons remain to tell us how they perceived themselves, or their place in the world, or their relationship with the invaders. The story must be completed by the evidence on the ground, the detritus of life, the objects that remain. These shards of life cannot lie in themselves, though in their interpretations of objects and places, archaeologists are indelibly marked by the prejudices of their own times, just as are historians.

The history of Roman Britain is, like one of its shattered mosaics, reconstructed from its pieces by each successive generation; each generation makes a slightly different pattern from the fragments. 'Britain' was an idea for the Romans. For us, 'Roman Britain' is also an idea, as well as a time and a place. Because it has always been, from the first classical accounts, so slippery, open to so many contradictory interpretations, 'Roman Britain' has become an imaginative space in which some of our darkest anxieties and fantasies have been rehearsed. Fifteen centuries on, it is printed on our landscape, physical and imaginative. As Elizabeth Bowen wrote of Rome: 'What has accumulated in this place acts on everyone, day and night, like an extra climate.'

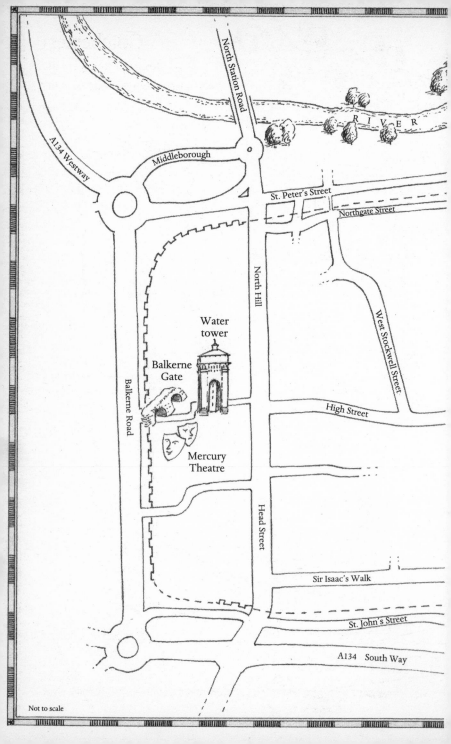

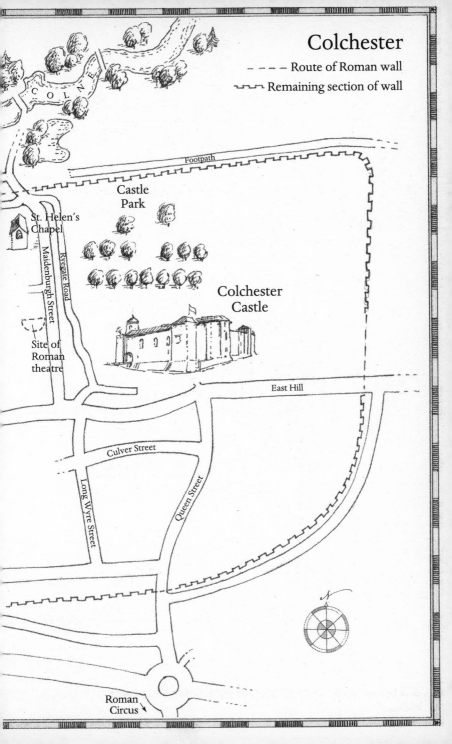

I

Kent and Essex

If you stand at the end of the modernist concrete pier in the Kentish town of Deal, you can lean into the sea breeze, as fresh to the face as a dousing of cold water, and look back to the shoreline, where toffee-coloured waves crackle against the pebbled beach. It was between this point and Walmer, a few hundred metres south on Kent's blunt, east-facing edge, that Julius Caesar is thought to have landed. And so, with its first securely dated and recorded event, the story of Britain slipped from prehistory into history.

There is no trace of this event to be seen now. Nor, in fact, is it certain that Caesar landed here. Rather, Deal beach is the spot around which an uncertain consensus has gathered, working from the general's own account of his two incursions into Britain, in the summers of 55 and 54 BC. Even without reading too closely between the lines of Caesar's self-justifying narrative, it is clear that they were inglorious affairs. In 55, the troops were impeded by their heavy arms and armour as they tried to disembark in swirling deep water. 'Terrified by the situation, and completely inexperienced in this kind of warfare, they did not act with the same vigour and commitment as they usually did in battles on dry land,' wrote Caesar in his *Commentaries on the Gallic War*. The standard bearer of the 10th Legion encouraged his hesitant fellow soldiers by leaping out of his ship, crying: 'Jump out – unless you want to betray our eagle to the enemy – I at least will do my duty for the republic and my general.' An indecisive battle on the beach was followed by a disaster for Caesar. As in 1588, when Spain sent warships against England, the weather came to the aid of the islanders: a storm destroyed the ships transporting the Roman cavalry, and badly damaged those lying at anchor off the Kentish shore. Eventually, after some danger that the invasion force would end up cut off from the continent, Caesar returned to Gaul. The following year's expedition was a similar stalemate, ending with diplomatic hostage-taking and mutual face-saving rather than conquest.

The sole municipal recognition of these events (any physical traces of which, as the eighteenth-century antiquary William Stukeley pointed out, are 'many ages since absorpt by the ocean') is an inconspicuous plaque set into the grass near the lifeboat station at Walmer, with Caesar's craggy profile rendered in concrete relief. As I examined it one sunny, cloud-scudded April morning, an elderly man walking his spittle-flecked Alsatian wandered up to see what I was doing. 'Could do with a clean-up,' he remarked – indeed, it was lichen-crusted and the inscription was almost illegible. But there were moves afoot to commemorate Caesar's landings more forcefully. In a camera shop on the high street, the proprietor, Peter Jull, told me about his campaign to erect a memorial to the landings. He envisaged, he said, a complicated bronze assemblage, with Julius Caesar in the prow of his galley, the standard-bearer of the 10th about to leap, and the Britons, in their war chariots, poised to attack. 'It would be high-profile, and photogenic,' he said. 'It would be good for tourism to the town. And as an event it ought to be better recorded, not just for Deal people but for people everywhere in the country.' Jull also claimed he could trace his own ancestry back to the Kentish Queen Bertha, who welcomed St Augustine's mission in AD 597. Out on the seafront, I encountered a philosophical street-sweeper, catching the sun on a sheltered bench, his rubbish cart beside him, who said that he had found perfect happiness by way of his job: 'I wish I'd done it in 1956 when I left school.' I asked him if he knew about the campaign for the sculpture of Caesar. 'It'll be between him and Norman Wisdom,' he said drily. It turned out there was a rival campaign under way to memorialise the Deal-born comedian.

As holidaymakers bicycled along the promenade, and children queued for ice cream despite the chill wind, it was hard to imagine the English Channel as the implacable, terrifying barrier classical writers described. The Romans' world was a generous sphere. The Mediterranean lapped comfortably at the shores of its more familiar regions, with Italy snug at its centre. Far, far away, where no civilised man ventured, roared the Ocean, girdling the world's inhabitable regions – or so Homer had written, and so it was generally maintained. In this liminal realm between the Earth and the void, in this frighteningly distant zone, lay Britain. Here, even the laws of nature could not be relied upon. Tacitus, writing in the dying years of the first century AD about his father-in-law's stint as governor of Britain, reported tales of curious gelatinous waves in the northern seas that were 'sluggish and heavy to the oars, and not set in motion as much as other seas even by the winds'. If for Shakespeare the 'silver sea' around Britain served it 'in the office of a wall' or as 'a moat defensive to a house', then the Romans thought about it in not dissimilar vein – but as outsiders.

Caesar tried his hand at Britain after he had conquered his way through Gaul. According to his own account, taking the island was the natural extension of his gains on the continent, since (he claimed) the Britons had close links with their neighbours across the Channel; alongside this practical justification came the kudos attached to campaigning on the very fringes of the known world. Britain stayed on the Roman agenda, on and off: Caesar's successor, the emperor Augustus, mooted, but never carried through, an invasion. As Britain crept into political focus for Rome, so it began to be harnessed as a literary metaphor for extremity and isolation. A poem by Catullus, a contemporary of Julius Caesar, is addressed to two friends, Furius and Aurelius, who are, says the poem, so loyal they would accompany the author even to India or Arabia, or to the steppes of Scythia, or Parthia, or Africa – or to the 'Britons at the margins of the world'. In Latin, the phrase is '*ultimosque Britannos*', and the word '*ultimosque*' is split awkwardly between two

lines: these Britons drop over the world's edge. The poet Virgil's first
Eclogue, composed during the civil wars that ended in 31 BC with the
accession of Augustus as emperor, is a pastoral set in a mythical landscape inhabited by shepherds and nymphs; Tennyson's 'the moan of
doves in immemorial elms' is inspired by one of its lines. But the poem
also seems to have a demi-life in Virgil's own turbulent era of civil strife,
aristocratic power struggle and land confiscations. One of its characters
has received the right to continue his bucolic existence; the other has
been cast from his land and is forced into exile – perhaps, he says, he
will be banished to the steppes of Scythia, perhaps to Britain '*toto divisos
orbe*', 'quite cut off from the world'.

Herodotus, the Greek historian of the fifth century BC, had been
sceptical about what could be known of the 'extreme tracts of Europe
towards the west'. It is possible, he wrote, that there were islands
called the Cassiterides (meaning 'tin islands'), but 'I have never been
able to get an assurance from an eyewitness that there is any sea on
the further side of Europe.' Nevertheless, he acknowledged, 'tin and
amber do certainly come to us from the ends of the earth', and there
is surely some echo here of a trading route linking Herodotus's world
with the far west, for the Baltic was the source of amber and Cornwall
did indeed, suggests the archaeological evidence, export tin. But for
Herodotus, these are fanciful travellers' tales, to be doubtfully brack-
eted with what he describes next – a race of one-eyed men inhabiting
the far north, who obtain gold by stealing it from griffins.

So much that we could know about the ancient world is tantalisingly out of reach. For every book that was cherished, copied and
passed down through the uncertain ages between antiquity and the
Renaissance, dozens were carried out of existence by a myriad possible
mischances. So it is with the work of Pytheas, a Greek of the fourth
century BC from the western colony of Massilia – modern Marseilles.
He was the author of a book called *On the Ocean*, which we know
about only in so far as it was quoted by later writers, such as the
Roman geographer Strabo, who was working during the reigns of
Augustus and Tiberius, and the Roman natural historian of the first
century AD, Pliny the Elder. When *On the Ocean* was quoted at all, it
was usually witheringly, for (so it seemed to his readers in antiquity)
Pytheas was obviously lying when he claimed to have sailed into the
perilous Ocean and actually to have circumnavigated Britain. He

reported a yet further island called Thule – perhaps the Shetlands, or Iceland, or Norway. He claimed to have visited a a promontory called Belerium, where tin was quarried, which might signify Cornwall; and an island called Ictis nearby, which could be reached on foot at low tide, just possibly St Michael's Mount. I would give a great deal to be able to read *On the Ocean*.

In the first century BC, Pytheas's book was drawn on by the Greek writer Diodorus Siculus, author of the *Library*, an immensely ambitious work gathering together the history of the entire known world, from the deep mythological past to the exploits of his contemporary, Julius Caesar. Fifteen of its forty books survive, and they include a description of Britain, in his Greek rendering Pretannia – the first surviving use of the word. Tantalisingly, he promises to return to the subject of Britain in more detail when he comes to describe the actions of Caesar, but that part of the book is lost. His description begins – oddly touchingly, to me – with his likening Britain's triangular shape to that of his familiar native Sicily. He names a region called Cantium, which is our Kent. As for its people, writes Diodorus, Britain 'is inhabited by tribes which are native to the land and preserve in their ways of living the ancient manner of life. They use chariots, for instance, in their wars, even as tradition tells us the old Greek heroes did in the Trojan War, and their dwellings are humble, being built for the most part out of reeds or logs . . . they are simple and far removed from the shrewdness and vice which characterise the men of our day. Their way of living is modest, since they are well clear of the luxury which is begotten of wealth.'

And so emerged another trope in classical writing about Britain. Untouched by the modern vices, suggests Diodorus, these people are instead tinged with the ancient glories of Homer's heroes. There is a moral flavour to this account that will be much more fully developed by the historian Tacitus in the next century: the thought is that at the edges of the Roman empire a certain kind of simple nobility flourishes. For the writers of such ethnographic descriptions, the world was parsed as if it was a series of concentric circles: at the centre, Rome, civilised (though, perhaps, corrupt). As the encircling bands become larger, so the people become less civilised, more savage (though also, sometimes, virtuous). The rule works in microcosm: for example, Julius Caesar's *Commentaries on the Gallic War* insist that the people of

Cantium, geographically the closest in Britain to the Roman world, are the island's most civilised. And for Strabo, the inhabitants of the unimaginably remote Ireland are even 'more savage than the Britons'. They eat, he says, their dead fathers, and have sex with their own mothers and sisters – the triumph of the seething, unfettered id.

What the Britons thought about themselves, and their place in the wider world, is a matter of speculation. It is clear, though, that just as Britain was becoming a reality for Rome in the first century BC, so was Rome looming larger for the Britons. There were trade links: luxury goods from the Roman world began increasingly to be placed in the graves of the British elite; there are finds of glass vessels, of fig pips, of amphorae once filled with Mediterranean wine. According to Strabo, Britain was an exporter: of hides, hunting dogs and slaves. And even if Caesar emphasised Britain's exoticism, claiming that it was a land of almost complete mystery to the invaders, he noted that it was visited by merchants, at least 'the maritime shore and those parts facing Gaul'. For the potentates of southern Britain, the presence of Rome could not be avoided.

Britain, during the period when it came to the focused attention of the Roman world, was an Iron Age Celtic society with much in common with its neighbours over the Channel. Roman authors tell us that the inhabitants were grouped in regional 'tribes' led by male or female rulers (Boudica is only the most famous of the queens; Tacitus also writes of Queen Cartimandua of the Brigantes tribe in northern England). Archaeological evidence tells us – though there are wide geographical variations – that the Iron Age Britons lived in settlements largely consisting of groups of thatched roundhouses. Some of them inhabited hill forts – settlements on a high point in the landscape, encircled by mighty ditches. The most impressive example is perhaps Maiden Castle in Dorset, which looks down upon Dorchester and its satellite, Poundbury, from its windy heights, the centre girdled by a tangled coil of earth ramparts. Towards the period of Roman conquest, powerful settlements known as 'oppida' also seem to have been established, especially in the south. Archaeologists are gradually hypothesising a more and more sophisticated modus vivendi for the Iron Age Britons, undermining traditional views, propounded since the Renaissance, that the Romans brought civilised ways to an entirely untutored race of savage

natives. In 2011, by way of example, the wooden foundations of a
metalled, cambered road in Shropshire long thought to be Roman were
carbon-dated to the second century BC. The craftsmanship of Iron Age
Britain also suggests a sophisticated culture, or at least a wealthy elite:
not only the obvious splendour of the gold torcs, thick as my wrist,
from the Snettisham hoard (now to be seen in Norwich Castle Museum
and the British Museum), but myriad other exquisitely designed and
crafted objects, such as the grave goods found in 1879 near Birdlip in
the Cotswolds and now in the Gloucester Museum. Along with a necklace of thick, chunky beads of Baltic amber and Kimmeridge shale was
discovered a beautiful bronze mirror engraved with complex, sinuous
abstract patterns and inset with enamel.

In the years before the reign of the emperor Claudius, a new power
base seems to have emerged in the south-east of Britain. Rulers of
the Catuvellaunian tribe, from north of the Thames around modern
St Albans, had started minting coins in Camulodunum, now Colchester,
the *oppidum* at the heart of the Trinovantes' tribal lands. A south-
eastern power, one can infer, was growing. Examples of these coins
can be seen in the museum at Colchester: tiny, shining gold discs
sitting alongside their original moulds, like jam tarts sprung from a
baking tin. On one side: a leaping horse and the letters 'CUNO', for
the ruler Cunobelinus (Shakespeare's Cymbeline). On the other, an
ear of corn and the letters 'CAMU', for Camulodunum. This is a
British ruler harnessing Roman modes of power projection (coinage,
Roman letters). The coins were almost certainly not money – exchange-
able for goods within a currency system – in any meaningful way.

Cunobelinus was indeed sufficiently powerful to be referred to as
'king of the Britons' in Suetonius's second-century biography of the
emperor Caligula, Augustus's successor-but-one, who ruled Rome from
AD 37 to 41. And he provided Caligula with a justification for an invasion
of Britain, too: according to Suetonius, he expelled one of his sons,
Adminius, who then sought political sanctuary with the Romans. In
Suetonius's account – which, in common with the other biographical
sketches in his *Twelve Caesars*, is coloured by his generalised animosity
towards the Julio-Claudian emperors – Caligula received Adminius's
'surrender' with an absurd degree of ceremony, and planned an invasion
in AD 40. But the adventure ended ignominiously on the shores of Gaul,
with Caligula commanding his troops to gather seashells to bring back

to Rome as spoils. Whether this story is sheer malicious invention, or evidence of the emperor's mental instability, or even a sarcastic gesture intended by Caligula to humiliate troops who had been unwilling to venture across the treacherous tidal wastes of Ocean, we shall probably never know. The second- to third-century Roman historian Cassius Dio – whose eighty-volume *History of Rome*, written in Greek, survives partly through the abridgements, or 'epitomes', prepared by medieval Byzantine monks – has the emperor embarking from Gaul in a trireme, then doing a sharp about-turn, mid Channel, without so much as touching the British coastline.

Caligula, whose eccentricities blossomed into a full-blown reign of terror, did not last. His own elite troops, the Praetorian Guard, assassinated him and inserted his uncle Claudius in his place. But the position of Claudius – who had a reputation for physical and mental decrepitude – was deeply insecure. A military victory was required, and he chose Britain as the theatre for his exploits. The symbolic value was clear: to complete a conquest that had eluded even Julius Caesar, the greatest general of them all, would provide a much-needed boost to his shaky regime. There may have been other reasons in play, too. Cunobelinus's sons and successors, Togodumnus and Caratacus, seem to have been pursuing an aggressively expansionist policy that may have threatened the balance of power in Britain and, by extension, Roman interests in Gaul. Dio recorded that 'a certain Berikos' had been driven out of the island, and had sought asylum in Rome. 'Berikos' was possibly Verica, of the Hampshire and Sussex Atrebates tribe, whose name is recorded as '*rex*', king, on coins; his expulsion may have come about as a result of the rise of Togodumnus and Caratacus. At any rate, his appeal to Rome provided a reason, or pretext, for invasion, according to Dio. What is clear is that Claudius will not very likely have been impeded by moral scruples. We may take it as a fair articulation of Roman imperial ideology when, in the first book of the *Aeneid*, Virgil has Jupiter grant Rome '*imperium sine fine*' – empire without limit.

Most historians believe that the Roman fort of Rutupiae at Richborough, a few miles north of Deal, near Sandwich, is the best contender for the Romans' main invasion point in AD 43. Sandwich is an insistently picturesque town, where even the building housing the local branch of Barclay's is dated 1610. But when I walked around it, its air of prosperity seemed fragile. The independent bookshop had closed, and Pfizer, the big pharmaceuticals firm based a few miles away – famous for producing Viagra – was winding down, shedding 1,500 jobs. I walked along the reedy river Stour, its edges clumped with houseboats. Occasionally a patch of the otherwise scrappy bank had been tended into suburban neatness by its riverine inhabitants. There was no one around. At length I climbed up over an old railway line, through nettle beds, and emerged into the fort.

I was surrounded on three sides by forbidding grey-white rubbly walls, some a full eight metres high. Inside the enclosure formed by the walls, and not quite parallel to them, ran a series of three deep concentric ditches, also forming three sides of a rectangle, their corners rounded off into sinuous curves. They looked as if they might have been made by a fashionable modern landscape architect. However, none of these things, dramatic as they were, were built by the Claudian invaders: instead, I had to search to find the traces of the shallower ditches that indicated the first defences built here to shelter the influx of perhaps 40,000 troops under the command of the general Aulus Plautius. The first walls would have been timber, the ramparts earth. Both the deeper ditches and the high flinty walls were made, it is thought, as defences against Saxon raiders in the third century. The fort holds great layers of Roman history between its walls. At the centre, for example, is a cruciform platform, its sides grass-covered, its top scabbed with flint. This is the base of a monumental arch of Carrara marble from Tuscany, which stood twenty-five metres tall. Built in the AD 70s or 80s, it was once caparisoned with sculptural reliefs and blazoned with inscriptions: it marked the triumphal seaward entry to a young province, and was a piece of architecture, with its sharp classical angles and its shining Italian stone, that would have been visible from the sea and the low-lying land for miles around, a complete contrast to the single-storey thatched roundhouses of the Britons. The arch was deliberately demolished in the late third century, for reasons that are ill-understood. As I looked north from the fort towards Thanet, the land stretched away as a sea of waving grass, through which the wind thrummed and sighed. When Aulus Plautius landed here, Thanet was properly an island, and Richborough was bounded by water on three sides. Later, the wide channel, the

Wantsum, that separated Thanet from Richborough and the mainland, gradually silted up. When I looked out on to the green ocean, the only vessel riding it was the giant hulk of a concrete power station. Its triple cooling towers no longer breathed steam. This, too, stood as a wreck in the landscape.

If you pause by the foundations of the monumental arch and look west, you can trace a line that turns into Watling Street: the Roman road that heads for Canterbury and London, where it becomes the Edgware Road, and, at length, reaches Wroxeter in Shropshire. Kent, from Julius Caesar on, has been a zone of national entrances: the first Saxon settlers, Hengist and Horsa, were supposed to have settled on Thanet; St Augustine's mission landed nearby. Turn the other way, east and south-east, towards the Stour, and you face towards land that during the First World War was busy once more with soldiers. Here were built seagoing barges to transport munitions to France; eventually a great shipyard and workshops were built, with sonorously named camps ('Kitchener', 'Haig') to accommodate 14,000 people. In February 1939, the by now derelict Kitchener camp was brought back into use, this time as a transit camp for 5,000 German- and Austrian-Jewish male refugees. Here was a communal university, with scientists and scholars giving lectures. Here was a band, directed by a former conductor of the Stuttgart Radio Orchestra, which was in demand in the Kent seaside resorts that summer. A Mr Hernstadt – who later anglicised his name to Hearn – performed turns as the magician 'Harun al Rashid'. The camp was nicknamed Anglo-Saxon-Hausen by its inmates, a dark joke on the Sachsenhausen camp in Germany from which many of them had come, and perhaps also on the historical associations of the area. Signs in the camp proclaimed 'England expects every man to do his duty. You are not Englishmen, but you should do your duty.' Most eventually enlisted in the British army.

Suetonius sniffed at Claudius's military record. 'He undertook but a single campaign, and a minor one at that.' It was not so minor, it seems, to the soldiers. According to Cassius Dio, the troops were unwilling to venture outside the known world – 'exo tes oikoumenes' – and almost refused to leave the coast of Gaul, until Claudius's powerful henchman Narcissus (a freedman, Greek to judge from his name) harangued them. This from a civilian and a former slave was too much for the troops, who shouted him down with a derisive chorus of 'Io, Saturnalia' – the traditional cry of the Roman festival of misrule, at which slaves and masters swapped clothes and roles. At any rate, the troops were shamed into action. Whether true or not, the story gives a powerful indication of the fascination and terror exerted by the idea of the Ocean and its mysterious islands.

Aulus Plautius's troops, writes Dio, met no immediate resistance – not the hordes that had confronted Caesar on Deal beach – but found themselves tackling an elusive enemy with a habit of melting away into swamps and woods. Plautius caught up with them in dribs and drabs, defeating forces under each of the brothers Caratacus and Togodumnus. An indecisive battle took place on the shores of a river – most likely the Medway. The Romans engaged with the British charioteers over a two-day battle, in which, notes Dio, Vespasian fought with distinction (twenty-six years later, this young officer became emperor). Somewhere in this or an earlier melee, Togodumnus perished – which, according to Dio, caused the Britons to unite to avenge him. Aulus Plautius, meanwhile, sent for Claudius himself – presumably to allow the emperor the credit of a now assured victory, though possibly also to rally the fatigued troops. At any rate, if Dio is to be believed, the arrival of the imperial train, and the advance upon the great power base of Camulodunum, was the cause of what must have been one of the more astonishing sights in Iron Age Britain: war elephants in Colchester.

According to Dio, Claudius advanced north of the Thames and captured Camulodunum in short order. Here he received the surrender of many tribes – some by force, some voluntarily. His stay was brief: after sixteen days, he began his journey back to Rome, where he was promptly granted permission by the Senate to celebrate a Triumph, the ritual procession through the streets of Rome undertaken on the occasion of a great – or allegedly great – military victory. In fact, despite Claudius's moment of shock and awe in the south-east, the work of subduing a respectable chunk of the island turned out to be painful, bloody, and the work of decades: it was not until forty years later that the governor Agricola at least claimed to have completed the conquest of the whole of the island, and even then the northern highlands were let go almost at once. Suetonius's biography describes Claudius's Triumph: the emperor riding in a chariot while his wife, Messalina, followed in a covered carriage. Also in the parade were provincial governors, specially allowed permission to leave their posts for the occasion, and officers from the campaign, clad in purple-bordered togas. There would likely, too, have been captives, advancing ahead of the emperor in his chariot as the procession snaked its route from Mars Field to the Capitoline Hill, the steps of which Claudius climbed on his knees, according to Dio. There would perhaps also have been displays of booty: though unless the invaders had got their hands on some really spectacular Celtic gold, one imagines it may have been rather frugal – at least compared with what had been brought back from earlier campaigns in the rich eastern Mediterranean. One can only imagine the state of these putative British captives, presumably chained and unwilling actors in this piece of public ritual, yet paradoxically its star attractions, as they wended their way to an uncertain fate – perhaps death, perhaps imprisonment, perhaps slavery. And then there were other lavish celebrations mounted by Claudius in Rome's theatres: horse races, bear baiting, athletics, and boys brought from Asia to perform the Pyrrhic dance, a war dance in full armour. Claudius was given the honorary title Britannicus, as was his son, who came always to be known by the name. (Britannicus was to die just short of his fourteenth birthday, reputedly poisoned at a dinner party by his elder stepbrother Nero, who by then had succeeded Claudius as emperor.) The triumphal arch Claudius erected in Rome in AD 51 records that he received the surrender of '11 British kings'. Britain had turned Claudius into what he needed to be: a great military leader.

One crucial aspect of Claudius's conquest that it is sometimes convenient to brush over from the Roman side, and perhaps even more so from a later, British, patriotic viewpoint, is the extent to which, in different parts of the country, the Roman takeover was, if not actually welcomed, then greeted with alliance-making and acceptance rather than military resistance. The great northern fastness of the Brigantes tribe, ruled by Queen Cartimandua, was friendly to Rome; so too was the East Anglian territory of Prasutagus, king of the Iceni – at least to begin with. There is an intriguing, if speculative hint of what might have become of such friendly client rulers, as these allied but subservient figures are known by historians. At Fishbourne, a little outside Chichester in Sussex, a workman cutting a water-main trench across a field in 1960 happened upon a mass of ancient building material. The following summer, and until 1968, the site was excavated

by a team led by the young archaeologist Barry Cunliffe (now Professor
Sir Barry Cunliffe).

The result of the investigations was the discovery of a stupendously
large and palatial villa building, begun in the AD 60s and reworked,
altered and extended on successive occasions until, in the late third
century, a wing of the villa burned down. It is anomalous in the history
of Roman Britain because, unlike so many of the other great villa
complexes of the province, most of which flourished in the fourth
century, it is so early: it was begun barely twenty years after conquest,
on the site of what was probably a military depot or supply base
dating from the time of the invasion.

More strikingly still, it is simply not the kind of building that anyone
had expected to find: there is nothing provincial at all about these
buildings. At their height, they ranged round elegant central gardens
in the Mediterranean style: one of the most striking aspects of
Fishbourne is the fact that the elaborate geometric bedding trenches
for formal hedges were discovered (and indeed have been replanted
– they are the kind of complex arrangement that would not do a
French chateau disservice). A tiny fragment of painted plaster survives,
suggesting that the western wall of the garden was painted with a
beautiful *trompe l'oeil* design of plants and foliage; also in the museum
at Fishbourne is a shard of frescoed wall, showing a landscape with
the sea in the background. The last time I had seen such work was
in the Roman houses of the Bay of Naples, their exquisite interior
decoration preserved by the catastrophe of Mount Vesuvius's eruption.
This is imperial glamour in all its Mediterranean splendour.

Despite the wealth of the mosaics in the palace, the evident scale
and majesty of the rooms, there is no clue as to who lived here. Any
guess is just that: a guess. Some think it must have been an official
building belonging to the Roman administration. But others are
convinced that Fishbourne belonged to a British client king called
Tiberius Claudius Cogidubnus (or Togidubnus); he makes an appearance in Tacitus's *Agricola* and on an inscription recording the building
of a temple to Minerva and Neptune that was found under Chichester's
North Street in 1723 (it is now fixed to the side of the town's Assembly
Rooms, not far from its beautiful medieval market cross). Fishbourne
is perhaps Britain's most magnificent recent example of the capacity
of the sleeping earth to throw up anomalies, puzzles that disrupt the

sense of what should be found. Perhaps one day a piece of evidence will arise to tell us more about those who used this array of rooms. Until then, the notion that it belonged to a client king is an intriguing but unprovable hypothesis.

The reverberations of Claudius's victory were meant to be felt far beyond Britain, and far beyond Italy. Coins were minted, showing his no doubt idealised profile on one side, and on the other a British war chariot. The victory was marked right at the opposite end of the empire, in the Sebasteion in the city of Aphrodisias, in modern Turkey. The Sebasteion was a grand collection of edifices: a temple to the deified emperors and to the goddess Aphrodite, flanked by two long porticoes. It was probably begun under the emperor Tiberius, Claudius's predecessor-but-one, and finished under his successor, Nero. The porticoes were decorated with relief panels: of gods, mythological scenes and emperors. One of them shows Claudius. He is heroically naked but for the sword belt strapped across his chest and a cloak that swirls dramatically behind him. One arm is lifted above his head, poised to strike the figure he is pinioning to the ground with his knee: Britannia, the female personification of the fledgling province. She is naked, too, or nearly – her dress falls off her shoulders in tatters – but this is the forlorn and abject nakedness of the defeated, not the glorious nudity of the hero: The Aphrodisias relief is Britannia's first-known appearance, a far cry from the figure who was reclaimed as ruling the waves by a later age, and who graced the coinage from the seventeenth century until her image was removed from the fifty-pence piece in 2008. (She still has her discreet place on the paper money issued by the Bank of England.) As an image, she is double-edged – both for the Sebasteion sculptor, in whose hands she is rendered far from contemptible; and in her modern incarnation, when she will always be Britannia who was once ravished and ruled.

'More than Britain's oldest recorded town,' proclaim signs at the railway station. Modern Colchester wears its antiquity self-consciously. It has little choice. Its Roman remains are everywhere; the encircling Roman wall, built probably in the early second century AD, binds the town to itself. Over the centuries, portions have been rebuilt or heavily patched; much of it, though, is still the original Roman heft, with pinkish layers of brick tiles sandwiched through the grey stone at regular intervals. During the English Civil War, the town, playing reluctant host to a Royalist army, was besieged within these walls by Fairfax's forces for eleven weeks. By the end, all there was left to eat were horses, dogs and tallow candles.

Colchester people are forever, and inescapably, walking over, through and past the wreckage of their history. The Roman Balkerne Gate through the town walls still has twin arches standing, and people hurry beneath them on the way to the shops or the Mercury Theatre. I imagine the gates as they might once have been: proud, and marble-faced. Now their straight lines have fallen in on themselves, the angles collapsed into softness like a face in old age. Standing under the arches is a little like being in a grotto or a cave. Ferns have sent out roots in the Roman mortar. Next to the gate is a pub called The Hole in the Wall, which is an accurate description of its position. A friend of mine, a Colchester native, remembers sitting in this pub in her punk years, 'engulfed in a miasma of Players No. 6', flirting with the soldiers. If Roman Colchester began as a fort, and in AD 49 became a colony for Roman army veterans, then it has also been a garrison town since the Napoleonic wars. I imagine my friend with her barbaric hair and forbidding facepaint, teasing the squaddies: a woad-covered Briton.

Walk through the Balkerne Gate, and all the architecture around seems to want to echo it: the arches of the red-brick water tower that loom above; the rather sad pastiche of Roman angles and curves that is the entrance to Balkerne Gardens, a gated housing development. Down the high street the arches march: here in the facade of a bank, there in that of a bookshop. At the bottom of the high street, in the park, stands the Norman castle, now Colchester Museum. It is a solid, comfortable building in warm sand-coloured stone. After the First World War, the archaeologist Mortimer Wheeler, excavating in the vaults, discovered that the foundations of the castle were Roman: they are thought to be the base of the temple that, according to Tacitus, was erected to the deified Claudius. It was only in the eighteenth century that Colchester was confidently associated with ancient Camulodunum; Maldon, some miles to the south-east, had been an early contender. In 1748, the antiquary Philip Morant argued: 'By laying all the circumstances together, it may appear to any unprejudiced person, that Colchester hath a better right to reclaim Camulodunum than any other place where it had been fixed by writers ancient and modern.'

The authority on Colchester's archaeology is Philip Crummy, a small, wiry Scot with a bleakly pessimistic sense of humour belying his ferocious commitment to the town's Roman history. As we stood together outside the castle, he told me he imagined Eudo Dapifer, companion knight to William the Conqueror, ordering the temple ruins, perhaps still substantial, to be cleared away and then his castle built from the existing masonry. 'It is,' he says, 'a building hewn out of the Roman ruins. It's a statement that he's the new boss around here. This is the traditional centre of power, and he's appropriating it.' He pointed out the rubbly grey material at the base of the building: Roman. Then, about two thirds of the way up the walls, a line of vertical tiles stuck together with pink mortar. These are, says Crummy, pilae stacks on their side – pilae stacks being the little pillars supporting a Roman floor, around which the hot air of a hypocaust heating system would swirl. So many of these stacks were reused in the fabric of the castle that they must have come from a large public baths complex, he thinks – and a town like Camulodunum will certainly have had big public baths, though they have never been discovered.

In the museum is the tombstone of a centurion of the 20th Legion, a northern Italian called Marcus Favonius Facilis: he stands staring out of his niche, an elegant figure in full armour, his left hand resting on his sword hilt. Nearby is a memorial to Longinus Sdapeze, an officer of the first cavalry regiment of Thracians from Sardica – modern Sofia. It is altogether less polished, less classical in its form, than the northern Italian's gravestone. The officer sits proud on his high-stepping horse, his armour rendered roughly, so that it resembles a coat of feathers. Trampled beneath the animal's hooves is a naked, cowering bearded man, the barbarian – the Briton? – whom the Roman has brought low. I was transfixed, too, by a case of luxurious marbles, brightly coloured and exotically named. Here was giallo antico from Africa; pavonazetto from Asia Minor; green porphyry from Greece. Elsewhere were wine jars from Crete and Gaza, a fish-sauce container from Spain, chalcedony beads from Hungary. In assuming Roman-ness, Camulodunum had become a small vein in an arterial system of commerce and trade that stretched from here to Tunisia to Palestine.

Crummy took me to Colchester's Victorian army garrison, where he and his team have been able to excavate because the barracks – with their imperial-sounding names, such as Hyderabad and Meanee – have been sold off for housing. One day Crummy and his team came upon the foundations of what seemed to be a road – and another identical one, running parallel with it, some seventy metres away. It was only when a press officer for the housing developer made a joke about the chances of their finding a chariot (which would be good PR, as opposed to roads, which are too dull to make headlines) that, said Crummy, 'the penny dropped'. The identical stretch of 'road' was, he surmised, in fact the opposite side of a chariot-racing track. His hunch turned out to be right – or, rather, was eventually established after nearly two years of slow and steady work. Beneath the garden of the now empty sergeants' mess, where, when Crummy walked me here, beds of overblown roses bloomed amid the untamed grass, two of the perhaps eight starting gates for the chariots had been discovered. Towards the centre of the track, up against the turning posts, the soil was found to be compacted and rutted: evidence, thought the archaeologists, of the charioteers' tactics of angling around them as tightly as possible. A local campaign had secured some of the land on which the circus stood, and there were plans for an interpretation centre and a café. 'Ben Hur in Colchester?' ran the headline in the *Guardian* when the discovery was announced.

Back inside the walls of Colchester, I wandered down Maidenburgh Street in the Dutch quarter – where Flemish weavers settled in the sixteenth century – and peered through a window in one of the buildings partway down the street. Here were low walls, carefully preserved for public view, that described a gentle curve: the foundations of a Roman theatre. Further down the lane was a little Saxon chapel built on the line of the theatre wall; indeed, built out of its very bricks and masonry. I pushed open the door and found myself in an anteroom full of flower-arranging impedimenta. Opening a second door, I was suddenly drenched in incense-laden air, facing an iconostasis. This Saxon chapel, with its Roman foundations and its Roman bricks, which had been restored by the Normans, and later by the Victorian Gothic architect William Butterfield, is now a Greek Orthodox church. It is dedicated to St Helen, the mother of Constantine the Great. In local folklore, Helen was the daughter of King Coel, whose stronghold was Colchester Castle. The story is told in Geoffrey of Monmouth's twelfth-century work *A History of the Kings of Britain*: Coel, who rules from Colchester, sues for peace when the great Roman senator Constantius arrives on British shores. After Coel dies, Constantius marries his daughter and seizes the throne, later becoming the ruler of all Rome.

Geoffrey of Monmouth's work, though regarded as authoritative until well into the Renaissance, is a repository of myth rather than fact. His version of Britain's early history – the source for which he vaguely and dubiously claimed was a nameless 'very old book' – provides some compelling narratives, stitched through with the threads of legends, many from his native Wales. He tells the tale of the giants Gog and Magog who once roamed the land; the fate of King Arthur; the story of Lear. He claimed that Britain was named after a man named Brutus, a grandson of Aeneas, the Trojan prince who fled his home city to Italy after the Greeks' sack, and whose descendants founded Rome. It is telling that Geoffrey needed to give Britain a classicising foundation myth, ascribing to it grand legendary origins on a par with Rome's: the literary equivalent, perhaps, of building your castle on the ruins of a Roman temple. It is a story that nobody tells any more.

Monmouth's story of Coel is a fairy tale, perhaps born from some false etymology relating to the name of the town. In fact Colchester is more likely to have got its name from the word *'colonia'*, the Roman veterans' colony, added to '-chester', the Saxon corruption of *'castrum'*, the Latin for camp. (The official Roman name of the town was Colonia Claudia Victricensis – the Claudian Town of Victory.) The story does, however, have one or two facts woven through it: Constantine the Great and his father, Constantius Chlorus, were indeed both in Britain. Constantine, who made Christianity the official religion of the empire, was proclaimed emperor in York in AD 306. But there is no evidence that the historical Helen, who is much more likely to have come from the eastern Mediterranean, ever set foot here, let alone was born here; and no evidence for a Coel at all. But the Helen myth stuck for a long while in Colchester: the town's coat of arms, first used in the fifteenth century, has an image of the True Cross and its nails, fragments of which St Helen supposedly found on her pilgrimage to the Holy Land. It also bears three crowns, to suggest the Magi, whose graves she is also said to have encountered on her travels. The Orthodox chapel's priest has written about St Helen: he reluctantly admits that the story of her connection to the town has no historical foundation. And yet, he argues, the tradition itself is what matters. She cannot be unstitched, now, from its history. Indeed, as a venerator of fragments from the past, and as a finder of the graves of those who died long ago, she might make rather a suitable patron for those who seek the revered objects of a lost Britain.

In fact, St Helen has, for the past century, had a serious rival as an ancient heroine for the town: Boudica. From the frontage of the town hall on the high street, which was built at the turn of the twentieth century, loom statues of famous figures from Colchester history. Here is a sculpture of Eudo Dapifer, and Edward the Elder, the son of Alfred the Great, who took Colchester from the Danes in 917. Tucked round the side of the building we see Boudica, gesturing portentously down a narrow side street. It is said that the spot occupied by the British rebel was meant for an image of Cunobelinus. Then, unannounced, in 1902, a sculpture of Boudica appeared in his niche – and not to universal acclaim, though perhaps the anonymous donor was inspired by the example of Thomas Thornycroft's bronze sculpture, *Boadicea and Her Daughters*, which had recently been erected at Waterloo Bridge in London.

Boudica is, at best, an ambiguous heroine for Colchester, since her
sole connection is that in AD 60 or 61 she and her men took and burnt
the town, and massacred its inhabitants. And yet she has, from her
appearance on the town hall facade, been embraced. In 1909, she was
one of the stars of the Colchester Pageant – a grand event, running
over six days, and involving a cast of 3,000, that staged tableaux from
local history. One of the posters showed Boudica as a Wagnerian
heroine, a horned helmet upon her head, borne along in her chariot
by fiery black steeds. Another promised the re-creation of BOADICEA'S
VICTORY – ON THE ACTUAL BATTLE GROUND, among other
attractions. In the modern successor of the Colchester Pageant, the
annual Colchester Carnival, another Boudica, face daubed with blue,
rides through the town in her chariot. When I enquired whether there
had been a St Helen in the last carnival, I was told by its organiser
that no one had come forward to take her on, and that Boudica was,
in any case, 'far more representative of an important event in
Colchester's history than the fictional St Helen'. I saw that there was,
too, a new school in Colchester called Queen Boudica Primary. It
seemed that this bloody queen had been adopted as a secular saint,
feminist role model and an example to the young. I felt sorry for St
Helen, her piety out of tune with the times. But it was time to go in
search of Boudica – in her homeland.

2

Norfolk

. . . and a woman,
A woman beat 'em, Nennius; a weak woman,
A woman beat these Romanes.

John Fletcher, c.1613

Caratacus and Boudica are the first British characters in history. They are entirely Roman creations. There is no convincing archaeological evidence that they existed at all, beyond a few finds of Iron Age coins marked 'CARA'. They are written into being, as figures of the British resistance against Roman rule, by Tacitus in his *Annals* – his last work, a now incomplete history of Rome from Augustus to Nero, composed around AD 117. He tinges them with a dangerous glamour and a subversive nobility; they are tools in his often cynical, always penetrating, critique of the values of the Roman empire.

Caratacus, the son of Cunobelinus and brother of Togodumnus, had slipped out of the grasp of the Romans at the time of Claudius's initial conquest in AD 43, and we next hear of him seven years later, leading the Britons in south and then north Wales – where no doubt the hilly, inaccessible territory helped him and his men as they slipped from wood to cave to mountain. But he was finally brought to ground by the relentless Roman war machine, and defeated in battle at a great hill fort, somewhere in Ordovician territory in north Wales. Caratacus himself escaped from the melee and sought protection in northern England with the Brigantes tribe, but Cartimandua, as a Roman ally, handed him over to the conquerors. As Tacitus has it, in the years that had elapsed since Claudius claimed Britain at Camulodunum, Caratacus had become a famous name in Italy. And so the capture of this elusive guerrilla leader, 'whose name was not without a certain glory', offered the opportunity for a spectacular public-relations exercise in Rome (as well as leading, according to Tacitus, to a false sense that Roman troubles in Britain had ended). 'There was huge curiosity to see the man who for so many years had spurned our power,' he wrote.

And so Claudius laid on a show, carefully stage-managed to make the capture reflect as gloriously as possible on himself. A parade was organised, with Caratacus's splendid gold torcs and war booty carried aloft, and his companions, wife and children forced to follow. Finally came Caratacus himself, who, according to Tacitus, was the only prisoner-of-war who walked with his head held high. Approaching the tribunal on which Claudius sat, he boldly addressed the emperor on equal terms, saying that under different circumstances he might have been welcomed to Rome as a friend, rather than dragged there as a captive. He added: 'I had horses, men, arms, riches: is it any wonder that I should lose them unwillingly? If you wish to rule the world, does it follow that everybody else should accept slavery? If I had been dragged before you having surrendered immediately, nobody would have heard of either my defeat or your victory: if you punish me everybody will forget this moment. But if you save me, I shall be an everlasting memorial to your mercy.'

Claudius was convinced by this shrewd appeal to his reputation, and pardoned the Briton and his family: nothing is heard of them again, though there was some (rather wishful) speculation in the nineteenth century that a woman whom the poet Martial mentioned some forty years later – Claudia Rufens, 'caeruleis . . . Britannis edita', 'sprung from the woad-painted Britons' – might be a descendant, suitably named after the merciful emperor. At any rate, Tacitus's description of these events is remarkable: the historian has the Briton employing the quintessentially Roman skill of rhetoric and using it to best the emperor himself. Not for the first or last time, a Roman writer was using the figure of a defeated enemy – one who is shown to possess true Roman virtues – to launch a bitter attack on the imperial project. It is precisely this treatment of Caratacus that allowed the character to be created, by later British readers, as a heroic figure. The carefully described moment of the Briton standing before Claudius lent itself to artistic depiction: George Frederick Watts, for example, submitted a painting of the scene for a competition held in 1843 to select artists to decorate the new Palace of Westminster. But Caratacus seems now to have drifted out of fashion and out of memory. There is no place for him in Colchester's annual carnival, though you might argue that he has a better claim to inclusion than Boudica. It is probable that more modern Britons have, thanks to the *Asterix* comics, heard of Vercingetorix, the Gaul who rebelled against Julius Caesar, than Caratacus.

In any case, it was Boudica whom I was now seeking: the other great British rebel leader, who, in AD 60 or 61, a decade after Caratacus's capture, rose up against the young Roman administration. Under the rule of her husband Prasutagus, the Iceni had been a Roman ally. But when he died, leaving his kingdom and property equally divided between the emperor Nero and his own daughters, things went badly wrong. The Roman military, according to Tacitus, seized Iceni property, flogged the queen, raped her daughters. The flagrant abuses and grotesque humiliations were too much. With the brunt of the Roman forces far away, tackling a Druid stronghold on Anglesey, Boudica and the Iceni seized their chance. They rampaged through the south-east, and took on Camulodunum, where the behaviour of the Roman colonists – driving Britons from their land, treating them like slaves – had sparked outrage. Terrifying portents were witnessed by the Romans: in the town, the sculpture of Victory spontaneously toppled and the theatre rang with the sound of hideous supernatural shrieks; in the Thames estuary, the sea took on the appearance of blood, and people saw an image of the colony overthrown. Those who could took refuge in the temple of the deified Claudius, which itself had become a hated symbol of foreign rule. The Romans sent to London for help, but the procurator (or chief financial officer) sent only 200 ill-equipped troops. Camulodunum was otherwise entirely undefended. The temple held out for just two days before the town was captured and burnt, the inhabitants massacred. Finally, the 9th Legion arrived, but the rebels defeated it, slaughtering its entire infantry and forcing its commander, Petilius Cerealis, and the cavalry to ignominious flight. The procurator, or chief financial officer, fled to Gaul from his base in London. Finally, the Roman general Suetonius Paulinus marched back to the south-east from Anglesey and, despite the appeals of the inhabitants, decided to sacrifice London for the sake of the province as a whole. Everyone from the city who could

not follow in his baggage train – the old, the sick, children – were left
to be slaughtered by the Iceni and their allies. Verulamium, the Roman
town beside modern St Albans, met the same fate. Finally Suetonius
Paulinus engaged the rebels on a battlefield of his own choosing,
somewhere near London. His victory was total. Fleeing Britons were
trapped by their wagons, which ringed the battlefield. Women were
not spared. Dead pack animals bristled with spears. Eighty thousand
Britons (or so wrote Tacitus) were slaughtered; 10,000 more than had
been killed by the rebels. Boudica took poison and killed herself.

Matthew and I were heading to the Iceni heartlands of Norfolk. As we
trickled south from Yorkshire, the camper van's engine, instead of
emitting its usual musical gurgle, began to roar and cough. Finally,
with an unpleasantly acrid stench, it gave out, and we were obliged to
continue by the less romantic means of a hire car. It was a relief, at
least, to be in a vehicle that could comfortably travel at more than fifty
miles an hour. The road into Norfolk, sweeping us east into England's
rump, was not designed for gentle puttering, but was a great trunk
route, with lorries hurtling through the flat agricultural heartlands.
Finally, in the market town of Swaffham, we ate a picnic in the graveyard – then ran for cover inside the church as a sudden downpour
came. Its medieval ceiling was carved with phalanxes of angels, wings
outspread. I lay on a pew and gazed upwards, soaring with them.

Past Swaffham, we came upon a sign inviting us to visit something
called the 'Iceni Village'. Since it was Iceni country we had come to
see, and the Iceni Village promised us a reconstruction of an Iron Age
British settlement, we each handed over our £6. We crossed over a
wickerwork drawbridge stuck with plasticky heads on poles. Inside
the enclosure was a clump of sketchily made roundhouses. Within,
they were dripping from the rain. A few garden-centre ceramic pots
were scattered around. Sinister-looking shop mannequins, with blue-
stained faces, bad wigs and some distant approximation of Iron Age
dress, leered at drunken angles through the gloom. They reminded
me of the Ugly-Wuglies, the creatures made of pillows and old suits
that come alive in E. Nesbit's story *The Enchanted Castle*. Wherever
Boudica was, she was certainly not here.

We retreated, out of sorts, to the village of Castle Acre, through
which runs the Roman road known as the Peddars Way – now a

footpath that can be followed from the north Norfolk coast to Suffolk. Grateful for something solid and true instead of the Iceni Village fakery, we wandered through the ruins of the village's Cluniac priory: the chevrons and diapers carved into the Norman arches were so crisp they looked as if they had been cut from paper. As the June evening elongated into dusk, we meandered along the river Nar, past fields drenched blue by oceans of prickle-stemmed viper's bugloss. As we rounded a corner of a tree-arched lane, we saw a barn owl bowling along towards us, low to the ground through the dark-green tunnel. Its impossibly wide wings shone white in the gloaming. It was perfectly silent, and perfectly uncanny, like a bird in a dream.

The following day we went east again, and drove to the village of Caistor St Edmund, a couple of miles outside Norwich. In a field on its outskirts lie the remains of a Roman town. Some 400 years before, the scholar William Camden had come here too, researching his magisterial work, *Britannia*, a county-by-county description of Britain that drew on his acute topographical and antiquarian observation as well as his learned knowledge of the classical texts that, thanks to the printing press and the great surge of humanist learning on the Continent, were now in circulation. First published in Latin in 1586, it had already run to multiple editions by the time it was translated into English by Philemon Howard in 1607. By way of its learned and beautifully written descriptions of Britain's towns, cities and antique remains, it was the work that, more than any other, began to wrest British historiography out of the grasp of Geoffrey of Monmouth's mythography. Camden's aim was, he wrote, to 'restore antiquity to Britaine, and Britaine to his antiquity'.

Camden thought the ruins at Caistor were those of the Roman town Venta Icenorum (meaning 'the marketplace of the Iceni') mentioned by the second-century Alexandrian geographer and astronomer Ptolemy. Most people since have agreed, not because there is any firm evidence that this was its name – no Roman inscription has been found on the site that definitively identifies it – but rather because there is no other settlement discovered in Iceni territory that has such a good claim to be 'the marketplace of the Iceni', the region's administrative or '*civitas*' capital. Now only the town's walls can be seen above ground: where it once stood is sheep-grazed pasture. As Camden wrote, 'It hath quite lost it selfe. For beside the ruines of the walles, which containe within a square plot or quadrant about thirty acres, and tokens appearing upon the ground where sometimes houses stood, and some fewe peeces of Romane money which are now and then there digged up, there is nothing at all remaining.'

We walked around the walls, taking in the scale of the place: assuming it really were Venta, it would be the smallest known *civitas* capital in Britain, a backwater. Not far to the west, trains streaked past en route to Norwich, and the main road thrummed away, a bass line to the cawing of irritable rooks. The south-facing wall was covered in plants: the alkaline Roman mortar, which bonded together the flints when it was built in around A D 200, had created a narrow strip of chalky habitat, an anomalous island amid the plain green pasture for lime-loving flowering plants. And so the ancient wall was covered with blooms: gentle mulleins, with their silvery furred leaves and tall spikes of yellow; buttery ladies' bedstraw; delicate pink convolvulus creeping low along the turf; lipstick-red field poppies. We wandered down to the river Tas, now a gentle stream ambling through cattle fields; once, it is supposed, a busy artery to the North Sea, with goods loaded and offloaded at Caistor's wooden quay. In the dry summer of 1928, aerial photography – then a brand-new archaeological technique – showed the complete plan of a Roman town marked out in neat lines of parched grass where the foundations of buildings were buried shallowly under the soil. Excavation then brought to light traces of a basilica, baths, a forum and two temples. But even a recent dig has discovered no evidence of an older, Iron Age settlement that might have been Boudica's, despite the fact that Roman towns in Britain were often built over, or near, their native predecessors. Boudica had slipped away again.

We drove on to Norwich. The website for the Castle Museum talks of 'East Anglia's very own Queen Boudica'. The stars of the show were the Iceni torcs: fat arcs of gold, formed of twisted wires and with intricately decorated ends, the products of infinitely patient craftsmanship and vast wealth. They are part of the hoard of gold, silver and bronze late Iron Age objects found between 1948 and 1990 at Snettisham, near King's Lynn. There are so many of these shining items that even with the finds split between Norwich and the British Museum, each display looks lavish. Nearby, children could take a ride in a simulated Iceni chariot. I saw an Iron Age sword, its hilt in the form of a human figure, and some brightly enamelled metal fixing for horses' harnesses: perhaps it was battle gear like this that the Iceni took up when they defied the Romans. A film showed a group of small children, dressed in putative Iron Age costume, being told the story of the rebellion by an actor playing their grandmother, who explained that the rebellion was brought down by the Romans' superior technology ('a solid line of shields like a living wall'). The story of Roman Britain told in this museum is the story of the heroic failure of the Iceni. There was little doubt whose side we were meant to be on. For someone who was so elusive, Boudica seemed to have been very thoroughly claimed.

As with Caratacus, everything that we know about Boudica and her heroism is begun by Tacitus. As with Caratacus, he puts into her mouth an extraordinary speech, delivered to her troops before the final, fatal battle. Speeches by great statesmen or leaders, set down in their entirety, are alien to history writing of the modern age: and since there can have been relatively few occasions in antiquity when it would have been possible to record speeches verbatim, their status as straightforward historical evidence of what was said is frequently fragile. And yet they are a constant of ancient historiography, from Herodotus onwards, reflecting a centrality to intellectual life in classical antiquity of rhetoric, of face-to-face spoken-word argument, of the dialogic batting back and forth of ideas. There is virtually no chance that Tacitus was drawing on knowledge of what Boudica said to her troops, if anything at all. (Nor would she, it hardly needs saying, have used Latin.) Boudica's speech, and the oration that Tacitus carefully sets up to balance it, given by Suetonius Paulinus to the Roman soldiers, are opportunities for the reader to step back from the forward motion of the narrative and to examine the moral meaning of events. They are opportunities for the author to create character, and bring us vividly into the midst of a dramatic episode. For Tacitus, above all, Boudica's speech is about vocalising the enemy. An enemy who speaks is already, in some ways, your equal. When an enemy speaks as well as Tacitus has Boudica speak, there is a danger she may be your superior. When your enemy is a woman there is, on top of all of this, something shiveringly unnatural afoot – but perhaps also something horribly fascinating and terribly impressive. Could a barbarian woman really have brought the virile Roman troops so low?

Boudica addresses her comrades from her battle chariot. Like Suetonius Paulinus's exhortation that follows, it is not rendered as direct, but rather reported, speech. She is not, she says, speaking as the scion of a great royal house, but as an ordinary woman avenging her lost freedom and her violated daughters. They had already destroyed a legion, and they could do it again – or die trying. Such was her resolve as a woman: as far as she was concerned, the men could live on and become, in a ringingly assonant phrase, slaves – 'viverent viri et servirent'. (The phrase is cruelly and cleverly punning: she seems to be hinting that the word for men, 'viri', is related to the word for 'become slaves', 'servirent'.) Suetonius Paulinus's speech is not obviously given any stronger a claim to the reader's sympathy than the Briton's, except perhaps by way of an appeal to the military discipline of his army as against Boudica's ragtag assemblage of barely armed troops, more women in the ranks than men. (Though that itself seems ambiguous – an army of women may not be quite a worthy enemy.) Whose side are we supposed to be on at this moment? Ultimately, for certain, the Romans'. But in the thick of the moment – as Boudica cries revenge for her raped girls and death or glory for her troops – it is hard to to tell.

The trope of the female warrior besting male troops goes back to Herodotus, who had the Persian king Xerxes remarking, 'My men have turned into women and my women men,' when he observed Queen Artemisia's superior naval manoeuvrings at the Battle of Salamis in the Persian Wars, in 480 BC. But the ambiguities in Tacitus's treatment of Boudica remind me particularly of the way the Roman poet Horace dealt with the Egyptian queen Cleopatra, in his supposedly triumphal ode celebrating her defeat by Augustus at the Battle of Actium in 31 BC. The poem treats her army as a dangerously exotic rabble – and yet the figure of Cleopatra, never named, seems to exert a strange fascination, even sympathy: after a triumphalist, hostile opening, the poem's tone changes, and Horace compares her to a dove chased by a falcon, or a hare by a hunter. And this of a woman who had almost torn Rome apart. She goes to her snake-bite suicide calmly and bravely: 'voltu sereno', 'with a serene expression'. For the Romans, suicide was an honourable death, a dignified way out of extreme humiliation. In Tacitus's account, Boudica, like Cleopatra, takes poison after her defeat by Suetonius Paulinus, and her suicide is, significantly, mirrored by that of a Roman: the camp prefect of the 2nd Legion, who kills himself because he has missed out on the glory. Horace calls Cleopatra '*non humilis mulier*', one of those ringing poetic phrases that struggles for adequate translation into English – perhaps 'a woman not to be brought low'. Boudica, too, is '*non humilis mulier*'.

Tacitus's account of the Boudican revolt has cast a long shadow. Cassius Dio, writing around a century later, embroidered the events, gilding Tacitus's phlegmatic account of the scene with a darkly glamorous physical description of the queen. He made her tall and grim, rough-voiced and piercing of eye. Blonde hair falls down her back; she wears a gold torc and a cloak fastened by a gold brooch. Her speech is crude but telling – at least in relation to Roman commonplaces about the world that lay at the edge of its empire. Even though, she says, we Britons are cut off from all other men by the Ocean such that most people believe we live in another world, under another sky, we have been despised and trampled underfoot by the Romans. But we are superior. If we are beaten, we melt into swamps and mountains. We can endure hunger and thirst: they, on the other hand, die without their bread and wine and oil. She prays to the victory goddess Adraste, woman to woman, to bring her triumph. But the real woman in all this, she says, is the emperor Nero, playing the lyre back in Rome, smeared in make-up. Free us from these Roman men, she begs – if indeed they are men at all, with their warm-water bathing, their wine-imbibing, myrrh-perfumed homosexuality. The speech taken as a whole is an almost comical ramping-up of the notion of the luxurious, decadent Roman set against that of the brave, self-denying Briton – all put into the mouth of this savage, primitive, terrifying woman. In this other world, under this other sky, everything is turned on its head.

How do we, the later readers of Tacitus and Dio, read all this? Whose side are we on? Who are 'we'? Are we to applaud Boudica's patriotism and bravery, or condemn her atrocities? Is Britain to be redeemed from her barbarity by the civilising force of the Romans – or enslaved? In *Holinshed's Chronicles*, the late-sixteenth-century histories frequently used as a source by Shakespeare, the account of Boudica's revolt leans heavily on Dio, revelling in its specifically female-directed atrocities committed by this woman-led rabble. 'Women of great nobilitie and woorthie fame they tooke and hanged vp naked, and cutting off their paps, sowed them to their mouthes, that they might seeme as if they sucked and fed on them.' These were, related the *Chronicles*, 'dredfull examples of the Britains crueltie'. Here female rule and especial barbarity are grotesquely clamped together.

This edition of the *Chronicles* was published in 1587, the year before Elizabeth I's appearance before her troops at Tilbury. In a domestic history notably devoid of models for female rulers, it is not surprising that James Aske, in his 1588 poem *Elizabetha Triumphans*, celebrating the defeat of the Armada, compared his monarch to Boudica, 'once England's happie Queene'. But Boudica, with that 'dredfull crueltie' in the background, could never be a straightforward model for Elizabeth, just as her own role as simultaneously virgin queen and 'prince' remained troubling to her subjects. At Tilbury, she addressed her troops from her horse, just as Tacitus's Boudica spoke from her chariot. But the confusions of sex pile up in Elizabeth's famous speech: she has the 'body of but a weak and feeble woman' but also 'the heart and stomach of a king', as if she were a man 'on the inside'. Finding a rhetoric adequate for the expression of female rule was difficult, almost impossible. Boudica, perpetrator of massacres, was precisely the figure you might choose to express your gravest anxieties about being ruled by a woman, rather than to reassure yourself.

Shakespeare's *Cymbeline*, first performed sometime before 1611 (but certainly several years after the death of Elizabeth in 1603), is set in ancient Britain on the cusp of Roman invasion. It is a play with many threads and many generic affiliations – it seems at once to be tragedy, comedy, pastoral and history play. The main setting is the court of Cymbeline, who is, via Geoffrey of Monmouth, *Holinshed's Chronicles* and a thousand Shakespearean imaginative twists and turns, a version of the real Iron Age king in the south-east, Cunobelinus. His wife, simply called the Queen, is the ultimate wicked stepmother, whose machinations include attempting to marry off her own son, the vile Cloten, to the virtuous Imogen, Cymbeline's daughter. The Queen seems to contain echoes of the figure of Boudica, for it is her primal savagery that must be neutralised before the play unravels its many tangled strands. Only with her death can the nation move towards a new future, with Britons in harmony with Romans. Native savagery, suggests the play, is an especially female savagery; the Romans, by contrast, bring male, civilised virtues. It is hard not to think of the significance here of the accession of James VI of Scotland to the English throne. Shakespeare is drawing on a myth of ancient Britain (rather than, specifically, England) that treats of two peoples coming together in harmony – after the death of a queen. *King Lear*, too, is another play premiered early in the reign of James (1605) that harks back to a British, rather than English, Geoffrey-inspired mythology. That same year the playwright Anthony Munday devised a pageant for the mayor of London called *The Triumphs of Re-united Britannia*, which dramatised Geoffrey of Monmouth's myth of Brutus, and had personified rivers foretelling the unification of the island under 'our second Brute, Royall King James'.

John Fletcher's play *Bonduca* was premiered at almost exactly the same time as *Cymbeline*. Scholars disagree on which came first; but it is not hard to argue that, whichever way round they came, they are closely related, and not just by way of their ancient British settings. Fletcher's play begins after the first great victory of Bonduca, as he names her: she gloats at the defeat of the Romans, but her general, Caratach (a version of Caratacus, whom Fletcher imported to the later story), warns her they are not to be underestimated. A subplot concerns a Roman officer, in love with one of Bonduca's daughters, who tricks and taunts him: all three women of the play are, in their way, brutal (and, of course, played, like Shakespeare's Queen, by men or boys in the original productions). As the climatic battle approaches, it is Caratach, not Bonduca, who addresses the British troops. Defeated, Bonduca and her daughters kill themselves, the elder daughter having given a grand speech of self-sacrifice that causes the Roman officer Petillius to fall in love with her. The women are all dispatched well before the end of the drama, as if, as in *Cymbeline*, the play's tensions can be resolved only once they are out of the way. The action comes to a close when the more moderate Caratach is captured and sent to Rome. And yet Fletcher seems to follow Tacitus – the ultimate source for his story – in balancing the arguments between the Romans and Bonduca. His Romans are by no means universally virtuous: there is dishonesty among them, and sexual violence. Bonduca herself seems to invite sympathy. About to die, she condemns Rome as 'vicious'. It is fitter, she says, that she should revere

> The thatched howses where the Brittans dwell
> In careless mirthe. Where the blest houshold gods
> See nought but chaste and simple purity.

As she takes her own life, she suggests that Rome will prosper only if it adopts British virtues: 'If you will keepe yor lawes and Empire whole/ Place in your Roman flesh a Brittaine soule.' I am reminded of Camden's ringing phrase in the first English translation of *Britannia*, which was published around the time of these theatrical premieres. He claimed that 'the Britans and Romans . . . by a blessed and joyfull mutuall ingrafting, as it were, have growen into one stocke and nation'. It is as if the resolution offered at the end of *Cymbeline* – Romans in harmony with Britons, as one people – has been worked through, historically as well as imaginatively. And yet nothing in these resolutions is particularly comfortable; in *Cymbeline* it feels very much as if the myth of Britain comes less easily to Shakespeare than his rhetoric about England, so ringingly articulated in plays such as *Henry V* and *Richard II*. But then the great lines of John of Gaunt in *Richard II* elide the truth. 'This England' was never, quite, a 'scepter'd isle'. National myths have a habit of tripping up on the truth.

Boudica and Caratacus both seemed to come once more into focus at the end of another long female reign: that of Queen Victoria. In October 1898, Edward Elgar, then aged forty-one, dedicated his choral cantata *Caractacus* to the monarch. (A year later, he would produce the *Enigma Variations* and achieve, for the first time in his career, widespread acclaim.) The cantata's libretto was commissioned from Harry Arbuthnot Acworth, a former member of the Indian civil service, and collector and translator of Indian Marathi ballads. Acworth's libretto begins with Caractacus preparing to face the Romans in battle; he also provides the tale with a romantic subplot, giving the British hero a daughter, Eigen (named after one of the Elgars' neighbours in Malvern), who is in love with a young Druidic bard.

The Britons having been defeated, the scene changes to Rome. Addressing the emperor, Caractacus appeals not to Claudius's reputation, as in the Tacitean original, but to his more delicate, romantic feelings, pleading on behalf of 'my guileless daughter' and her lover. Claudius pardons the family, and the cantata ends with a chorus fore-telling the glories of the British empire, taking its cue from the prophe-cies of Rome's future greatness in the *Aeneid*. In early versions of the piece's vocal score, Elgar had even used as an epigraph a quotation ('a land pregnant with empires . . .') from the sixth book of Virgil's epic.

But jingoism is not the only mood in the work. By far its most affecting passages relate to the defeated Caractacus, with whom Elgar strongly identified. While writing the cantata, he and his wife, Alice, stayed in the shadow of the Herefordshire Beacon in the Malverns, which – with its impressive Iron Age hill fort – local antiquaries thought was the site of the rebel's final battle. Elgar marinated himself in the landscape, walking the hills and the woods. When Caractacus makes his final appeal to Claudius, he sings:

> We lived in peace, was that a crime to thee,
> That thy fierce eagle stoop'd upon our nest?
> A freeborn chieftain, and a people free,
> We dwelt among our woodlands, and were blest.

The word 'woodlands' is repeated when sung – a moment of shat-tering poignancy. Elgar wrote of it to his friend A. J. Jaeger: 'I made old Caractacus stop as if broken down . . . & choke & say "woodlands" again because I'm so madly devoted to my woods.' It is as if, for Elgar, Caractacus is sprung from the land – from the very woods and the mountains. The unpleasant sentiments of the last chorus mask, in truth, a complicated web of potential sympathies and allegiances (was not the British empire the 'fierce eagle' of its day, swooping upon other nests?). In the end, Elgar's Caractacus will not be pinned down.

Thornycroft's bronze sculpture group, *Boadicea and Her Daughters*, which gallops along the Embankment at Westminster Bridge in London, was finally erected in 1902, after decades of toil and fund-raising. The horses had been modelled on some of Prince Albert's – they rear up terrifyingly, their ears pinned back against their heads, their eyes wild. Boadicea stands, arms raised in victory, the fine fabric of her dress pressed back against her body by the onrushing wind. Her daughters lean to each side of her. Scythes flail from her

wheelhubs. The gold-lettered inscription on the plinth is from William Cowper's poem 'Boadicea: An Ode', which was written in 1780.

> Regions Caesar never knew
>   Thy posterity shall sway,
> Where his eagles never flew,
>   None invincible as they.

It is a fascinating harnessing of an earlier text. The statue itself is a not-very-occluded reference to Queen Victoria (an association aided by the fact that Boudica's name is derived from the Celtic word for 'victory'). The co-opting of the lines, in the context of the sculpture, is clear: they vatically proclaim that the Romans may have had a great empire, but Victoria's is greater still. Boudica is harnessed as a kind of ancestor figure for the later queen and empress. But she is a puzzling, troubling model: for after all, like Caratacus, she was on the losing side.

Cowper's poem is set just after Boudica's flogging: she is 'bleeding from the Roman rods'. She seeks counsel from a Druid, 'sage beneath a spreading oak', who foretells the destruction of Rome: 'Rome shall perish – write that word/ In the blood that she has spilt.' But at length,

> Other Romans shall arise,
> Heedless of a soldier's name;
> Sounds, not arms, shall win the prize
> Harmony the path to fame.

These 'other Romans', these Britons, are a progeny sprung 'from the forests of our land'. As for Elgar and his Caractacus, it is the British woodlands that are the womb and nursery for this new people. They shall be greater than the Romans: 'they shall a wider world command'.

The poetic model for this Druidic foretelling is the prophecy of Rome's future greatness in Virgil's *Aeneid* – just as it is for the final chorus of Elgar's *Caractacus*. In the sixth book of the *Aeneid*, the hero – Aeneas, another warrior from the deep past on the losing side, fleeing Troy after its sack by the Greeks – descends to the Underworld. Here he encounters his father, Anchises, among the shades of the dead. Anchises maps out the future for Aeneas's descendants, right up to Virgil's present. A great city will be founded; a great empire will grow. 'Remember,' says Anchises, 'it is for you to rule over nations with your power. These will be your arts, to impose law on peace, to spare the conquered and to war down the proud.'

The layering of time in the Virgil, and in the Cowper, and in the Cowper as recycled on to the Thornycroft sculpture, and in the Elgar–Acworth, seems to revolve in my mind. Magnificent destinies are foretold by poets and artists ventriloquising imagined figures from the deep past. The poems of great lost empires are plundered to make poems on great future empires. The stratified layers of time seem to have come loose, to have clashed and mingled. And these empires – the Roman, the British – have passed away.

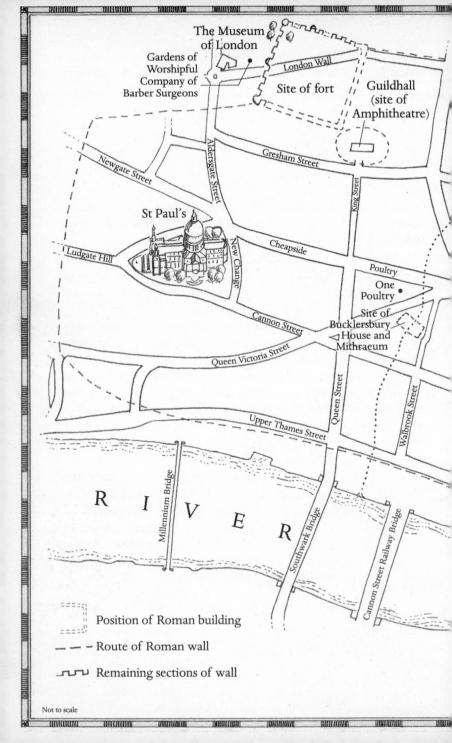

The Museum
of London

Gardens of
Worshipful
Company of
Barber Surgeons

London Wall

Site of fort

Guildhall
(site of
Amphitheatre)

Gresham Street

Newgate Street

Aldersgate Street

St Paul's

New Change

Cheapside

King Street

Ludgate Hill

Poultry

One
Poultry

Site of
Bucklersbury
House and
Mithraeum

Cannon Street

Queen Victoria Street

Queen Street

Walbrook Street

Upper Thames Street

R I V E R

Millennium Bridge

Southwark Bridge

Cannon Street Railway Bridge

Position of Roman building

Route of Roman wall

Remaining sections of wall

Not to scale

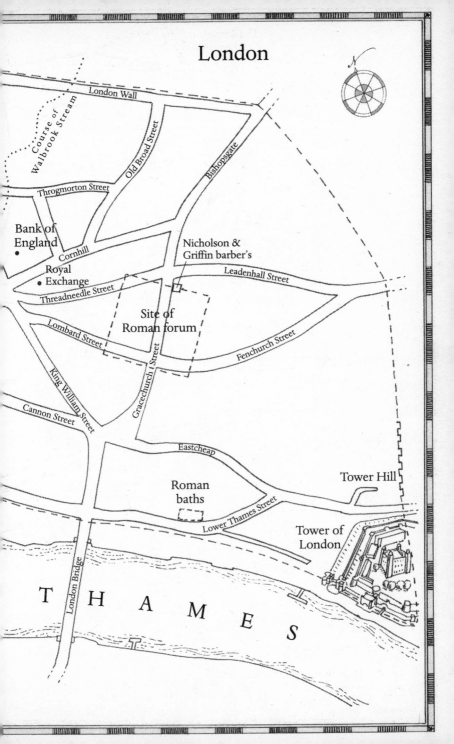

3

London

Tot campos, Sylvas, tot regia tecta, tot hortos
Artifici destra excultos, tot vidimus arces,
Ut nunc Ausonio Tamisis cum Tybride certet.

(So many fields and pleasant woods, so many princely Bowres,
And Palaces we saw besides, so many stately towres,
So many gardens trimly dressed by curious hand which are,
That now with Romane Tyberis the Tamis may well compare.)

William Camden, 1607

Very soon trees will be thrusting through the empty window sockets,
the rose-bay and fennel blossoming within the broken walls, the brambles tangling outside them. Very soon the ruin will be enjungled,
engulfed . . .

Rose Macaulay, 1953

Unlike Rome, where antique, medieval, Renaissance and modern buildings jostle each other, where past and present are in energetic, fractious
conversation, Roman Londinium lies buried beneath modern London.
The borders of Londinium still, more or less, mark the borders of the
City of London, because the Roman walls became the medieval city's
boundaries, entered and exited by those long-perished portals that have
a ghostly presence through their medieval names: Cripplegate, Newgate,
Aldersgate, Bishopsgate, Aldgate, Ludgate. All these were Roman gates;
only the seventh, Moorgate, was a medieval newcomer. The Thames
– wider then than it is now – was crossed almost exactly where our
London Bridge is, over to marshy, island-dotted Southwark with its
mudflats and creeks, its gardens and baths and inns.

Londinium lies between six and eight metres below London. In Naples, you can take tours to 'Napoli Sotterranea', underground Naples. You can climb down steps under a church, and be in the Roman streets. Or wander through the Greek city, older still, which was once the new city, the *'nea polis'*. You cannot 'be' in Londinium, though you can, if you are persistent, seek it out and glimpse it in the crypt of a church, in the cellar of a shop, in an underground car park, behind a locked door in an office basement. If Londinium is the city's dark ancestral place, its unconscious, then it is, for the most part, occluded. It is in the City's nature to prefer the bright, sunlit, angular surface of things, the hard edges of its supermodern architecture with its false promise of prosperity. Why would you want to go down there, to the dank, dark places of the imagination? To the past? The *katabasis* – the Greeks' 'going-down', the descent to the Underworld, is a dangerous journey. You might not return with what you set out to find.

Londinium was probably a Roman creation, built at the first bridgeable part of the Thames that could also be used as a port, in the years following Claudius's conquest. The Romans were punctilious about assigning different categories to towns, depending on their administrative functions. No one knows for sure precisely what category Londinium was, but it became, de facto, the principal city of Britannia, *'copia negotiatorum et commeatuum maxime celebre'*, extremely famous for its many traders and goods, according to Tacitus. There are plenty of signs of life before the Romans – just no town, no great Iron Age settlement as at Colchester. In the British Museum there is, for example, an Iron Age artefact known as the 'Battersea shield', a shining sheet of bronze with whorls of raised decoration, studded with scarlet enamel. Like other ancient objects in the museum, the shield came from the Thames – perhaps because it was placed there, or flung there, to fulfil some unknown religious impulse. The waters are full of ancient things: in the long-ago culverted Walbrook Stream – whose course is marked by the street named for it, running from Bank to the Thames, and whose shores were lined with shrines and workshops in its Roman heyday – the archaeologist Augustus Pitt-Rivers found numerous human skulls in the late nineteenth century. He thought they might be the heads of Romans massacred by Boudica. In the twelfth century, Geoffrey of Monmouth seemed to know about the heads: he fashioned a tale about a Roman legion whose soldiers were decapitated by a besieging British army, their heads flung into a stream called by the Saxons 'Galobroc'. Archaeologists now speculate they were placed there by Britons for some ritual purpose. For Geoffrey, London was the town founded by Brutus: it was Troynovant, or Trinovantum, the new Troy – later to be renamed Lud's Town, and so London.

The first notable event in the history of Londinium was its destruction. The name of the city first appears on the page in Tacitus's account of the rebellion of Boudica. There is a line of black in the archaeological layers that is said to be the charred matter from her flaming of the fledgling city. That was the first great fire of London. The second – another layer of black – came in about AD 120. The third was in 1666. The fourth, 1940–1, was the Blitz.

For centuries, people have speculated about where Suetonius Paulinus finally defeated Boudica, after he took the tactical decision to abandon Londinium. There is no evidence; but there has always been plenty of fantasy. John Nelson, in his 1811 history of the parish of St Mary, Islington, wrote that Battle Bridge – now called King's Cross – 'is supposed to have been so called from its contiguity to the spot where the celebrated battle was fought'. He added: 'The opinion that the scene of this dreadful conflict was not far distant from this spot, is further strengthened, by some considerable remains of an encampment, which may yet be seen in the neighbourhood, and which exhibits sufficient evidence that the situation was an important military post.' Nelson's 'Roman camp' was in Reed Moat Field, which became Barnsbury Square a decade or so later when the area was developed.

I live within sight of the square. It is no longer thought to be an old Roman camp, but rather the site of a moated medieval manor house. When I cycle to King's Cross, to the office where I work, or to the British Library, I follow this mythical route of Suetonius Paulinus. I pass through the 'camp', and as I speed down the long hill of Copenhagen Street, I pass a turning to Boadicea Street. In the office, I sit at a desk overlooking a canal basin that remembers the old name for King's Cross: Battle Bridge Basin. There is a persistent myth that Boudica is buried beneath platform eight of King's Cross railway station. None of this has the least foundation, but I enjoy the accretion of story – like a thickening in the air. In the early nineteenth century, industrial, filthy Battle Bridge was notorious as a haunt of low-lifes and criminals. And so, when the area was redeveloped in 1830, in an attempt to banish all the unpleasant associations of the past it was renamed King's Cross, after 'a ridiculous octagonal structure crowned by an absurd statue of George IV', according to Walter Thornbury's 1878 history, *Old and New London*. That structure – which at various times contained a police station and a public house – was pulled down in 1845, and so there is no longer a king's cross at King's Cross. I prefer one of the other names that was mooted in 1830 and discarded: Boadicea's Cross.

If Londinium was burned almost at its birth, it now reveals itself only through London's destruction. When Christopher Wren set to work remodelling the City – which had been rendered, as he put it, a 'great Plain of Ashes and ruins' by the 1666 fire – he found a number of Roman remains, including 'the most remarkable Roman Urns, Lamps, Lacrymatories and Fragments of Sacrificing-vessels, &c' near Cheapside. When he was working near Ludgate, a tombstone set up to one Vivius Marcianus by his wife Januaria Martina was dug up: it can now be seen in the Museum of London. On the site of St Paul's, according to his son's memoir, Wren found 'to his Surprise . . . a Roman Causeway of rough Stone . . . He concluded then to lay the Foundation of the Tower upon the very Roman Causeway, as most proper to bear what he had design'd, a weighty and lofty Structure'. He searched in vain for the temple to Diana, or Apollo, that reputedly lay beneath the burned-out ruins of the old St Paul's. 'Having rummaged all the Ground thereabouts, and being very desirous to find some Footsteps of such a Temple, I could not discover any,' he wrote.

Wren wanted to build a rational city, in spirit like the regularly gridded Londinium: he envisaged a central piazza radiating streets like a sunburst, with the Exchange at its centre, 'the Building to be contriv'd after the Form of the Roman Forum, with double Porticos'. But he was thwarted by 'the obstinate Averseness of a great Part of the Citizens to alter their old Properties'. Not for the first time, London resisted rationalisation: no new Rome was to be built here. Even on Roman Londinium's grid, laid out with sergeant-majorish precision, archaeologists have found the foundations of British roundhouses. Not everyone, it seems, wanted flat-fronted. As Nikolaus Pevsner wrote in his 1957 architectural guide to the cities of London and Westminster, the City's keynotes were, and remain, 'ever-recurring contrasts of tall and low, of large and small, of wide and narrow, of straight and crooked, the closes and retreats and odd leafy corners'. At least the improving Wren was allowed to build St Paul's, he said, 'after a good Roman manner'.

There is a map of Londinium, published by the Museum of London. The Roman city's streets and buildings are all marked, as far as they are known, which is incompletely. Roman towns are predictable. From Spain to Syria they came with a more or less full complement of forum, basilica, baths, amphitheatre, theatre. When Londinium's amphitheatre was discovered under the Guildhall in 1988, the surprise was that it had been located, not that Londinium turned out to have had one. On the map of Londinium there are large gaps. But you can be sure there are Roman things in these lacunae, perhaps tunnelled through by sewers or Tube lines, or crushed out of existence by London's foundations, rooting down. Or perhaps still intact, waiting to be discovered by some fracture of the city's surface. On the museum's map, Londinium is shown in solid black lines. It is modern London that is rendered as a faint grey shadow, behind. Looking at it, I have the impression that the Roman city has risen up to the surface and engulfed our own.

I started out at the museum. My reading of the map was complicated further by Chamberlin, Powell and Bon's post-war architecture for the Barbican, in the purlieus of which the museum stands. The architects' vision was for a multi-level city, with gardens and walkways that ran above the streets. So I was now hovering on a raised path – Bastion Highwalk – above both London and Londinium. From here, I could see the line of the Roman city wall marked by the medieval brick bastions in the gardens below the Barbican. And on the other side of the Highwalk, I could see, marching down Noble Street, craned over by post-war blocks, the Roman wall itself – or, rather, a medieval wall that is Roman at its base. It was revealed when a great slice of the city, from here down to the Thames and east of St Paul's, was destroyed by the bombs of the Blitz. In her memoir, *Jacaranda, Oleander*, the novelist Penelope Lively recalled a happy childhood in Egypt that came to an end with the war and a return to England. One day a family friend took her to see the blitzed City. 'The effect was not one of destruction but of tranquil decay, like some ruined site of antiquity,' she wrote. I imagine them looking at their map, wondering at how little it resembled what they saw in front of them; like my plan of Londinium, it was a map of the past. Then he showed her a bastion of the Roman wall. She was amazed: she knew about the Romans, they were in Egypt, but 'how could there be Romans right up here, in England?' All of a sudden, she wrote, 'amid the wreckage of London and the seething spires of willowherb', there seemed to be a 'sense of relevances and connections which were mysterious, intriguing and could perhaps be exposed'. The City's deconstruction, the revelation of its secret parts, became a personal metaphor: 'It was as though the exposure of the chunk of wall had also shown up concealed possibilities. I sniffed the liberations of maturity, and grew up a little more . . .'

She was not the only writer to be struck by London's appearance of antique decay after the Blitz. Rose Macaulay, in a postscript to her 1953 book *The Pleasure of Ruins*, wrote vividly of 'the new ruins', summoning up 'the lane of tangled briars that was a street of warehouses'; the 'jungled caverns' where 'stood a large tailor's shop . . . Tomorrow or tonight, the gazers feel, their own dwelling may be even as this.' The fronds and branches of untameable vegetation are simply waiting their chance, biding their time: they will take over, in the end.

I went down to street level, opposite the glass-and-steel of 88 Wood Street, a Richard Rogers building, which, with its blue-and-red funnels emerging from the pavement in front of it, resembled an ocean liner. Following a sign to the Museum of London's goods entrance, I descended a ramp, which took me below street level, to the medieval bastions. Here was the entrance to an underground car park, where there is another chunk of the Roman wall, exposed during the bombing and preserved by the Corporation of London. As I entered, the attendant gazed at me glassily, as if, like Charon, he expected a coin. The chunk of wall is parked in bay 52, next to the motorbikes and scooters, past the BMWs and the Mercs of the City workers. It stands two and a half metres tall, and is thickly made from Kentish ragstone, sliced through with three layers of tile courses. I was beset by the headachey smell of old petrol. Every few seconds came a sound as of a blasting wind: a heavy vehicle passing overhead. I ascended gratefully, not looking back. By the entrance, through a forbidding metal door marked 'Private', there are the remains of an early-second-century fort gate. Once in a while, the Museum of London organises viewings. Otherwise, you would never know it was there.

I climbed back up on to the Highwalk and this time went on into St Alphage Gardens: a knot garden of bloomless wintry roses and beeches bristling with dead foliage. This – one of Pevsner's 'odd leafy corners' – had been created by the bombs, and through it runs another chunk of the wall. You can read its history in the stone and brick: it is Roman at the base and medieval at the top, the brick battlements built when it was restored during the Wars of the Roses. Behind are the ruins of the medieval tower of St Alphage Church, bombed. To read the 1957 London Pevsner is to read a war memorial (restrained, taxonomical) for the city churches. St Alban, Wood Street: 'a grievous war loss'. St Augustine, Watling Street: 'The graceful lead spire of 1695 is destroyed.' St Lawrence Jewry: 'burnt out. The glorious woodwork is all perished.' St Nicholas Cole Abbey: 'Burnt out and now standing surrounded by devastation.' St Swithin, Cannon Street: 'burnt out'. Dutch Church: 'destroyed by a direct hit'. Many of the losses were Wren churches. The City of London had been reduced once more to a 'great Plain of Ashes and ruins'. Later, in the British Library, I leafed through a Corporation of London report produced just after the war. There was page after page of photographs of the shattered city. Sometimes a lonely classical column, perhaps from one of Wren's churches, still stood amid the rubble.

I descended from the heights and entered the yard of the Guildhall, the headquarters of the Corporation of London. In the paving on the ground was picked out a wide circle in dark-coloured tiles. It marked the outline of the ancient amphitheatre, which was discovered when the Guildhall Art Gallery was being built to replace its bombed prede-cessor. Go into the art gallery and head downstairs, beneath the Rossettis, the Alma Tademas, and the bronze head of the young Prince Charles, and you can enter the east gate of the amphitheatre, with its walls still there – low, but legible. It was built around AD 70: a timber drain was dated using the technique of dendrochronology, in which tree rings are counted to determine the precise year the tree was felled. It was rebuilt in stone about AD 120, perhaps to coincide with the visit of the architecture- and engineering-loving Emperor Hadrian to Britannia. The stone amphitheatre was embellished with Egyptian marble, its walls lined with painted plaster. The excavators found the traces of what could have been trapdoors, lifted to let animals into the arena – perhaps wolves, bears or boars. In the amphi-theatre's drains were excavated a gold-and-pearl necklace clasp, coins, a hairpin: the curious archaeological business of finding lost property that has outlived its owners by millennia. One day I watched modern performers re-enact gladiatorial games in the Guildhall yard. It was skilfully done, and jovial: the master of ceremonies threatened to drag into the arena anyone whose mobile phone rang. We in the audience gamely spread our hands wide to indicate mercy, or clenched our fists and extended our thumbs to communicate 'death' (a system regarded as more historically authentic than the Hollywood thumbs-up, thumbs-down routine). The fighter I liked the best called herself Achillea: in real life she was an art and design teacher in a secondary school. She found beating her husband in single combat, she told me, 'a great stress-buster'.

From the Guildhall, I walked down Gresham Street to Bank. Here once stood what was arguably Sir John Soane's masterpiece, the Bank of England. In the 1930s, it was drastically remodelled. This repre-sented, according to Pevsner, the City's most egregious architectural loss, Blitz notwithstanding. During the work, Roman mosaics were found nearly eight metres below the ground. One can be seen in the

bank's museum, and the other is viewable by appointment, preserved where it was discovered. I followed a uniformed attendant as she walked me through marble-floored corridors and down a great canti-levered staircase into the bowels of the building. I joked that we must be near the vaults – she inclined her head seriously, to suggest that that was indeed precisely where we were. The mosaic was right at the bottom of the staircase, a simple but attractive guilloche design with a labyrinthine border. I thought of poor Soane. In the museum were drawings of the bank being eviscerated during the pre-war rebuilding work. The curious paintings Soane commissioned from his pupil Joseph Michael Gandy, envisioning it as a classical ruin in some long-distant future, had been prophetic.

I left the bank and crossed over to James Stirling's postmodern ark of a building, 1 Poultry. When it was being built, in 1994, archaeolo-gists found a writing tablet. The wax covering the 'page' of silver fir, preserved by the damp of the nearby Walbrook Stream, had nearly worn away, but the stylus had scratched through the wax, leaving faint marks on the wood. Dr Roger Tomlin, a papyrologist at the University of Oxford, was with difficulty able to decipher them. It was a legal document: a deed of sale for a slave called Fortunata (or 'Lucky'), a woman of an obscure Gaulish tribe. She was being sold to Vegetus, 'the slave of Montanus the slave of the August Emperor and sometime assistant slave of Secundus'. Montanus, in the service of the emperor, might have been a figure in the financial administration of the province. Roman slaves such as he – bureaucrats in the imperial service – could easily have owned slaves of their own. Fortunata was 'guaranteed healthy, and warranted not to be liable to wander or run away'.

I emerged from Poultry on to Queen Victoria Street. It was between these two roads that the Bucklersbury mosaic was revealed in 1869 – an endlessly sinuous combination of strict geometry and trailing, stylised foliage that is now on display in the Museum of London. A picture in the *Illustrated London News* of the time shows ladies and gentlemen, all crinolines and toppers, being shepherded by bobbies as they queued up to look at it. Until recently, you could see the London Mithraeum here too. When it was excavated in 1954, and identified as a temple by the archaeologist W. F. Grimes, 'only a mild interest was taken', recalled Ralph Merrifield in his 1968 book *Roman London*. It was the discovery of a delicately carved marble head of Mithras that changed everything. The 'unveiling of an ancient mystery cult in the workaday world of the City seemed to touch a chord of imagination and romanticism', he wrote. Sixty thousand people came to see the new discovery over three days. Public opinion wanted it preserved and displayed. But building work on the new Legal and General building, Bucklersbury House, was about to start, right on top of the excavations. To replan the arrangement of somewhat featureless, but essentially pleasing modernist slabs would have cost £300,000 – no small sum in 1950s austerity Britain. So the temple of Mithras was moved, wholesale (though not with great accuracy or precision) to the Queen Victoria Street side of the new building, where it sat for half a century in a forecourt between the blocks, a slightly gloomy and unexciting ruin: a rectangle of squat grey walls, apsidal at one end, all encased in concrete. It was quite hard to imagine it serving as the temple for a men's mystery cult, its barrel-vaulted ceiling deliberately low, the room cavelike and dark, the benches lining its nave thickly packed with men enacting scenes of Persian-inspired ritual.

Bucklersbury House is no longer there; it was pulled down in 2011. On my visit in the chill January of 2012, I was stopped short by the new gaping space, the unexpected view of sky and steeples. The Mithraeum was no longer to be seen. The life cycles of this constantly self-destroying, self-renewing city are shrinking: it is now the turn of the post-Blitz buildings to be flattened and replaced. Norman Foster is the architect for the next iteration of Bucklersbury House, this time to be called Walbrook Square. The Mithraeum is to be moved – again – and displayed in the new development.

The fortunes of Londinium's remains are inextricably linked with the economic fortunes of the City of London. When the property market sinks, Londinium is more likely to lie undisturbed. When it booms, the archaeologists move in, ahead of the builders. One day, Roy Stephenson, the head of archaeological collections at the Museum of London, took me to the museum's store and study collection in Shoreditch: the home of the less glamorous, less attractive cousins of the objects on public display. Inside, it was dark and almost window-less. The occasional shaft of light illuminated researchers rustling about among the lines of shelving. You could find bricks here that had been charred by the Great Fire; but we turned to the Roman section. Here were 150,000 archive boxes containing the relics and shards of Roman London, stacked on ten kilometres of shelves. They were blandly labelled ('bone'; 'tile') and arranged according to their year of discovery. You could read London's boom and bust in these boxes. For overblown 1988, I counted twenty-two shelves of finds; for 1989, the year of the crash, fourteen; for recessionary 1990, six, for 1991, two and a half.

Perhaps, though, I was being sentimental about Bucklersbury House. Londinium, no less than London, could be cavalier about the past. Romans inscribed their deaths and their reverence to the gods in stone, and we expect with that monumentality to come permanence. But Romans pulled down Roman monuments and did what they liked with them. Christopher Wren's tombstone to Vivius Marcianus had been built into the Roman city wall at Ludgate. Another memorial sculpture in the Museum of London shows a man wearing a sword and cloak, holding a set of writing tablets – presumably a military man seconded into administrative work for the governor. His tomb was recycled into a tower wall at Camomile Street, up near Bishopsgate.

The break-up and reuse of monuments has set numerous puzzles for antiquaries. Charles Roach Smith is one of the most intriguing figures in the history of Londinium's rediscovery. He was a pharmacist who kept a shop on Lothbury, near the Bank of England. His chief

delight was to range over the City's building sites, picking up antiquities from the construction workers employed in building London's
sewers in the 1830s and 40s. It must have been a useful source of extra
income for the navvies, some of whom must surely have developed
an 'eye' for coins or Samian ware. His diaries show the level of his
commitment: for his entry of 28 June 1838, he briefly noted that today
was 'the Coronation of Victoria'. But he was more interested in his
visit to Leadenhall Street. 'Fragments of Samian Pottery . . . were
lying about and the men told me some good things had been found
there,' he wrote. 'On my return found that in Bartholomew Lane a
fine tessellated pavement had been found about 15 feet deep, and
broken up by the workmen . . .' He fought a long and difficult battle
with the Corporation of London, condemning its indifference to the
antique city that was being broken up so carelessly, without any
attempts at preservation or even record-keeping. His diary entry for
13 December 1838 railed against 'the great want of energy in the society
in regard to their obtaining correct . . . information on discoveries
made in various parts of the kingdom which . . . are too often suffered
to remain unrecorded'. Londoners were so transfixed by the quotidian
demands of profit and loss, he lamented in his 1859 book *Illustrations
of Roman London*, that they were blind to their own history. In
describing a portion of the Roman wall at Tower Hill, he adopted a
typically mournful tone. 'Although the wall was . . . saved from immi-
nent destruction, it could not be preserved from the effects of the
prevailing spirit of the day, which cannot recognise the utility of
ancient monuments except in the ration of their applicability to the
necessities of trade, and the common, practical purposes of life; and
the wall is now a side wall for stables and out-houses, and, of course,
is hidden from public view.'

There is still a length of wall at Tower Hill, and Roach Smith might
be pleased to see that it is no longer crowded in by 'stables and out-
houses', but stands in its own patch of garden, through which the
City workers hurry on their way to the Tube. It was at Tower Hill,
in 1852, that Roach Smith made one of his most significant discoveries:
a tombstone built up into a bastion of the city wall. It is now in the
British Museum. With it, he recalled in *Illustrations of Roman London*,
were 'a great number of broken cornices, shafts of columns, and
foundation stones of a building or buildings of magnitude'. The slab

was inscribed with the words '(D)IS MANIBUS FAB(I) ALPINI CLASSICIANI'. Interpreting fragmentary inscriptions can be a difficult business. The first part was all right: 'dis manibus' means 'to the shades of the dead', indicating that it was indeed a tombstone. The next bit looked easy enough, too: the genitive case of what was clearly a name. And not any name, but Classicianus – a figure actually mentioned by Tacitus in his *Annals*. Gaius Julius Alpinus Classicianus was the Gaulish procurator of the province of Britannia immediately after Boudica's revolt – brought in to replace the hapless official who had fled in the thick of the violence.

It must have been an extraordinary moment for Roach Smith when he recognised the name, enabling him to line up archaeological and historiographical evidence in a rare, and thus no doubt extremely satisfying, way. Perhaps it is just as well, then, that by 1928 – after a retirement writing treatises on pomology among his beloved Kentish orchards – he was long dead. For that year, R. G. Collingwood, one of the great historians of Roman Britain, as well as one of the most significant philosophers of his day, flattened Roach Smith's hypothesis, writing that 'Roach was obviously wrong to think of connecting [the figure in the inscription] with Julius Classicianus in Tacitus, *Annals* XIV, 38.' He instead conjectured that the inscription might have something to do with the word '*classis*', fleet – it could mean 'Fabius Alpinus, formerly of the navy'. Perhaps he believed that the connection with Classicianus was simply too good to be true. So the matter rested until 1935, when the missing chunk of the monument was found during the construction of an electricity substation, also at Tower Hill. The extra jigsaw piece added the crucial words 'procurator of the province of Britain', and the information that his wife Julia Pacata Indiana, a Gaul from an important tribe, had erected the tomb in his honour. Roach Smith had been right after all.

From the Mithraeum, I turned to walk down Walbrook and reached Cannon Street, where I found the object known as the London Stone, set into the facade of a boarded-up 1960s office block. Underneath the modern railway station, on the other side of the road, impressive Roman buildings once stood, perhaps offices for the provincial or city administration. One theory, first propounded by Wren, is that the London Stone is a remnant of these buildings. At any rate, it is an object to which many myths cling (such as the fantasy that it was a

Druid's sacrificial altar, as in Blake's 'They groan'd aloud on London Stone'; or even that it is the boulder into which King Arthur's sword was once plunged). Camden thought it might have been a Roman milestone, marking distances to other parts of the province, 'considering it is in the very mids of the City'. In the nineteenth century, it was moved from an inconvenient spot in the middle of Cannon Street into the wall of Wren's St Swithin's Church. And when St Swithin's went in the Blitz, the stone was moved again to its new home. When I visited it, it was surrounded in its niche by fag ends and discarded train tickets, and what seemed to be grains of wheat and a couple of almonds (as if in obscure offering). It was awaiting more glamorous quarters: there were plans to display it with the Mithraeum in the new Walbrook Square building, though what sense anyone would make of this obscure chunk of rock, I couldn't tell.

At any rate, I felt self-conscious as I squatted in the street to examine the London Stone, and so I continued along Cannon Street and turned left up Gracechurch Street, which, as it becomes Bishopsgate, then Shoreditch High Street, and then Kingsland Road, is really the beginning of Ermine Street, which would take you all the way to York if you kept going. But more immediately, Londinium's forum stood exactly in my path. The point where Fenchurch Street crosses Gracechurch Street marks, more or less, the southern edge of Londinium's forum; the crossing with Cornhill its northern boundary. It was vast: 170 square metres (each side just short of the length of St Paul's). A three-storey basilica, holding law courts and the city's senate, ran the length of the forum's north side. It was the biggest building this side of the Alps: its nave was 100 metres long. It is shiveringly hard to conceive of anything so grandiloquent in this patch of the city, even as Richard Rogers's Lloyd's building looms down, just beyond the old forum's north-east corner. Now, the only thing that can be seen of it is in the basement of Nicholson & Griffin, a barber's at 90 Leadenhall. When I visited, the place was deserted but for a group of cheerful hairdressers folding towels. One of them was on the phone discussing hair dye. Another moved a few handbags so that I could sidle up to a glazed wall, through which I squinted to see one of the pier bases of the old basilica. It was hard to make anything of it: it was as if a cathedral had been reduced to a garden wall.

I headed down to Lower Thames Street, the north side of which marks the Roman shoreline, though there's another block to go before you reach the modern riverside. The Romans themselves started inadvertently to narrow the Thames. As they built up their wharves and revetments, the banks gradually silted up, moving the land outwards. A clue to the original whereabouts of the water's edge is the sharp slope of the little street called St Mary-at-Hill – the top of the steep ancient riverbank. Nearby, under a 1980s office block called Centurion House, was excavated a timber wall and riverside warehouses with their wooden shuttering intact.

On the corner of St Mary-at-Hill and Lower Thames Street is Centennium House, another City office block with a cod-classical name. In its southern frontage there is an unmarked opaque-glass sliding door. Here I met Jenny Hall, the now retired curator of Roman antiquities at the Museum of London. She unlocked it; behind was a second portal, more utilitarian, with signs forbidding smoking and warning of trip hazards. We stepped through and entered a kind of bunker with bare breeze blocks for walls and a large poster describing the necessary first aid after an injury to the eyes. There was a staircase leading downstairs. 'Let's make plenty of noise to scare away any other visitors,' said Hall; it was a minute before I realised she meant rats. At the bottom, fluorescent strip lighting flickered into life and we saw London's best-preserved Roman remains – the fragments of a luxurious waterfront villa and bathhouse. Hall said they were a miraculous survival – extraordinary that the builders who stumbled on them thought to preserve them, forty years before they were formally protected under the first Ancient Monuments Act of 1882.

Hall showed me the walls of an east and north wing of a dwelling, and between them, a suite of baths. Its entranceway was flanked by two semicircular rooms for warm and hot bathing, with the little pilae stacks that give away the presence of underfloor heating. In one corner a portion of the floor itself survived: hefty terracotta tiles that might have been overlaid with an elegant mosaic. From the baths' entrance, a few steps lead down to a frigidarium, or cold room. The house gave right on to the river; Hall said she believed it was either a luxurious private home, or an inn with bathing facilities for riverborne travellers. Despite their wonderful legibility and good state of preservation, these

ruins are not open to public view, except on special open days organised by the Museum of London.

The house was built in the late second century and the baths added
in the third; but at some point later the north wing collapsed and
became a waste ground, covered, said Hall, in brambles, and inhabited
by frogs, mice and snails. The east wing and the baths continued in
use; and over 200 coins dated AD 388 and later were discovered in the
furnace room, as well as late Roman glass and an amphora from
Palestine. These were the very dying years of Roman rule in Britain:
had the coins been hidden against future collection? Offered to some
god? Already, by this time, great swathes of Londinium were abandoned. There is a strip of loam in the archaeological layers, which
some scholars believe means this now-vacant land was cultivated, by
its later Roman inhabitants, as market gardens. Others believe the
land became waste ground, and simply gave in to rot and decay: grass,
brambles, weeds and scrub making their final, inevitable conquest of
the ruins. This layer of soil is called by archaeologists 'dark earth'.

After the end of Roman rule in AD 408, Londinium, it is thought,
was completely abandoned. When, later in the century, Anglo-Saxon
settlements sprang up, they were dotted around the edges of the city,
not inside it, in what are now London suburbs: Croydon, Battersea,
Tulse Hill, Kingston, Upper Norwood. The Saxons established a port
where the Royal Opera House now stands: but that was away to the
west. It was only 400 years later, in the late ninth century, that Alfred
the Great moved into the old city and made it his capital, taking
advantage of its still-standing walls as a defence against the Vikings.

I think of Richard Jefferies' novel of 1885, *After London*, which
imagines a future Britain after some nameless disaster has depleted
its population. London is contaminated and uninhabitable. Scrub and
forest have greedily devoured the once cultivated countryside, so that
it is a land of frightening, impenetrable forests. What remains of
civilisation has lapsed into feudalism. Jefferies' hero, Felix, ventures
forth to a 'dreadful place, of which he had heard many a tradition':
the 'deserted and utterly extinct city of London'.

Jefferies writes: 'For this marvellous city, of which such legends are
related, was after all only of brick, and when the ivy grew over and
shrubs sprang up, and, lastly, the waters underneath burst in, this huge
metropolis was soon overthrown.'

In around AD 450, half a century after the end of Londinium, someone had reason to walk over what is now Lower Thames Street, picking a path through the treacherous, collapsing old buildings and the undergrowth – an adventurer, like Jefferies' Felix, in a lost city. Who was it? I want it to be a woman. So let it be a woman; a woman from over the German sea. Who knows what brought her here. Whatever she sought, she also lost something: a Saxon brooch was dropped here, among the fallen roof tiles, among the shards of other lives.

4

Silchester

Heu Veii veteres! et vos tum regna fuistis,
et vestro posita est aurea sella foro:
nunc intra muros pastoris bucina lenti
cantat, et in vestris ossibus arva metunt.

(Alas, ancient Veii! You too were a kingdom once, and a golden throne
was placed in your forum: now within your walls sounds the horn of
an unhurried shepherd, and over your bones they gather the harvest.)

Propertius, *c.* 14 BC

Like the medieval city of Dunwich, which the North Sea claimed
from the Suffolk coast and whose ghostly submerged church bells are
still said to ring, Roman Silchester is a lost town, buried not by the
grey eastern waves but by soil and an ocean of tall grass, through
which the wind sings and sighs. Near Reading and Basingstoke, and
a few miles from Aldermaston and the forbidding triple-fenced enclo-
sures of the Atomic Weapons Establishment, Silchester hardly promises beauty or isolation by way of its setting. Yet it is tucked away at
the heart of a deep labyrinth of narrow, high-hedged lanes that seem
to stretch away to infinity when you are caught in their pleasant wind-
ings. To be here in midsummer is to witness the absolute triumph of
nature over street and stone. The air is sickly-sharp with the scent of
elderflower. Goldfinches stream brightly between hedgerows; swallows foregather on a wire; and high above, higher and higher, the
singing specks in the sky are larks.

Merely finding Roman Silchester feels like unlocking a charm. Roger
Wilson's *Guide to the Roman Remains in Britain* grumbles that it is ill-
signposted – which it is, and as the camper van nosed its trundling

way through the lanes, my head was buried in the map. We asked directions from the man who had come to empty the bins in the little public car park; he appeared to gesture all around. This seemed to be the typical experience of entering Silchester. When one Norris Brewer wrote up his trip here for the *Monthly Magazine* in 1810, he recalled: 'I trod, with increasing ardor, and believed the object of our expedition yet distant, when my companion suddenly arrested my progress, by exclaiming: "We are there!"' And when John Plummer and George Nelson visited in 1879, compiling a pamphlet optimistically entitled *Silchester: the Pompeii of Hampshire*, the same happened to them. 'We wind our way through a succession of those lovely lanes which are so peculiarly the charm of our English land . . . and we wonder where the famous "city" which we have come so far to see, is to be found. We hail a country lad, who is engaged in agricultural pursuits, upon the other side of a hedge, and who, in answer to our question, "When shall we get to the 'city'", replies briefly, but very much to the purpose, "You be there now."'

If Silchester is now an invisible city, as Calleva Atrebatum it was once one of the most important towns in Britain. Roads sprung off it: from here you were connected directly to London, Chichester, Winchester, Bath, Cirencester, Dorchester. Before the Romans, it was the tribal capital of the Atrebates; traces of its Iron Age defensive ditches can still be seen if you peer through the undergrowth in the right places. The earliest coins found here are marked to 'Eppillus rex', king, with the mark CALLE or CALLEV. He is described as the son of Commius, known in Julius Caesar's *Commentaries* as a Gaulish leader who left his native territories for Britain in the 50s BC, after rebelling against Caesar. The current archaeology takes Calleva's origins back only to the 20s BC – but it is speculated that Commius may have been the original founder of the town, some thirty years earlier.

Excavations at Silchester are now reaching deeper and deeper into the pre-conquest town: in the summer of 2011, an olive stone was found in these Iron Age layers, suggesting that its inhabitants had Mediterranean tastes well before Claudius came to Britain with his elephants. (A weakness for effete foreign snacks is perhaps not quite what we might expect from the Iron Age Britons – but then, if we think of them as sturdy, hardy and simple in their tastes, the Romans are at least partly responsible for that. Cassius Dio, in the speech he has Boudica give to her troops, contrasts the sophisticated gastronomy of the Romans with the frugal food of the Britons: 'They need bread and wine and oil, and if any of these things fails them, they die. For us, on the other hand, any grass or root serves as bread, the juice of any plant as oil, any water as wine.')

After the invading general Aulus Plautius took the south-east, the future emperor Vespasian probably forged west this way, presumably with naval vessels shadowing his progress along the south coast, for he is said by Tacitus to have taken the Isle of Wight, as well as twenty hill forts. The Roman town eventually built here to replace its Iron Age predecessor had fine walls, a primly angular gridded street plan, a forum with a stone basilica twenty metres tall, baths, inns, temples: the whole busy thrum of Roman town life. In the *Agricola*, Tacitus wrote in his typically barbed way of the policy of transforming Britons into good Romans. 'Agricola gave private encouragement and public help to the building of temples, forums and houses, praising the energetic, and criticising the idle. And so compulsion was replaced by an honourable rivalry. He also provided an education in the liberal arts for the sons of the chiefs, and showed such a preference for the talents of the Britons over the hard work of the Gauls that those who had recently sneered at Latin now desired its eloquence. So, too, a liking sprang up for our style of dress, and the toga became fashionable. Little by little they were led to things which encourage vice: porticoes, baths, elegant supper-parties. All this in their ignorance they called civilisation, when it was only a part of their slavery.'

All of this – porticoes, temples, forum, baths – now lies under pasture except for the city walls, which still stand high and proud. The only buildings within them are an old farmhouse and a medieval church. The site was never much built over: not, it is thought, because of some powerful *genius loci* that bred suspicion against the old Roman town, but rather because the ground, bearing hundreds of years' worth of rubbish and waste, was known as fertile farmland, better for crops than the surrounding fields. The emptiness, though, does not quite explain the curious atmosphere of this place, the uncanny, held-in-check silence of it. I thought of Robert Browning's poem 'Love Among the Ruins', in which the narrator contemplates a 'plenty and perfection' of grass that 'o'erspreads/ And embeds/ Every vestige of the city, guessed alone,/ Stock or stone.' A friend had once said to me of Silchester: 'It's pure *Puck of Pook's Hill*.' He was right.

The wind-smoothed, cattle-grazed grass is bisected by a drover's path, which cuts over the town at a blindly non-Roman angle. Stare at the pasture long enough, though, and pale stripes in the green become visible – then disappear as you change the angle of view. This is the ancient street plan, revealed like subaqueous hints of a wreck seen from the surface of the sea. The land was cultivated when Camden came here, but he encountered a similar effect: 'Although the ground bee fertile and fruitfull inough, yet in certaine places crossing one another, the corne doth not thrive so well, but commeth up much thinner than else where, by which they suppose the streets of the citie went in old time.' He also wrote of the country people's stories about the place. The 'great store of Romane coine' dug up here, he said, was known locally as 'Onions pennies. For they dreame that this Onion was a Giant and dwelt in this citie. There are digged up also many times inscriptions, of which the unskilfull rurall people envie us the having.' The antiquarian Thomas Hearne described a visit to Silchester in a diary entry for 22 May 1714. He thought that 'Onion' was a misreading of 'Constantine', which the local people might have seen inscribed on coins. Onion was also supposed, wrote Hearne, to have thrown a rock called the 'Imp Stone' to Silchester Common. The word 'Imp' might have derived from the common contraction of *'imperator'*, emperor, seen on numerous Roman inscriptions.

In the 1720s, another pioneering visitor came to inspect the remains of Silchester. This was William Stukeley, an intriguing character in the history of antiquarianism, who has left us voluminous writings both published and unpublished, as well as a prolific correspondence in a nicely rounded copperplate hand. Born in Holbeach in Lincolnshire in 1687, he was a polymathic man of his age, studying classics, theology and science at Cambridge – where he set up a room for experiments and 'sometimes surprizd the whole College with a sudden explosion'. In 1720, he became a fellow of the Royal College of Physicians, and during the course of his long and fruitful life his interests ranged across geology, astronomy and the history of religion, as well as anti-quarianism. He was Newton's first biographer – and though his manu-script remained unpublished for 200 years, his was the first telling of the famous apple-and-gravity story. He startled his friends by taking holy orders and in 1730 becoming the vicar of Stamford, in his native Lincolnshire, despite some intriguingly heterodox religious views. Though many of his ideas can now appear rather fanciful (and did so even during his lifetime, especially his enthusiasm for Druidism), he was a crucial figure in the history of antiquarianism, pioneering the accurate measuring and recording of ancient monuments. When he came to Silchester in the 1720s, he was working on his *Itinerarium Curiosum*, published in 1724 and again, in a new edition, in 1776. The book was a programme for a kind of anti-Grand Tour, in which the glories of the Continent (which he never visited) were eschewed in favour of a series of journeys around Britain. In the preface, he argued that the conventional Grand Tour had 'led infinite numbers of its admirers through the labours and dangers of strange countries, through oceans, immoderate heats and colds, over rugged mountains, barren sands and deserts, savage inhabitants, and a million perils; and the world is filled with accounts of them . . . while our own country lies like a neglected province. Like untoward children, we look with contempt upon our own mother.'

Silchester, he wrote in the *Itinerarium*, 'is a place that a lover of antiquity will visit with great delight'. He noted that the 'walls of this city are standing, more or less perfect, quite round' – adding, with customary (and misplaced) national pride, that they were 'perhaps the most intire of any in the Roman empire'. Matthew and I followed Stukeley's lead, and walked around them. Ash trees, their thick trunks grey and wrinkled and their branches bearing bunches of fresh green keys, pulled their way out of the flint. Camden had been impressed by the trees: not ashes, but oaks, that seemed 'bredde with the verie stones, with such huge boughes all about, that it would make the beholders to wonder thereat'. Stukeley too described the walls as 'quite round crowned with oaks'. Michael Fulford, professor of archaeology at the University of Reading, who has dug at Silchester for more than thirty summers, remembers the oaks here in the 1970s: many of them died, he said, in the drought summer of 1976. Perhaps the ashes will soon be gone, too.

A little to the north-east of the town walls was, Stukeley wrote, 'another great curiosity, which the people think was a castle: I presently discerned it to be an amphitheatre . . . The whole area or arena within is now covered with water, but they say it is not much above three foot deep . . . it is a most noble and beautiful concave, but intirely over-grown with thorn-bushes, briars, holly, broom, furze, oak and ash-trees, &c, and has from times immemorial been a yard for cattle, and a watering-pond.' He provided an illustration: a pool fringed around with trees, two gentlemen fishing at the water's edge. It is telling of Stukeley's mixed reputation, as well as the sometimes brutal intellectual atmosphere of the time, that Hearne wrote, in a diary entry of 10 September 1724, that Stukeley was 'a mighty conceited man' who 'addicts himself to fancy altogether . . . He pretended to have discovered a Roman Amphitheatre at Silchester, a draught of the walls thereof he shewed me. This is again fancy. I have been at Silchester, there is nothing like it.'

But Stukeley was right. Today the amphitheatre is no longer a 'watering-pond' but an elliptical gravel-floored space with earth banks rising around it, and Roman walls marking the edge of the central arena. Into them are set niches, which may have been for images of Nemesis and Fortuna, one pulling the combatant towards reckoning and death, the other to luck and life. Several thousand people might

have sat here watching. The anonymous author of a short work called *The History and Antiquities of Silchester in Hampshire*, published in 1821, imagined it to have been the stage for 'disgusting sights and barbarous exhibitions'. 'The lion's roar, and the tiger's howl, have echoed through these woodlands. The shrieks of the torn victims have rent the air while the shouts of the multitude, as cruel as the beasts which afforded them such sanguinary pleasure, were still more awful.' He (assuming it was a he) went on: 'How thankful should we be for milder punishments, and more rational pleasures. The Gospel has thus ameliorated our conditions.' The barbarity of the amphitheatre has long been regarded as the epitome of Roman brutality (all the more so because of lurid tales of Christians flung to lions). In fact, current evidence suggests that the Silchester amphitheatre lay empty for long periods of its history; and it is unlikely that anyone took the trouble to bring lions and tigers to Hampshire.

From the amphitheatre, Matthew and I walked back to Silchester's walls, and came to the only building, aside from the church, that breaches them: the farmhouse. Despite his horror of gladiatorial combat, the author of *The History and Antiquities of Silchester* was disapproving about the inhabitants' lack of antiquarian sensibility: 'We deeply regret that the occupiers of the farm do not make frequent researches for the numerous curiosities of antiquity which might easily be found, and that when found, we wish they would carefully preserve them. Even now at the door of the farm house, a horseblock is constructed of a portion of the shaft of a Roman column, on the top of which is placed the mutilated fragment of a capital [sic].' The authors of *Silchester: the Pompeii of Hampshire* were similarly struck by the sight, in the farmyard, of 'several massive stones which are apparently portions of a stately column or columns, which were formerly the support and glory of some stately temple'.

A little digging was done in Silchester in the eighteenth century: unusually, not by a gentleman antiquary, but by a working man – a local cobbler, John Stair of Aldermaston, who measured the basilica and mapped out the basic street plan. In 1817, after the Battle of Waterloo, the Duke of Wellington was given the local stately home, Stratfield Saye, by a grateful nation; and in 1828, the parish of Silchester was added to his lands. It was the second duke who was the enthusiast for the remains on his doorstep. Under his auspices, the splendidly named Revd James Joyce undertook the first concerted excavations, in the 1860s. He found many wonderful things, including two mosaics fit to be removed and relaid in the entrance hall of Stratfield Saye, where they are still. He kept careful notebooks of his excavations, with delicate watercolours of his finds, which can be seen at the Reading Museum. More archaeology was undertaken by Edwardian excavators. For many years afterwards, it was supposed that Silchester had offered up all its secrets.

That was not, it turned out, quite the case. For Professor Fulford – a merrily round-cheeked figure in his sixties – Silchester has been his scholarly mainstay. 'I've published more on it than everything else put together,' he told me, as we drank coffee at the Reading Museum. 'Silchester is a virtually untapped archaeological resource, for the early excavations only got to its upper layers, to the third- and fourth-century town. The Victorians barely touched the tip of it.' What makes it so rich for Fulford is that it was continuously occupied in both the pre-Roman and Roman eras, and may have continued as a community after the end of Roman rule too. Equally, it wasn't occupied afterwards: there is no modern town above it to negotiate. In the 1970s and 80s, along with an ever-changing army of volunteers and students, he re-excavated the town defences, the amphitheatre, and the forum basilica. For the past sixteen summers, he has been working on the same large plot, fifty-five metres square. Slowly, painstakingly, he and his team have peeled back successive layers of Calleva's history: the project is to try to piece together something of the whole history of the town.

Fulford told me a little about their recent work. Beneath the regular grid of the Roman town – the one that you can see from the grass, with luck and a steady eye – his team found traces of an earlier, Iron Age street plan. The better to explain what he meant, he took my notebook and drew a series of diagrams. First he sketched a neat Roman grid, with a hefty Roman timber building on it – perhaps part of the fort built immediately after the conquest. But he then drew dotted lines running at opposing angles, representing the earlier Iron Age street layout. The Roman building had been 'plonked down', he said, on this earlier crossroads, but with a new orientation. He then drew another Roman grid, square and neat, showing the streets as they were in about AD 80–125, and sketched in a series of dwellings that he believes were standing at the same period – a thatched roundhouse, a longhouse with a tiled roof, and a clump of other, smaller buildings. But he planted them at a wonky angle: although they related to each other, they completely ignored the Roman grid. In fact, he told me, they seemed rather to be aligned to the midsummer solstice sunrise, and the midwinter solstice sunset. According to Fulford, the evidence suggests that there were people in Calleva who were persistently ignoring the neat system of Roman roads in favour of an orientation of their own – just as the Roman town had utterly disregarded the old tracks of the earlier Iron Age settlement.

Just as the drover's path of the modern meadow cuts blindly across the grain of the Roman streets, so beneath and between the lines of the Roman grid lie the ghosts of other paths. What does it mean? Were the British inhabitants clinging on to pre-Roman property boundaries? Was there a religious significance in the orientation of the buildings, with their alignment to the solstice sun? Or are the shape of the streets and the angle of the houses telling us of deliberate resistance, a refusal to align physically and perhaps also mentally to the Roman plan? Equally, there may be some entirely different explanation; or some overlooked factor or misinterpretation of the evidence. Someone may look back on the data in a century, with new methods and new technologies, and contradict Fulford's conclusions. Archaeologists may dive down into the depths of the earth, but they can only bring back what they have eyes to see. Archaeology feels its way along: it deals in the provisional, not in certainties.

I asked Fulford what mental picture he had drawn of Calleva: what he believed the town might have 'been like'. He talked about a shanty town of incomers from the countryside, 'drawn into it to benefit from the economic advantages, the trading opportunities with the Roman world'. He said he thought there would have been 'plenty of rickety wooden buildings that let the rain in: life would have been pretty hard'. Then he wondered aloud about these economic migrants: 'Would you even understand what people were saying? If others spoke Latin, or Celtic with a Gallic accent?' (He was thinking of Commius and his putative community of immigrants from Gaul.)

At the same time, Calleva would have been cosmopolitan, he argued. Every Roman soldier heading towards the great Welsh garrisons from London would have passed through Silchester. At the south gate there is evidence, he said, for what might be a *'mansio'* – a kind of inn where couriers on imperial business would put up for the night. The connectedness to the world outside was reflected in the imported goods. Wine had come into the town from the Mediterranean, and oil, and garum (the ubiquitous Roman sauce, impossible to imagine for the modern palate, since it was made from rotten fish). Amphorae have been discovered, containing traces of dried dates and raisins from Turkey and Palestine. Among the timber buildings there were also rich stone-built mansions: the archaeologists have found mosaic floors, and traces of Egyptian porphyry and Tuscan marble. Fulford is particularly fond of a bronze figurine of a lady wearing a high tiara on her elaborately dressed hair, holding a flute. A few summers ago, the excavators discovered a tiny bronze statuette of the god Harpocrates, who was adopted by the Greeks from the Egyptians: he was a hellenisation of the deity Horus, child of Isis and Osiris. In Egyptian iconography, the god holds a finger to his lips, a reference to the form of the hieroglyph for 'child'. The Greeks, and after them the Romans, misinterpreted the gesture, and made Harpocrates into the tutelary spirit of secret and silence: an appropriate find in this city that keeps so much to itself. Among all this, said Fulford: 'I am struck that we are finding what I would call "Iron Age things" even in the layers relating to the third and fourth century.' He told me about the curious business of the Calleva dogs. Canines turn up regularly, deliberately buried, he said. Recently, they found the remains of a puppy that had been buried in a pit in about AD 250–300. Nearby was found an ivory-handled knife, carved with an image of two dogs mating. 'Perhaps the dog was sacrificed, perhaps with that knife,' he offered. There were nicks in the bones of the dog, as if it had been flayed.

After our conversation, I went upstairs into the Roman galleries of the Reading Museum. Here was a little eagle cast in bronze, one of the museum's most celebrated objects. Its beak was cruelly curved, its feathers exquisitely described in the surface of the dully glowing metal. It was also about the size of a pigeon and lacking wings, such that its grandeur was a little undercut. James Joyce found it in 1866, while excavating beneath the basilica. A mystery: how had this creature, which he thought must be an eagle from a Roman legionary standard, ended up here? There are so many unanswered questions in ancient history, questions that the novelist, where the historian may hesitate to advance a theory, can fearlessly answer with invention. It was this bronze eagle from which Rosemary Sutcliff made her children's story *The Eagle of the Ninth*, first published in 1954.

The Eagle of the Ninth tells of the young Marcus Aquila, a centurion on his first command. Injured terribly during a skirmish with Britons flamed to rebellion by a wandering Druid, he must forfeit his military career. But then rumours begin to circulate of sightings of the standard of his father's lost legion, the Ninth – north of Hadrian's Wall. If he can find it, he will recover the honour of the disgraced legion, and of his father.

I call it a children's story; my copy, with its gorgeous line drawings by C. Walter Hodges, bears my name on the title page in barely joined-up handwriting. But Sutcliff claimed her books were readable by anyone from nine to ninety. In an interview given in 1992, the year she died, she said: 'I don't write for adults, I don't write for children. I don't write for the outside world at all. Basically, I write for some small, inquiring thing in myself.' Aged two, she had contracted Still's disease, a form of arthritis, and for most of her life she used a wheelchair. That, and an itinerant childhood as the daughter of a naval officer, meant that when young she was educated at home by her mother, and did not read until she was nine. By way of compensation, the learning she got at her mother's knee was surely the perfect training for a storyteller: she was told tales from the Norse and Celtic legends, fairy tales, Icelandic sagas. There was Malory too, and the Mabinogion. Her first attempts at writing were retellings of her mother's tales.

I have read *The Eagle of the Ninth* dozens of times; and as the reading self changes, so does the book. When I last read the story, it was the sheer quality of the prose that delighted, the utter rightness with which Sutcliff gives life to the visible world. She attended art college from the age of fourteen, and specialised in miniature painting. She told an interviewer: 'Fortunately, I have got a very good memory. And it's a visual memory: I was taught how to look at things. And I've found this really useful because I know . . . how the colour of sunlight gleaming off a sword will change, depending on whether it's a warm sky or not.' A miniaturist's visual skill, then, but deployed on a generous imaginative canvas: desperate moorland chases on horseback; a fort subject to a vicious attack; strange and wild native rituals practised by night.

Marcus, then, invalided out of the army, joins his uncle Aquila, a retired army officer, at his house at Calleva Atrebatum. Here he 'comes face to face with the wreckage of everything he knew and cared about'. He is lonely, in pain and homesick, enduring 'the wind and rain and wet leaves of exile'. Gradually, though, he forges friendships – not with soldierly young Romans, but with a slave, a wolf cub and a young British girl. All four are deracinated, parentless creatures. Esca, a Briton of the Brigantes tribe, has lost his family to Roman slaughter as well as his freedom; Marcus buys him after watching him fight in the Calleva amphitheatre. Cub has been plucked during a hunt from the lair of his mother. The proudly British Cottia has been sent to live with her aunt and uncle, whose comically overeager adoption of a Roman lifestyle she despises.

Sutcliff here, as in her later books on Roman Britain that spiral out of the *Eagle*, is greatly interested in questions of identity. What does it mean to be British? Where is home? Can friendship trump tribal loyalties? *The Eagle of the Ninth* speaks deeply of its time of writing, during Britain's post-war era of decolonisation. Reading half a century on, when the the imperial age is viewed in a more critical light, Sutcliff has Esca relate to his master in a way that we might now find troubling. A moment at which Cub is offered his freedom – but then comes trotting back home, humbly offering his muzzle to Marcus – is echoed by a parallel scene in which Marcus offers Esca his liberty, only for the Briton, just like the potentially savage wolf cub, to declare his continued allegiance and devotion to the Roman.

What Sutcliff achieves above all in *The Eagle of the Ninth* is a world that is entirely credible; a world that could trick you into believing in it as historical truth. She once said: 'I think that I am happiest of all in Roman Britain. I feel very much at home there . . . If I could do a time flip and land back in Roman Britain, I would take a deep breath, take perhaps a fortnight to get used to things, then be all right, for I would know what was making the people around me tick . . . I have a special "Ah, here I am again, I know exactly what they are going to have for breakfast" feeling when I get back into Roman Britain.'

I envy Sutcliff and her supreme confidence that she could feel at home in Roman Britain. Even if I know that some people in Calleva, at some point in the day and in some unknown combination, were eating celery and dill and coriander and mutton and goose and oysters (for these are some of the food remains that have been found here), Roman Britain seems to me an alien, irrecoverable place. Yet I love Sutcliff's imagining of it. I want very much to believe it, and in fact for as long as I am reading *The Eagle of the Ninth*, I always do: which is the storyteller's gift.

The 9th Legion last left its mark in Britain when it raised an inscription in York, in AD 108. Its abrupt disappearance from the epigraphic record, and absence from historiography, has long been a mystery, leading many to speculate that the entire legion was wiped out somewhere in northern Britain. But there is no evidence of such a disaster, and it is now thought to have been simply withdrawn from the province. It may have been transferred to Germany, where a bowl and a horse brass marked with its name have been found. Possibly, even, it was the nameless legion that Cassius Dio recorded as having been destroyed in Asia in AD 160. But there is no certainty about its fate; mystery still clings to it.

The eagle? It is now thought not to have been a legionary standard, but part of a bronze statue group. Clearly it was a precious and expensive object, perhaps part of a sculpture of Jupiter, or of an emperor. How it ended up under the basilica is a matter of speculation. Fulford told me he believes it may have been part of the wreckage and rubble of a building that was burned down, and later built over; and perhaps, just perhaps, the fire may have been part of the devastation caused by Boudica and her rebels. Fulford even wonders whether it may have come from Commius's (or his family's) household of luxurious and exotic possessions. Boudican burnings; dog sacrifice; olive-chewing natives; Egyptian cult objects; powerful Gaul-Britons with bronze sculptures of Jupiter: this is not Sutcliff's Calleva Atrebatum at all.

In another display case in the museum is a rather undistinguished piece of terracotta tile. Into the damp clay someone has scored words in a neat, schoolboyish hand: 'Pertacus Perfidus Campester Lucilianus Campanus conticuere omnes'. The first five words are all men's names. The last two, 'Conticuere Omnes', were written by Virgil: they are the opening words of the second book of the Aeneid. They mean, 'They all fell silent.' Who wrote this? A group of schoolboys, swearing secrets into the damp clay, sealing the vow with Virgil's magical words? The scene in the poem is this: Aeneas and his crew, exiles from the now-destroyed Troy, have arrived on the coast of north Africa at the court of the Carthaginian queen, Dido. Aeneas is welcomed as a guest. There is a feast. Wine is shared and a bard sings. Dido asks Aeneas many questions about the Trojan War; about Priam, and Hector, and the greatness of Achilles. Then she persuades him to tell the assembled guests the whole story from the beginning: to tell them about the trap that the Greeks set for Troy, about the calamity that befell his people. 'Conticuere omnes': everyone fell silent, and each face was turned intently, expectantly upon Aeneas.

'Conticuere omnes' is exactly half a hexameter. We have reached the point of the caesura, the tiny, subtle pause in the centre of the poetic line. Looking at the faint scratched words, I feel caught in an instant of suspense. The drinking cups have been refilled, the audience is still and expectant; it is that enchanted second when the singer breathes in deeply and the first note has yet to come. I am silent; I wait for the story to begin. But for me, the clamour of the people of Calleva

Atrebatum is forever stilled. I will not – I cannot – hear them. The silence is not the hush of expectation, but the chill of secrets. Harpocrates holds his finger to his lips.

Wales and the West

It is strange indeed that by merely peeling off a wrapper of modern accumulations we have lowered ourselves into an ancient world.

Thomas Hardy, 1885

Wroxeter: 'It lieth low near merry England's heart/Like a long-buried sin,' wrote Wilfred Owen, a Shropshire lad, who used to visit the site of the Roman town as a boy for happy afternoons digging up coins with his younger brother, Harold, or his friend Stanley Webb. I thought of him as Matthew and I chugged there in the camper van, in the heat of midsummer, poppy fields flashing by in a red haze. Wroxeter Roman City – as Viroconium Cornoviorum is now officially described – with its car park, visitor centre and English Heritage signboards, lacked the charm I imagine Owen found here, when he cycled along the lanes, urging his brother to 'Hurry, Harold, hurry. Think what we may be missing – the greatest find of the century.' But there is something indelibly particular about the way the ruins inhabit the landscape that cannot entirely be erased by the banality of their presentation. The Roman site has never been built over, and the medieval village of Wroxeter is a short walk away, through sheep-grazed pastures. There is a piece of masonry at the heart of the remains, called 'the Great Work', which dominates the skyline: a miraculously tall, pitted, scarred hulk of a single wall, once part of the wall of the *palaestra*, or exercise ground, of the town baths.

In the AD 50s, the soldiers of the 14th Legion marched here, northwest up Watling Street from London, and established a fort; in the 60s they were replaced by the 20th, which, in the early 80s, set off with Agricola to Scotland. When the soldiers finally left the fort for good in about 90, to be stationed in Chester, the town proper began to spring up: temples, baths, the basilica, the forum. It became, in all likelihood, the administrative capital of the Cornovii tribe. Soldiers from Faenza and Piacenza were buried here; and a woman called Placida, whose death at the age of fifty-five was marked by a stone set up by her nameless husband of thirty years. In Shrewsbury Museum, which Owen loved, is an inscription dedicating the forum to the emperor Hadrian. Charles Dickens visited Wroxeter in 1859, while the site was being excavated by the antiquary Thomas Wright, and he wrote up the trip for his magazine *All the Year Round*. He described the scene: 'There is a bright spring sun over head, the old wall standing close by looks blank at us; here and there a stray anti-quary clambers among the rubbish, careless of dirt stains; an attentive gentleman on the crest of a dirt heap explains Roman antiquities to some young ladies in pink and blue, who have made Wroxeter the business of a morning drive. An intelligent labourer, who seems to be a sort of foreman of the works, waits to disclose to the honorary secretary the contents of a box in which it is his business to deposit each day's findings of small odds and ends.' In the same issue of the magazine, one could read a chunk of the freshly written *Tale of Two Cities*.

Wroxeter lieth low, as Owen wrote, but it is fringed around by Shropshire's wild hills with their wild names: Abdon Burf; Wenlock Edge; the Long Mynd; Hoar Edge. They say you can see twelve Iron Age hill forts from the Roman town, if you know where to look and the day is clear. Massing greatest of all are the volcanic, gloomy heights of the Wrekin – whose name has a family resemblance to that of the Roman town, as William Camden noted. I used to see the Wrekin's hunched shoulders from a window in the house where I grew up in Staffordshire: a threatening, tempting presence on the distant horizon.

It was before the First World War that Owen used to come here, before his poetry was transformed into vatic, discordant outpourings by Flanders slaughter. It is tempting to imagine another reality for Owen, if there had been no war, as an amateur antiquary or even a professional archaeologist. One of his biographers, the poet Jon Stallworthy, wrote that as a sixteen-year-old, Owen 'enjoyed the company of his contemporaries less than the contemplation of the the long dead'. Sometime around 1913, he wrote a poem about Wroxeter, called 'Uriconium: An Ode'. It is a Keatsian outpouring into which thoughts and associations crowd freely as he reflects on the ruins; just as Keats's 'Ode on a Grecian Urn' contemplates the figures locked into stillness on an ancient vase. Walking over the streets of the ancient city, time collapses:

> I had forgot that so remote an age
> Beyond the horizon of our little sight,
> Is far from us by no more spanless gauge
> Than day and night, succeeding day and night,
> Until I looked on Thee,
> Thou ghost of a dead city, or its husk!

The ancient city, its bones revealed, allows him 'To lift the gloomy curtain of Time Past/ And spy the secret things that Hades hath.' The city becomes both a way of imagining a descent to the realm of the dead, and a means of contemplating the harsh, repetitive cycles of man's violence: 'Yet cities such as these one time would breed/ Apocalyptic visions of world-wrecks.' Owen would soon be experiencing his own apocalyptic visions: in his masterful battlefield poem,

'Strange Meeting', he indeed seems to spy the 'secret things that Hades hath' when he describes a dream-state descent through a 'profound dull tunnel, long since scooped/ Through granites which titanic wars had groined.' 'Uriconium: An Ode' seems to prefigure the later, greater poem.

In 'Uriconium: An Ode', there is also a sense of the countryside's continuity, indifferent to these minor human squalls: the Roman stones have rooted down into the landscape and become an inconspicuous part of a perfectly ordinary rural English life. 'The village anvil rests on Roman base', runs one line; the font in the church is 'a temple's column' (as it still is). He does not mention the pair of Roman pillars that still serve as gateposts for the churchyard. Owen kept up his interest in antiquities through the war years: in April 1918, a month after writing 'Strange Meeting', he walked from the Yorkshire town of Ripon, where he was serving at the Northern Command Depot, to Aldborough. There he found 'Roman Remains, and the finest tessellated pavement in Britain,' he wrote to his mother. He added: 'If in 1913 I used to wish to have lived in the 4th Century, how much more now!' The companion of his youthful outings to Wroxeter was already dead. 'I thought of poor Stanley Webb when I was among the "Remains".'

Owen was not the first poet to find in Wroxeter a poetic metaphor through which to express the brevity of the human span. A. E. Housman published his sequence of poems, A Shropshire Lad, in 1896. Its deceptively simple, ballad-like verses are shot through with a quietly tearing sense of loss. Critical studies of his work have suggested he was impelled to write it in the wake of the departure to India of his friend Moses Jackson, with whom he was probably in love. His poems of yearning, and of youth cut off in its prime, resonated deeply for readers during the First World War. It was A Shropshire Lad, with its feeling for the rhythms of the English countryside, that soldiers read in the trenches, not Owen's poems, whose creative flowering came at the end of the war and whose work found a public in the decades after it. Housman and Owen stand Janus-faced in relation to the war; Housman's poems seeming obliquely to anticipate it, Owen's posthumously shaping the public memory of it.

'On Wenlock Edge', Housman's poem about Wroxeter, which Ralph Vaughan Williams later set to tremulous, febrile music, has one constant feature: the lashing gale, the 'old wind' that has troubled English yeoman and Roman alike. The Roman, now, is ashes under Uricon. And you will be too, soon, implies the poem. But the wind, indifferent and ageless, will go on blowing.

On Wenlock Edge the wood's in trouble
His forest fleece the Wrekin heaves;
The gale, it plies the saplings double,
And thick on Severn snow the leaves.

'Twould blow like this through holt and hanger
When Uricon the city stood:
'Tis the old wind in the old anger,
But then it threshed another wood.

Then, 'twas before my time, the Roman
At yonder heaving hill would stare:
The blood that warms an English yeoman,
The thoughts that hurt him, they were there.

There, like the wind through woods in riot,
Through him the gale of life blew high;
The tree of man was never quiet:
Then 'twas the Roman, now 'tis I.

The gale, it plies the saplings double,
It blows so hard, 'twill soon be gone:
To-day the Roman and his trouble
Are ashes under Uricon.

In the summers before the outbreak of the war, the archaeologist J. P. Bushe-Fox was excavating at Wroxeter. A photograph shows him in knickerbockers and a straw boater, guiding visitors in plumed hats around the excavations: one of the little girls, with hair in long ringlets, looks like a character from an E. Nesbit story. One of the students at the dig was Mortimer Wheeler, who would later go on to become one of the most celebrated figures of twentieth-century British archaeology. He worked on numerous Romano-British sites, and on excavations in India; and, in co-founding the Institute of Archaeology at the University of London, was a crucial figure in transforming archaeology into an academic discipline. Owen and Wheeler almost certainly met at Wroxeter. In a letter to his mother dated 6 July 1913, Owen wrote: 'I've not been to Uriconium again. Perhaps because of those two Oxford Blues, whose colours are to me as red to a bull.' The 'Oxford Blues' were Wheeler's fellow student diggers.

Wheeler had a good war and emerged a major. But by 1918 his generation, he recalled in his memoir, 'had been blotted out'. He wrote: 'Of the five university students who worked together in the Wroxeter excavations, only one survived the war. It so happened that the survivor was myself.' The 'Oxford Blues' were dead. So was Owen, killed on 4 November 1918 as he crossed the Sambre-Oise canal in northern France with a raiding party. Wheeler experienced a profound sense of isolation, which, he wrote, became 'a dominant element' in the way he conceived of his life. 'As a survivor,' wrote his biographer, Jacquetta Hawkes, he felt 'he had been entrusted with a mission on behalf of the dead'.

Wheeler himself was not an 'Oxford Blue' but studied at University College, London, where A. E. Housman taught him Latin – the great man seemed often distracted, remembered Wheeler, 'though liable to rally unexpectedly in caustic comment, whether the subject were Martial's text or its luckless exponent'. Owen had himself passed the matriculation exam for U.C.L., but he failed the exam for a scholarship, without which his family could not afford to support him; which perhaps accounts for his bitterness towards the 'Oxford Blues'.

In time, Wheeler became the embodiment of the idea of archaeologist-as-hero, a swashbuckling figure and a household name, thanks to a broadcasting career in the 1950s and 60s. In the memorial address given after his death in 1976, he was uncompromisingly described as 'a fire-breathing giant . . . relentlessly, inflexibly driven to achieve his aim by a mechanism which enlisted the help of lesser mortals and compelled them to bow in his path'. An early cover for his autobiography, Still Digging, shows him in half-profile; Indian excavators toil away in the distance. His military moustache is as stiff as a banner in the breeze, and his gaze is intense, intelligent and just a shade devilish. 'Women were of immense importance to him and he enjoyed and made use of them in a marvellous variety of ways,' wrote Hawkes, who then provided a typology: 'young girls – including, I have been told, the domestics of at least one country house . . . women he met on his innumerable cruises and other travels . . . Any who were attractive, light-hearted and unlikely to interfere with his work . . . exceptional young women with fine looks . . . and with the character, vitality and temperament to offer the "resistance" – flint to his steel – that he needed to kindle his fires.'

In 1912, Wheeler had married a bright, small, charming young woman called Tessa Verney, who had grown up in Lewisham in the affectionate, if slightly unconventional, household of her mother and stepfather, who were not married to each other. She and Wheeler met at U.C.L. – they both served on the committee of the college literary society. If Wilfred Owen had passed his scholarship exam, he and Verney would have been exact contemporaries at the college. Verney threw over a scion of the building firm Mowlem to become engaged to the charismatic 'Rik', as he was known. She henceforth anchored her endeavours to his, setting her quick mind to the work of archaeology that so absorbed her husband. In 1920, he was appointed keeper of archaeology at the Museum of Cardiff, and the couple moved to Wales with their young son, Michael. Over two consecutive summers, 1924 and 1925, they excavated a remote Roman site at a farm near Brecon, simply known as 'Y Gaer' – the hill fort.

Y Gaer, slipped into a crook of the river Usk, is not easy to find. Roger Wilson's *Guide to the Roman Remains in Britain* gives meticulous instructions, a catalogue of 'unsignposted crossroads', and 'turn back hard on your right' and 'the second turning to the left, after crossing a stream'. We coaxed the camper van through the maze of minor roads; Wilson did not fail us. I knocked at the farmhouse door, asking: 'Do you mind if I look at your Roman fort?' The farmer did not: in fact he interrupted his lunch to give directions and advice ('the west gate's worth seeing'). I asked him what it was like, to have your own Roman fort. He shrugged. 'I have grown up with it,' he said, his voice the gentlest of Welsh melodies. 'I'm more interested in their engineering, in what they could do in that way. These days, we shall be going backwards if we are not very careful. There is a Roman drain out there that still works when it rains. Quite an epitaph, isn't it, really? Imagine the council doing something and expecting it to last two thousand years. It's all plastic piping now. People want it all done yesterday, this is the problem.'

Wheeler, remembering the excavation in *Still Digging*, described this fort as 'celebrated', something that seems unbelievable now. The farmer told me that there was 'a guidebook once', but today there was not a signpost, nor an information board, nor the merest hint that behind the swallow-nested barns of his neat farmyard there was anything of interest at all. The fort is in effect a large sheep field, set about with walls and still-fine Roman gateways. It was simply built in about AD 80 with timber buildings, and remade in stone in the middle of the next century. A cavalry force was garrisoned here – 500 Vettones, from north-west Spain – and it was one of Wales's most important forts, part of a network that dotted the hills between its twin fortresses of Isca (Caerleon, near Newport) and Deva (Chester), presiding over south and north respectively. Wheeler described the two summers of the dig as 'the happiest and least anxious of all my enterprises'. Flinders Petrie, the great Egyptologist, who had famously surveyed Giza, spent his summer holiday nearby, amusing himself, recalled Wheeler, by measuring stone circles using 'a single slender bamboo pea-stick and a visiting card' – the visiting card to provide a right angle, and the pea-stick a line for surveying. (On one occasion, he and his wife Hilda were 'treed' by a bull.)

Wheeler too regarded the excavations as something of a holiday, according to Nowell Myres, one of the student diggers, later a great historian of the Anglo-Saxon period. He would begin the day by issuing instructions to the students and the 'handful of unemployed Welsh navvies who comprised the labour force . . . and would then disappear, suitably equipped, in the direction of the river. In the evening he would return, not always overburdened with trophies of the chase, listen to what we told him of the day's work on the dig, and explain to us what he thought it meant.' It was Tessa who 'coped with all the organisational and administrative chores that a dig entails, including the provision of enormous picnic meals'. Later, Petrie would write to Wheeler remarking on the fact that the eventual site report 'effaced any record of the unfailing driving power of Mrs Wheeler, which seemed the back-bone of the carry-on'. It is hard to tell whether his tone is critical or approving.

At Y Gaer, it was pure pastoral. The air was filled with the plaintive baaing of the fresh-shorn sheep; a pair of red kites floated serenely on the hot summer thermals above us. The day blazed; Matthew and I picnicked under an oak, leaning on the Roman walls. It was an eclogue afternoon: made for lying, as Virgil wrote, *'lentus in umbra'*, leisurely in the shade.

It is a trope of Augustan Latin poetry to cast back to the distant past and imagine the thronged streets of modern Rome before it was built, when it was all meadows and bucolic. In the eighth book of Virgil's *Aeneid*, Evander, an Arcadian who has founded a kingdom in Italy, shows Aeneas round his domain: which happens to be the future site of Rome, to be founded three centuries hence by Aeneas's descendant Romulus. Evander points out the future Capitoline Hill, which in Virgil's time was the site of the greatest temple of the city, dedicated to Jupiter. The tree-fringed summit and its grove cause the local people to tremble in religious awe, Evander tells Aeneas. He says: some god lives there, but we don't know who. Virgil is giving the topography of Augustan Rome a numinous aetiology, suffusing its everyday modernity with the mythical.

The spot has its own ancient ruins, too. In tour-guide mode, Evander continues: *'Haec duo praeterea disiectis oppida muris, / reliquias veterumque vides monimenta virorum'* – 'Here you can see two buildings with shattered walls. They are the relics and monuments of ancient men.' The buildings, he explains, are citadels built by Janus and Saturn – deities who occupied this place in the deep past and ruled over it for *'aurea saecula'*, a golden age. The group approaches Evander's lowly dwelling, *'passimque armenta videbant/ Romanoque foro et lautis mugire Carinis'* – 'and everywhere they saw herds of cattle lowing in the Roman forum and the smart Carinae'. Virgil lets time collapse here, such that for a moment his contemporary readers would have been given the head-spinning image of cattle roaming the streets of their own busy city – a kind of double exposure, past and present in the same frame. Reading these lines in the twenty-first century, there is a different frisson again: the oleander- and cyprus-fringed Forum of our day is once more empty but for tourists and old stones. For us, a visit to the Roman Forum is more like Aeneas's tour-guided trip round Evander's ancient realm. Time has come full circle: from pastoral ruin to pastoral ruin. But in a curious way, our modern perspective is implicit in the passage: it is as though by conjuring the ruins of Saturn's old city, Virgil can foresee the ruins of his own Rome. Nothing lasts for ever; empires come and go. As I lay in the shade, lulled by the breeze-shifted canopy of leaves above, I felt how eloquently and sorrowfully realised were Virgil's lines, here in the pasture of Y Gaer.

In the sixteenth century, a Roman tombstone was found near the farm. In the Wheelers' day it was on the Roman road leading away from Y Gaer into the valley; now it is in the sleepy, agreeably tatty Brecknock Museum at Brecon (outside which stands a bronze sculpture, by John Thomas, of Boudica brandishing a sword as her daughters huddle in her skirts, which pre-dates Thornycroft's group at Westminster Bridge by almost half a century). Although the Roman tombstone is much worn and weathered, we could still clearly see the subject of the carved relief. R. G. Collingwood, the great authority on the inscriptions of Roman Britain, wrote it up for Mortimer's archaeological report on Y Gaer thus: 'Above, full-length figures of a man and his wife are cut in relief. The woman's left arm rests on her husband's shoulder, while her right arm seems to cross her body so that she may clasp her husband's right hand, but the weathering and flaking of the stone obscures all details and only permits us to see that the group has been a dignified and well-designed composition . . . The local name, Maen y Morwynion (Maidens' Stone) betrays the impression made by the group on the minds of passers by.' Of the inscription beneath, only the words *'coniunx eius h. s. e.'* can be made out – meaning 'her husband put this up'. (The abbreviated letters are short for *'hic situs est'*, or 'put this up'.) Though the image is worn almost to complete smoothness, there is something ineffably touching about it, as Collingwood betrays even through his objective epigrapher's description.

In July 1926, the summer after the Wheelers finished work at Y Gaer, Mortimer took up a new job, as the director of the then embryonic Museum of London. The *South Wales News* covered the leaving-party speeches: 'In Mrs Wheeler Dr Wheeler had a wonderful chief of staff . . . Mrs Wheeler, in replying, said she had always endeavoured to be a part of the shadow behind her husband.' Notwithstanding Mortimer's new job, there was still unfinished business to be attended to in Wales: he had already laid plans for another excavation, this time near the mouth of the Usk at Caerleon.

Caerleon had been the garrison of the 2nd Legion; now it is a small, pretty town, despite being jammed up against the motorway and the sprawl of Newport. The twelfth-century cleric Gerald of Wales described in his *Itinerarium Kambriae*, or *Journey Around Wales*, what he saw there. 'Caerleon is of unquestioned antiquity. It was constructed with great care by the Romans, the walls being built of brick. You can still see many vestiges of its one-time splendour. There are immense palaces, which, with the gilded gables of their roofs, once rivalled the magnificence of ancient Rome. They were set up in the first place by some of the most eminent men of the Roman state, and they were therefore embellished with every architectural conceit. There is a lofty tower, and beside it remarkable hot baths, the remains of temples and an amphitheatre. All this is enclosed within impressive walls, parts of which still remain standing. Wherever you look, both within and without the circuit of these walls, you can see constructions dug deep into the earth, conduits for water, underground passages and air vents.'

It is not quite as splendid now as Gerald described it 900 years ago, and his 'gilded gables' were surely something of a fantasy, but when Matthew and I visited, we still could see a fragment of the great baths with their swimming pool, and a portion of the pillared, naved exercise hall, once the size of a cathedral. And out on the town's edge was the great amphitheatre, traditionally known as King Arthur's Round Table, grassy-bottomed and high-banked. On the hot June day when we met my brother and his family here, boys were kicking a ball around the sheltered green enclosure. We walked in through the Roman gates and, like other visiting families, laid out a picnic, crowding into the sparse shade cast by the stone-supported seating banks. Tilda and Eleanor, my nieces, ranged around the amphitheatre, mapping the hunks and hollows of the structure as they made it their playground; we lazier adults dozed in the sun. Before he had accepted the job in London, Wheeler had announced his plans for excavating the amphitheatre, using the Arthurian associations as a hook to tempt the newspapers. The ploy worked. The *Daily Mail* was down in a flash, and offered to pay £1,000 towards the cost of the excavation in return for exclusive news from the dig. Archaeology had – as Wheeler wrote – 'acquired a new market value'. That was surely down to the sensational discovery of Tutankhamun's tomb three years before. South

Wales was not Egypt: but Wheeler, a journalist's son, was learning how to harness the power of the press.

By the time the dig was due to start, Mortimer was busy in London, so it was Tessa who excavated the amphitheatre at Caerleon, shuttling back and forth between the site and London, helped by her young friend and admirer, Nowell Myres. There is a to-do list in Verney Wheeler's firm, competent hand from that excavation, in which she notes the day's tasks – everything from archaeological matters on which to consult her husband, to 'draft an appeal', 'consider post-cards' and 'write to Archbishop'. It was in excavating Caerleon's amphitheatre that Verney Wheeler came of age as an archaeologist and scholar in her own right. On this project she published solo for the first time, and afterwards was elected one of the first female fellows of the Society of Antiquaries.

Two years later, in the summer of 1928, the Wheelers came west again to dig, at Lydney Park in the Forest of Dean – a tract of land in that stretch of Gloucestershire on the west side of the Severn estuary that seems to belong properly to Wales. The late-nineteenth-century house of the Bathurst family, the viscounts Bledisloe, is tucked into a little fold of its own deer park; and each spring its gardens are opened to the public to show off its exotic plantings of azaleas and magnolias – and its exquisite Roman-temple ruins. On the day I visited, a motley gang of us, children outnumbering grown-ups, drifted round the glades and avenues. The grass was carpeted with the downcast heads of early English bluebells; ferns unwound their new leaves. Through the grass nodded the slim, erect stalks of pink candelabra primulas, which grow wild in the Himalayas. My nieces and their friends lay in the thick grass on the banks of a pool to study the tadpoles squirming in the water. It was an unseasonably hot April day. Opposite the shrubbery of candy-coloured rhododendrons, the ground rose sharply.

I left the others eating cake on the lawn and climbed up the rise – Dwarf's Hill, as it was once known. Here, between the canopies of beeches, one with palest green leaves, the other a fiery copper, I came upon the remains of a late-Roman temple, dedicated to an otherwise unknown god called Nodens. Nearby were the fragments of a little bathhouse, and further along the hilltop, deep square holes in the turf: Roman mineshafts where men had dug for iron ore. Perhaps in some distant imagination the dwarves of the hill had toiled in these mines. When the Wheelers excavated the site in 1928, Mortimer was excited to see the marks of ancient picks on the stone walls of these shafts. From the low mossy stonework of the temple remains, the view opened out, down to the Severn. The excavation report – authored jointly by the Wheelers – called it 'a vista of luxuriant forest and spacious estuary which can scarcely be matched for beauty even in a county of pleasant park-lands'.

Back down the hill, in the old-fashioned little museum attached to the house, a room of which is devoted to shells and ethnographic objects collected by the Bathursts in New Zealand in the 1930s, I studied the finds from the temple. So many little canine statues have been found here that it is thought Nodens was particularly associated with dogs. The god remains something of a mystery: it was a young Oxford professor of Anglo-Saxon called J. R. R. Tolkien who was commissioned to speculate on the origins of the name for the Wheelers' report. He thought it might have parallels to words meaning 'catcher' or 'snarer' in ancient Germanic languages. My eye was drawn by an imperfect, slightly damaged figurine in milky-ambery alabaster: a hunting dog, elegant and leggy. It was lying down, its front forelegs folded underneath it, and I felt I could sense that utter gentleness and looseness that a large dog's paw has in repose. But its head was high and alert, its ears pricked and eager, its nose practically quivering, as if it had just been roused to wakefulness.

In another room of the museum was an album of photographs taken during the 1928 excavation, its pages much worn by use. I paused at a page showing two pictures of a young woman standing next to a range-rod, the striped pole used to show scale in archaeological photographs. In the first photograph she was in profile, eyes down; the picture's angle emphasised the lines of her neat bob. In the second, she was looking up into the eyes of the photographer. Her expression was striking, and hard to read: wary? pensive? resentful? As I looked at the pictures, the museum attendant said, 'Sir Mortimer Wheeler was of course notorious for bringing his girlfriends on digs.' I felt a sudden rush of illogical defensiveness towards her: this was no girlfriend, but his wife. One anecdote, told by Wheeler in his autobiography, seemed particularly telling of the way they worked together. Sitting eating lunch one summer's day on a wall of the Lydney ruins, he had contemplated a piece of fourth-century 'inferior cement' that had apparently been laid to mend a broken mosaic. 'Beside it lay a pick, and the conjunction of idleness and opportunity was too much for me. I drove the point of the pick into the cement patch.' The soil beneath the cement was 'freckled with minute green specks'. The specks turned out to be 1,646 tiny late-antique coins, probably dating from the mid fourth century. For Wheeler, these *minimi* were a 'veritable symbol of the Dark Ages'. A newspaper article romantically called them 'King Arthur's small change'. It was a find that would 'alone have justified our two seasons' work on that lovely spot', remembered Wheeler. It seems somehow entirely typical that while Mortimer had casually made the spectacular discovery, it was Tessa who followed patiently in his wake, cleaning and studying and classifying the tiny scraps of bronze.

It was on quite a different kind of day – when the wind was blowing strong, and rain threatened from a glowering January sky – that I went to Maiden Castle, in Dorset, one of Britain's most impressive Iron Age hill forts, which bears down from gloomy heights upon Dorchester and its satellite, Poundbury. I climbed up its high sides, which were twined round, at the summit, with a cat's cradle of sheer-sided ditches and earth ramparts. This may have been one of Suetonius's '20 hillforts' that the future emperor Vespasian took, when he fought his way west in the AD 40s after the defeat of Camulodunum. At the top, the gale blew so strong that you could lean right back into it and feel it cradling your body; but it scoured the skin on my face and wrenched my words away. In a corner of the plateau there were, like an after-thought, the foundations of a late Roman temple, dwarfed by the great scale of the older fortifications. It is not the only Dorset Iron Age hill fort to have been thus adopted: at Hod Hill near Blandford Forum, a Claudian-era fort was improvised out of a corner of British earth ramparts, so that two sides of it are regimented and Roman, straight lines marching over the hilltop, and two are formed by the great snaking curve of the Iron Age defences.

Thomas Hardy's short story, 'A Tryst at an Ancient Earthwork', describes the approach to Maiden Castle: 'The profile of the whole stupendous ruin, as seen at a distance of a mile eastward, is cleanly cut as that of a marble inlay. It is varied with protuberances, which from hereabouts have the animal aspect of warts, wens, knuckles, and hips. It may indeed be likened to an enormous many-limbed organism of an antediluvian time – partaking of the cephalopod in shape – lying lifeless . . .' The story, told in the first person, describes an ascent to Maiden Castle by night, as a storm rages. The narrator is to meet there an antiquary, whom he finds wielding a spade – against the law. 'I inquire why, as a professed and well-known antiquary with capital letters at the tail of his name, he did not obtain the necessary authority, considering the stringent penalties for this sort of thing; and he chuckles fiercely again with suppressed delight, and says, "Because they wouldn't have given it!"' The antiquary begins to dig, and at length discovers 'a pavement of minute tesserae of many colours'. He goes on with his spade, and draws from the earth 'a semi-transparent bottle of iridescent beauty, the sight of which draws groans of luxurious sensibility'. Then comes a skeleton; and then a bronze figurine of Mercury. The storm renews itself, more vigorous than before. At the end of the night, the antiquary reburies each of his treasures, though 'each deposition seems to cost him a twinge; and at one moment I fancied I saw him slip his hand into his coat pocket'. Against the backdrop of the lashing storm, and the unspeak-ably ancient sleeping beast that is Maiden Castle, the antiquary's desecration seems both arrogant, and deeply irrelevant.

It was here that the Wheelers undertook a major excavation that began in the summer of 1934. By this time, they had also worked together on Verulamium, the Roman predecessor of St Albans. (Here the *Daily Mail* had taken an interest in 'Girl Excavators', describing Tessa, in a piece of 9 August 1930, as a 'woman with dark wavy hair and smiling brown eyes, dressed in a business-like brown jumper and skirt, brown stockings, and Wellington boots', who is 'directing the important work of excavating the site of the Roman city of Verulam'.) But after St Albans, Wheeler had professed himself suffering from 'a satiety of Roman things'. Iron Age Maiden Castle was to make a change – though, of course, studying the remains of the Roman temple was part of the job. It was the largest dig the Wheelers had masterminded, with Mortimer as general, and Tessa the ever-efficient aide-de-camp, supervising the many students who came to dig, some of whom would go on to great archaeological careers. William Wedlake, who worked initially as the dig's foreman, recalled: 'I well remember Dr Wheeler's arrival at the site. My first impression was of his long striding legs with equally long arms . . . I soon noticed that Mrs Wheeler and the staff which he had brought with him from London were trained almost like commandos to carry out the Keeper's instructions.' Not for nothing Wheeler's war career. The digging was hard work, but there was also something of a holiday atmosphere. Tourists came and bought souvenirs: objects of the minor archaeological type, pieces of tile and slingshots. For the student excavators, there were amateur dramatics (including a pageant enacting the site's archaeological layers, with a pantomime mammoth), and, no doubt, affairs.

Before the third season of digging, in the spring of 1936, Wheeler set off alone on a trip to Egypt, Palestine, Lebanon and Syria, in order to acquaint himself with the archaeology of the Levant. He also, reported Hawkes, had personal reasons for taking the trip alone; the presence in Palestine of 'a remarkable young woman, the then reigning sovereign of his love life'. On his way back, six weeks later, he bought the *Times* at the Gare du Nord. Flicking through it on the train, a headline caught his eye: 'TESSA VERNEY WHEELER'. The article was an obituary. She had died three days earlier, at the age of forty-three, from a pulmonary embolism, the aftermath of a botched operation for misdiagnosed appendicitis. Wheeler pressed the bell-button and ordered a double brandy; a 'kindly numbness' spread through his mind.

The excavations at Maiden Castle continued that summer, but for student diggers such as Veronica Seton-Williams – an Australian who had been drawn to England to study archaeology with the Wheelers, and who had found in Tessa a beloved mentor – 'the magic of the great hill had gone'. Tessa's friends felt that her death had been hastened through neglect and overwork, and pain at Wheeler's infidelities. There was no pause in his pursuit of pretty girls.

In *Still Digging*, Wheeler describes his wife's death out of chronological sequence, placing it next to his account of Passchendaele. The battle, in October 1917, was 'the nadir of physical misery', but, he wrote, he felt its 'mental effect' only after his wife's death in 1936. Passchendaele, he wrote, was 'the definition of hell'. 'The cataclysmic rains and such shelling as never was before had churned the whole landscape into bottomless mud, honeycombed continuously with ever-renewed shell holes, every shell hole liable to be an actual grave or a pond of slime into which the wounded rolled from time to time and were choked to death.' As he picked his way across this deathly landscape, late at night, 'I flashed my torch to circumvent a shell hole; the thin light lit up an arm and half-clenched hand, thrust from the mud as though to clasp my ankle.'

The report on Maiden Castle was written up, at length, and dedicated to the memory of Tessa Verney Wheeler. The great discovery was of a 'war cemetery' at the fort's east gate, in which Wheeler envisaged Britons interred after bloody defeat by the Romans ('the fury of massacre rather than the tumult of battle'). He believed that the battle had taken place as the Romans marched west under Vespasian, flattening everything in their path. In a vivid passage in the report, he pictured the survivors of the dreadful onslaught creeping forth 'from their broken stronghold' as 'the ashes of their burned huts lay warm and thick upon the ground' to bury their dead 'hastily and anxiously and without order'. He wrote: 'The whole war cemetery as it lay exposed before us was eloquent of mingled piety and distraction, of weariness, of dread, of darkness, but yet not of complete forgetfulness. Surely no poor relic in the soil of Britain was ever more eloquent of high tragedy.'

The graves are not now thought of as a 'war cemetery'. Later archaeologists have judged the bodies to have been carefully placed, not hurriedly buried in the wake of a massacre. Even though a handful of them bear the marks of a violent death, there is no evidence that the people were killed by a single, cataclysmic war event. And yet

Wheeler, soldier and widower, dug into the soil of this Dorset hill and found violence, and untimely death. It was as if the three events – the death of his wife, the ghastly scenes of Passchendaele and the slaughter at Maiden Castle – had folded in on each other. As if the grief and guilt and devastation at Tessa's death could be exorcised only through his summoning up a vision of the dead of Maiden Castle. As if, too, the British dead themselves had been fashioned into imagined being – ghostly warriors – through a memory of the dread and darkness of his own war.

6

Bath

There's a lot of fine-boned, blue-eyed English madness in Bath, part
of its charm, a population with rather more than a fair share of occult-
ists, neo-Platonists, yogis, theosophists, little old ladies who have spirit
conversations with Red Indian squaws, religious maniacs, senile
dements, natural lifers, macrobiotics, people who make perfumed
candles, kite-flyers, do you believe in fairies?

Angela Carter, 1977

The city of Bath exists because of the hot sulphurous waters that
surge from the ground in almost appalling profusion. A quarter of a
million litres gushed through the Romans' sacred spring every day,
and fed in turn the medieval King's Bath that was built above it. If
you visit the Roman baths, you can see the ancient overflow pipe, the
stone around it stained orange from the metals in the water, still
carrying away the spuming, frothing excess to the Avon. This scalding
bounty is reckoned to pulse up from three kilometres beneath the
Mendips. The very water itself is ancient, even by Roman standards:
it fell as rain on the hills 6,000 years ago.

When I dunked myself in the open-air rooftop pool at the Thermae,
the city's modern spa, steam rose from the water, and hung in the air
like the breath of a giant. It was chill January, and snowflakes declined
gracefully from a swollen white sky. Even in the antiseptic environment
of the modern, hygienic bathing facility, I caught a hint of grandeur,
of mysterious chthonic forces titanically bound beneath the earth. It
was easy to see why the Celts' god Sulis lived here; and why the Romans
adopted the cult, merging Sulis with their Minerva, and building, from
the late first century AD, the city of Aquae Sulis. For the Romans, all
springs were bound to the gods, liminal places where the superficial

realm of the everyday and the great dark unknown of the Underworld collided. They were not to be taken lightly.

This was Bath's first heyday: its Roman period, when the great temple to Sulis-Minerva was built, in the late first century. Its magnificent pediment was carved with the image – held aloft by winged Victories – of a frowning, Gorgonesque deity, his face circled with snaky hair and beard. Beside the temple was the frequently re-elaborated complex of baths, including a rectangular pool that is now open to the sky and fringed around with fake-antique statues, but was once closed in by a barrel-vaulted ceiling. Altars, tombs and inscribed lead tablets hint that Bath was busy with tourists, or pilgrims, and locals with their curious Romano-Celtic names (Uricalus, Cocus, Oconea, Enica, Senicio). Here were hot baths, warm baths, cold baths – visitors still sling coins, without perhaps knowing why, into the elegant circular cold bath, just as the thousands of Romans flung coins into the sacred spring. A *haruspex* set up an inscribed stone here: Lucius Marcius Memor is the only priest known in Britain who dealt in the arcane Etruscan art of reading the future from the arrangement of the warm, bloody entrails of slaughtered animals.

At some point late in the Roman period, the flooding Avon caused the baths and temple area repeatedly to silt up. And so they were gradually abandoned. There is an Anglo-Saxon poem, from the collection known as the *Exeter Book*, that has often been regarded as describing the ruins of Bath. The poem is ruined itself, in fragments because the manuscript was badly scarred by fire. It is a lyrical meditation on a once great city, destroyed by *wierd*, fate, and it ends, or fades into fragments, thus:

> There once many a man
> mood-glad, gold-bright, of gleams garnished,
> flushed with wine-pride, flashing war-gear,
> gazed on wrought gemstones, on gold, on silver,
> on wealth held and hoarded, on light-filled amber,
> on this bright burg of broad dominion.
>
> Stood stone houses; wide streams welled
> hot from source, and a wall all caught
> in its bright bosom, that the baths were
> hot at hall's hearth; that was fitting . . .
> . . .
>
> Thence hot streams, loosed, ran over hoar stone
> unto the ring-tank . . .
> . . . It is a kingly thing
> . . . city . . .

Bath's second heyday was in the eighteenth century, when the dandy Beau Nash became the unofficial king of a newly glamorous, fashionable watering-hole, which burst through its medieval walls to become, through riotous bouts of speculative building, a great Georgian town, its architecture defined by classical qualities, as if it was reliving its Roman period. This was the era of the cure, of taking the waters – both by bathing in them and by imbibing them. '*Ariston men hudor*', is the Grecian boast inscribed above the door of the Pump Room: 'water is best', the opening words of Pindar's first *Olympian Ode*. Thomas Guidott's *A Discourse of Bathe, and the Hot Waters There*, first published in the 1670s, noted that the waters were good for the stomach, for they 'infallibly cleanse this useful Receptacle from any Impurities lodging in the Bottom or Plicatures thereof'. The water increased appetite and made 'those that drink it receive and enjoy their Food with more Delight and Satisfaction'. It was also 'of good Use in the Heart-burning, or Cardialgia, occasioned by the Sharpness and Acrimony of a bilious Humour'. Furthermore, 'It is of singular

Use in all Fluxes, whether with Blood, or without; Diarrhea's, Dysenteries, or bloody Urine.' Moreover, 'It is also of incomparable Use in the Diabetes, or pissing Disease.' For women, the water 'prepares them for Conception; so that in some kinds of Barrenness, no more effectual Medicine can be used'. A veritable panacea, then, with only one or two caveats: 'I doubt not also to commend it in the Dropsy, but Care must be taken that it pass well away, otherwise it may prove more prejudicial than advantagious. The like also may be said of the Gout.' These days, you can buy a little bottle of the stuff for £3.99 a throw in the Roman Baths souvenir shop, or drink a tepid glass (50p) straight from the source in the Pump Room. It is unpleasant enough to make you feel that it is doing you good: William Stukeley, in medical mode, reported that after drinking it, 'you find yourself brisker immediately' and that 'it is of most sovereign virtue to strengthen the bowels, to restore their lost tone through intemperance or inactivity'.

As well as enjoying the health-giving properties of the waters, visitors to Bath might also have rather less respectable experiences. According to a salacious soft-porn tome called *A Step to the Bath*, anonymously published in 1700, the town was both 'a Valley of Pleasure, yet a sink of Iniquity'. The author described first his journey from London, en route seducing a fellow coach passenger ('I lay'd her down on Nature's Carpet, and made bold with Mother Earth for a Boulster'). This activity caused him certain discomforts on the onward journey: 'Nor would I advise any who have been Sufferers in Venus sports, to Adventure the Fatigue of Coach to the Bath, least it dis-joint a Member or Two.' Once installed, he provided an unpleasantly graphic picture of those taking the cure – for syphilis, it seems – in the King's Bath: 'In a Corner was an Old Fornicator hanging by the Rings, Loaded with Rotten Humidity; Hard by him was a Buxom Dame, Cleansing her Nunquam Satis from Mercurial Dregs, and the remains of Roman Vitriol. Another, half-covered in Sear-Cloth, had more Sores than Lazarus, doing Pennance for the Sins of Her Youth . . . At the Pump was several a Drenching their Gullets, and Gormandizing the Reaking Liquor wholesale.' A satire after Juvenal's own sclerotic heart.

Since these heady days, Bath has been in a state of more or less genteel decline, punctuated by little peaks and troughs in its fortunes. When Jan Morris wrote about the town in 1974, she thought of it as 'hangdog', and on its way to ruin: 'There are houses never rebuilt since the blitz, or awaiting, year after year, planning permission or builders' cash. There are abandoned churches up for sale. Through the cracks of stately flagstone tufts of grass spring through, and sometimes the corner of a garden, the elbow of an alley, is choked with creeper and bramble, as though a civilization has retreated here, and the weeds are taking over.' Occasionally, Morris wrote, she fantasised about Bath's 'crescents peeling and unkempt under a philistine dictatorship, or forcibly converted into workers' holiday homes, and . . . the last of the admirals' widows scrubbing the floors of ideological museums'. But the town is seeing better days now, firmly established as smart, and as a place where overseas tourists go, on the little British grand tour that also takes in London, Oxford, York and Edinburgh. The Roman baths are paying their way, a major attraction. Bath is revived by the regenerative powers of the hot-water springs, just as it always has been.

The Royal Crescent and the Circus – two of the great Palladian set pieces of the city – were laid out by the architect John Wood, and finished off by his son, also called John Wood. The elder Wood was the most important of the Georgian improvers of Bath: he set the tone in the town for ever after, but he was thwarted in his grander designs. In 1725, he 'proposed to make a grand Place of Assembly, to be called the Royal Forum of Bath; another Place, no less magnificent, for the Exhibition of Sports, to be called the Grand Circus; and a third Place, of equal State with either of the former, for the Practice of medicinal Exercises, to be called the Imperial Gymnasium of the City, from a Work of that Kind, taking its Rise at first in Bath, during the time of the Roman Emperors'. The Circus is the only element of this grandiloquent piece of town planning that was realised, though it is doubtful whether it has ever been used for the 'Exhibition of Sports'. Wood, when he made his extravagant proposals, was about twenty-one years old.

With his schemes for imperial gymnasia and his talk of emperors, Wood was playing up to the city's Roman past. The temple of Sulis-Minerva had not yet in fact been discovered – that happened during the rebuilding of the Pump Room in 1790, well after Wood's death in 1754. But Bath was known to have Roman origins: as far back as the sixteenth century, antiquary John Leland had noted that 'There be divers notable antiquitees of the toune in hominum memoria engravid in stone that yet be sene yn the walles of Bathe.' He carefully transcribed some of the inscriptions on these tombstones, noting that they seemed to have been recycled into the town walls, rather than originally placed there. Later, William Camden noted, with typical penetration, that 'where the said Cathedrall Church now standeth, there was in ancient time, as the report goeth, a temple consecrated to Minerva'. He was not very many metres off target. The 'report', in all likelihood, was a passage from the third- or fourth-century Roman author Gaius Julius Solinus. His work *Collectanea rerum mirabilium, A Collection of Marvels*, had mentioned prodigious springs in Britain consecrated to the goddess: Aquae Sulis clearly had a reputation in antiquity that spread far beyond Britain. In 1727 – a couple of years after Wood had laid out his original proposals – workmen digging a sewer in Stall Street found a bronze head of Minerva: it is now one of the great objects of the Roman baths museum.

Wood's aim, however, was much broader than a simple desire to re-create the glories of the Roman city. He laid out the theoretical basis for his designs in his *Essay Towards a Description of Bath*, as masterful a piece of entertaining fairy tale, tortured logic, hard-headed architectural sales pitch and pure gossip as has ever been produced. It is remarkable that the result of this kind of thinking was what Angela Carter described as Bath's 'lucid and serene' streets, for the tone of Wood's book is quite the reverse. He even included a lurid account of the suicide of one of his tenants, one Sylvia, who hanged herself by a girdle 'of Silver Thread' owing him 'two and fifty Pounds three Shillings and four Pence for Rent'. The antiquary Roger Gale wrote to his friend Stukeley that *A Description* was 'a silly pack of stuff, collected together from our fabulous historians, & where their fictions or traditions are not sufficient to support his fancys, he never wants falsitys of his own invention to supply their defect', which is a fair review, but does not get across the fact that it is also an oddly enjoyable read.

Wood began by reasserting the mythical foundation story of Bath. In Geoffrey of Monmouth's *The History of the Kings of Britain*, in which the seeds of the story first appeared, the city was said to have been established by Bladud, father of Lear and descendant of the Trojan exile Brutus. This Bladud 'encouraged necromancy throughout the kingdom of Britain', according to Geoffrey, and, like Daedalus, constructed himself a pair of wings. But the experiment went wrong, and he was dashed to pieces on the temple of Apollo in Trinovantum, the city that would eventually become London. Over time, the story was elaborated. Bladud, as a youth, so the expanded story went, contracted leprosy, and was exiled from the royal court. He became a swineherd. One day his pigs went astray. At length he found a sow wallowing in some hot springs, from which she emerged cured of all her ailments. Bladud too immersed himself in the waters, and his leprosy vanished. He returned to the court and in due course became king. Around the muddy spot where he had been cured he built Bath. By the time Wood was a young man, this medieval story was already regarded as nonsense – though as it happens, Geoffrey of Monmouth's claim that Bladud founded Bath in 'around 863 BC' is stated as fact in the brochure for the Thermae spa.

Wood took the myth of Bladud, and, through some tortuous chronological comparisons with the Bible and classical history, adjusted Bath's foundation date from 863 to 483 BC. He also shifted the whole of Geoffrey's geography to the south-west. When Geoffrey talked of the Thames, he must have meant the Tamar, argued Wood. Trinovantum, where Bladud died, was clearly not in the south-east of England, as Geoffrey claimed, for the exiles could not have been 'skipping from one remote Part of the Island to another with a Handful of People and carrying New Troy into Middlesex'. Rather, it was Bath that was Trinovantum. (Geoffrey himself must have been drawing on a garbled memory of the ancient British tribe, mentioned in various classical texts, of the Trinovantes, who inhabited parts of Essex and Suffolk.)

The account became yet more involved. Wood claimed that Bladud was one and the same person as a figure of classical myth, Abaris, who flew about upon a sacred arrow 'in the Air over Rivers and Lakes, Forests and Mountains'. This character's existence, and airborne adventuring, were doubted even on his first literary outing in Herodotus's *Histories*, in the fifth century BC. But Wood ran away with the idea: Abaris/Bladud was 'received in Greece as the known Priest of Apollo', he decided. Furthermore, he restored the temple of Apollo at Delphi, consorted with Pythagoras, and very likely communicated the heliocentric model of the universe to Zoroaster. On his return to Britain, he established the priesthood of the Druids: 'King Bladud appears manifestly to have been their Founder, and to have made Bath their Metropolitan Seat; and part of what he taught them was first communicated to him by the great Pythagoras.'

Wood was not alone in developing a great interest in the Druids, an order of Celtic religious men of Britain and Gaul, known only through their brief mention in a handful of classical texts. The geographer Strabo wrote of their undertaking human sacrifice inside a 'wicker man'; Caesar and Diodorus Siculus described them as powerful religious figures, diviners of the future. The Romans, easy-going when it came to tolerating and appropriating others' religions, drew the line at both human sacrifice and anything with a whiff about it of organised resistance to Rome. In Suetonius's biography of Claudius, the Druidic religion was called 'dreadful and savage' – the emperor abolished its practice in Gaul, noted the writer. In Tacitus, Druids are mentioned as a focus for British resistance against Roman rule: Suetonius Paulinus was attempting to put down a Druid-orchestrated rebellion when Boudica struck. From the seventeenth century onwards, antiquaries such as John Aubrey and the Irish philosopher John Toland speculated that megalithic monuments including Stonehenge and Avebury were Druidic. (The architect Inigo Jones was in the minority when he argued that they were Roman.) That the Druids were connected to such monuments was, perhaps, not an entirely unreasonable stab in the dark when a biblical chronology for world history was still broadly accepted, before the archaeological system of Stone, Bronze and Iron Ages had been developed, when all there was to go on for prehistory were scant details about the Celts in classical authors. A wiser head than Wood's (the eighteenth-century antiquary Robert Sibbald) thought that prehistoric flint arrowheads were elf-bolts let loose from the heavens by fairies. William Stukeley was particularly notorious for his obsession with the Druids, even devising a temple in his vicarage garden, at its centre an 'antient appletree oregrown with sacred misletoe'.

Wood's enthusiasm for the Druids impelled him to survey the stone circles at Stanton Drew, near Bath. He did this in the teeth of superstitious opposition from the locals, who warned that everyone who had previously attempted to measure these still poorly understood monuments had been 'struck dead upon the Spot, or with such an

Illness as soon carried them off'. Surviving the encounter with the monument, he found the main stone circle (through a bit of jiggery-pokery) to be not only the precise diameter of the Pantheon in Rome, but also, when taken together with other standing stones in the vicinity, to 'form a perfect Model of the Pythagorean System of the Planetary World'. Stanton Drew was, concluded Wood, nothing less than a university for Druids. Bath and Stanton Drew had been 'founded by one and the same Person, and for the same Purposes, to wit, to cure the Diseases of the People, to honour the Gods, and to instruct Mankind in the Liberal Sciences'.

Though it is hard to synthesise Wood's ideas – contradictory and mercurial as they are – another of his works, *The Origin of Building*, brings some of these notions into the realm of what he felt he was doing architecturally. Like many of the intellectuals, architects and artists of the early eighteenth century (including, for example, Stukeley), Wood was a Freemason. One of Freemasonry's tenets was that the principles of true architecture had originated among the Jews. These principles, including the three classical orders, were then bequeathed to the Greeks. As Wood explained in *The Origin of Building*, it was the pillars of Moses's tabernacle that 'furnish'd the various Sorts of Building necessary for Man; as the Strong, the Mean, and the Delicate; and which, in Process of Time, were ranked under the Name of Order, with Grecian Names; to wit, Dorick, Jonick, and Corinthian'. In turn, according to the Freemasons, these principles passed to the Romans, and at length to the peoples whom the Romans had conquered. The Romans, wrote James Anderson in *The Constitutions of the Free-Masons*, 'communicated their Cunning to the northern and western Parts of Europe, which had grown barbarous before the Roman conquest'. Thinking of Britain's henges and standing stones, he also allowed that the ancient Britons might have produced 'a few Remains of good Masonry' before the Romans appeared. The keystone of Wood's shaky argument was to take Anderson's hint about 'a few Remains of good Masonry' and claim that the ancient Britons, in particular the Druids, had directly inherited true architecture from its Jewish source, bypassing the Greeks and Romans. 'If we were to scrutinize all the Works of the Druids, we shou'd find them to have been copied from the Works of the Jews,' he asserted. They 'bespeak a Parent of more Antiquity than the Romans'.

How does this theorising manifest itself in the streets of Bath? In the vast spaces of the Circus, each facade is decorated with the three orders of classical architecture, Doric, Ionic and Corinthian – the orders that Wood believed had adorned Moses's tabernacle, and had been disseminated by the Jews. The Circus is, very obviously, meant to be Bath's Roman Colosseum. But it is also a stone circle, its form and dimensions echoing the measurements Wood took during his survey of Stanton Drew. The frieze of the Doric entablature is decorated with hundreds of pictorial emblems, some of which – a hand reaching from the clouds holding a pair of compasses, for example – are overtly Masonic. And so Wood's masterpiece, generally supposed to contain all the neoclassical virtues of harmony, elegance and balance, is in fact a magnificently demented mingling of disparate thought-experiments, a glorious piece of architecture 'built brilliantly on theoretical foundations of some absurdity', as his biographers have put it. The Circus aims to re-create the glories of the Roman empire. But it also aims to be a specifically British, ancient architecture, echoing a megalithic monument and, in turn, casting back to Solomon's temple itself.

When I visited the Roman baths, I spoke to Romans. This was the claim: that history would 'come to life'. At the side of the great open-air pool now lurk costumed interpreters – each named for a real character mentioned on one of the Roman inscriptions found here. I met Flavia Tiberina: the wife, she said, of Gaius from the procurator's office in Londinium. She was wearing a high halo of a Flavian-period hairdo, just like the coiffure of one of the most striking carved heads from the museum. We talked about make-up, the plucking of her underarm hair ('Do you know, I actually think the slave enjoyed it') and the farewell dinner she was expected to enjoy that evening ('There will be dormice'). The interpreter was very good at what she did, and I enjoyed talking to her. The exercise seemed to be about finding that we had things in common. Beauty routines, dinner – if not the minutiae of the methods or the specifics of the menu. I was being invited to believe not only that the costumed interpreters were behaving like Romans – but that Romans behaved like costumed interpreters: friendly, unthreatening, familiar. I couldn't help feeling, as Flavia Tiberina and I chatted, that there were other stories that might be buried in the stones at Bath, stranger and more frightening ones. God knows what religious observances, rituals and sacrifices took place here. We did not discuss L. Marcius Memor, up to his elbows in animal gore. Nor the uncanny tin mask of a man's bearded face found in the sacred spring, perhaps (who knows) an emblem carried aloft in some ritual procession.

The sacred spring has borne many secrets. In 1978, a young girl died of amoebic meningitis after swimming in the waters. In the ensuing investigation, the pools were all drained, including the King's Bath – the medieval structure, topped with a seventeenth-century balustrade and statue of Bladud, that can be seen during a visit to the Pump Room or Roman baths today. Archaeologist Barry Cunliffe took the opportunity to excavate beneath the medieval bath, down into the Romans' sacred spring. As well as a number of beautiful carved intaglios from rings, his team found seventy-eight curse tablets. These are small, unprepossessing sheets of lead, many of which had been rolled into little sausages, just a few centimetres long, before being cast into the spring. They are incised with writing so faint and fragmentary that the untrained eye could easily miss it: it is indecipherable except by those expert in the sloping strokes of the hands known as old and new Roman cursive. The texts are appeals to the goddess of the spring to punish those who have done you wrong – the person who has stolen your blanket, your ring, your cloak, your money. The thing to do was to get the wording just right, as in a legal contract, so the goddess could not catch you out on a technicality. One tablet asks for the return of six silver coins from whomever has stolen them, 'whether pagan or Christian, whosoever, whether man or woman, whether boy or girl, whether slave or free'. No loopholes. This is the first occurrence of the word 'Christian' in any British inscription. The petitioner, Annianus, helpfully provided a list of suspects, a poem in itself: 'Postumianus, Pisso, Locinna, Alauna, Materna, Gunsula, Candidina, Euticius, Peregrinus, Latinus, Senicianus, Avitianus, Victor, Scotius, Aessicunia, Paltucca, Calliopis, Celerianus.'

Another tablet is on the subject of the theft of a cloak: 'To Minerva the goddess Sulis I have given the thief who has stolen my hooded cloak, whether slave or free, whether man or woman. He is not to buy back this gift unless with his own blood.' Sometimes the curses were brutal: the theft of one unknown object caused the petitioner to demand that the perpetrator, and his family, be prevented from eating, drinking, defecating or urinating. There is one tablet that is thought to have been written in British Celtic – using the Latin alphabet – which makes it unique, but untranslatable, without some kind of Rosetta Stone to unlock this usually unwritten language. Sometimes the curses were written right to left, as if to increase the magic, or the secrecy. There are a number of 'illiterate' tablets, random scratches on the lead, that those hurling them into the seething spring might have thought contained the enchanted power of writing. Dr Roger Tomlin, the scholar who has undertaken the delicate task of transcribing and interpreting the spidery, slippery handwriting of the tablets, thinks the curses may be the dark obverse of the goddess's power. If she can heal, then she can also debilitate; if she can help, she can also hurt, wielding that black strength from deep beneath the earth. He also thinks the curses worked: that is, sufficiently well for people to continue flinging them into the springs for two centuries.

Some of the curse tablets had turned up before Cunliffe's excavations. In 1904, Edward Williams Byron Nicholson, Bodley's librarian at the University of Oxford, settled on a very particular vacation project. He took with him on a Scottish holiday photographs of a tiny lead tablet, incised on both sides with what had hitherto been regarded as indecipherable letters. Roger Tomlin has written vividly of Nicholson: he was known to his deputy at the library as *diabolus bibliothecae*, the devil of the library; to others he was simply 'Old Nick'. Two of his board of curators, according to Tomlin, committed suicide under the strain of working with him. The sleeves of his voluminous gown used to dash the papers off desks as he swept like a tornado through the reading rooms. Among his many and varied interests, he attended spiritualist meetings, wrote on animal rights and was an antivivisectionist. He campaigned against plans to use the beautiful Jacobean entrance hall of the Bodleian Library as a bike shed. One of his many money-making schemes was an idea for selling biscuits imprinted with images of British beauty spots.

Nicholson's Scottish holiday was not idly spent. On his return, he published a pamphlet with a translation of the tablet's text:

Vinisius to Nigra: (? The grace) of the Lord Jesus Christ to thine also. (Thy) husband's faults Vinisia has related to Vilius's Similis. (? Do thou

be strong in Jesus and) with all thy strength (? in thee go counter).
Unless in just conflicts (lit. arenas) (? avoid jealousies more abundantly).
Christ's enemy has sent Biliconus from Viriconium that ye may take
(him) in the sheepfold, although a dog of Arius. Do thou pray Christ
for light. A(p)ulicus carries these sheets.'

This was sensational stuff. One of the great teases of Romano-
British history was then, and continues to be, precisely how widespread
Christianity was under Roman rule before Britain was subsumed by
the pagan Saxons. (Augustine's mission in 597 is the conventional date
for Christianity's official introduction to Britain, though in its original
Roman form it survived in the west and Ireland, whence it was later
reintroduced to Iona and then Lindisfarne and the north-east of
England.) As Nicholson put it in his pamphlet: 'Everybody . . . is aware
how very little we know of the history of Christianity in Britain during
the Roman occupation, and how scanty are its literary relics. There
are the texts of some writings of Pelagius in the early fifth century,
a blundered copy of the signatures of five British ecclesiastics at the
Council of Arles in 314, a few stones, rings, &c., with a Christian
monogram or motto – but that, I think, is the entire literary legacy
known to have been left by the British Christianity of that period:
there is not even a Christian inscription on a British tombstone which
can safely be ascribed to the first four centuries. Consequently more
than ordinary interest attaches to the fact that there exists in the Pump
Room at Bath a complete fourth-century Latin letter written by a
Christian man in Britain to a Christian woman in Britain.'

Nicholson's lead tablet referred not only to Christianity, but even
to the question of the Arian heresy, a non-Trinitarian position that
contended that God's divinity was stronger than that of Jesus, which
was debated at the First Council of Nicaea in AD 325. The same
controversy was mentioned in one of the very few near-contemporary
literary sources on the end of Roman rule in Britain, a polemical text
by the sixth-century cleric Gildas. In his *On the Destruction of Britain*,
he called the Arian heresy 'fatal as a serpent and vomiting its poison
from beyond the sea'.

Amid this paucity of evidence, Nicholson's reading threatened to
revolutionise knowledge of Christianity in Roman Britain. His translation was widely, and mostly warmly, covered in the newspapers. The

Scotsman was one of the few publications to express scepticism. 'In deciphering such ancient writings there is not a little danger of error,' wrote the paper's correspondent. 'Possibly the next interpreter may tell us that Vinisius and Vinisia, Nigra and her husband, Biliconus and Similis and Vilius, and Apulicus, the unfortunate postman who carried letters of lead from Viriconium to Aquae Sulis, are but shadows in the imagination of Bodley's Librarian. In the meantime we may accept his tale.'

Unfortunately for Nicholson, he had made one crucial error. He had read the tablet upside down. Tomlin turned the photographs over (the original sheet of lead is lost) and started again drawing his own copies of the text. He ended up with the following translation:

Whether (they be) boy or girl, whether man or woman, forgiveness is not to be given to the person who has stolen this unless [. . .] innocence. Forgiveness is not to be given to him/her, nor shall he/she sleep, except on condition that Euticia (?) sell a bushel of cloud, a bushel of smoke.

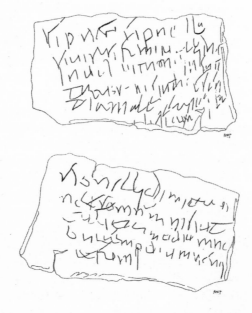

As Tomlin himself has pointed out, the text – while falling into the familiar formulae of the curse tablet – remains rather eccentric, with its bushels of smoke and cloud. You might even ask, why should we let Tomlin's reading pass without challenge? He himself would be the first to argue that deeply specialised palaeography of this kind is an insecure and provisional business. But what haunts me in this story is that Nicholson did not intend to deceive. He stared into the mirror of that dulled metal, and he conjured up visions, visions that were only reflections of himself. His Roman Britain was the purest, most perfect fantasy.

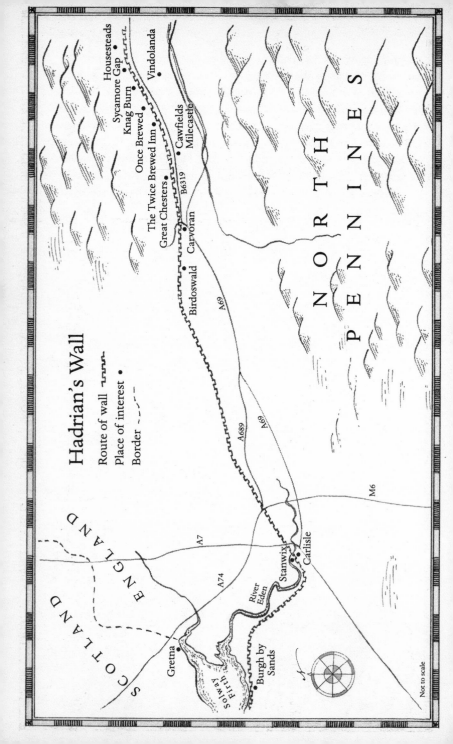

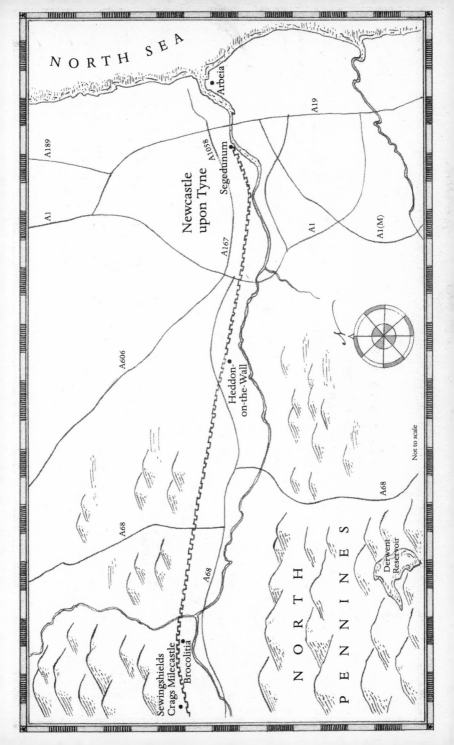

7

Hadrian's Wall

My laborious, my romantic, and even my Quixotic undertaking, the double tour of the Wall.

William Hutton, 1802

Still I hope that in our anticipated pilgrimage we shall not forsake the Wall a single yard in its course. Let us try to trace it over the whole of its length.

John Collingwood Bruce, 1885

A walk expresses space and freedom
and the knowledge of it can live
in the imagination of anyone, and that
is another space too.

Richard Long, 1980

From the summit of the wild and remote Sewingshields Crags, east of the Roman fort at Housesteads, you can stand next to Hadrian's Wall and see it snake away from you in either direction for miles, following a long, sharp ridge. That ridge is part of the Whin Sill, a tide of volcanic rock that forced itself up to the earth's surface 295 million years ago like (according to an unusually vivid local information board) the jam forcing its way through the bread in a sandwich. The landscape seems to stretch itself out impossibly luxuriously. There are no towns, no villages to be seen, just the occasional lough, hill farm and plantation, and (on this bright, blustery day) the clouds racing their shadows over the calm heights. Here, the wall might have been built on the crest of a wave frozen at the point of breaking.

It is hard to imagine this knobbly spine of stones as the implacable
barrier it once was, a structure two metres thick and five metres tall,
manned by infantry, its bulk blotting out the views that the steady
stream of walkers now comes to admire. It was built in AD 122 by order
of the new emperor Hadrian. His policy was to set the empire, peril-
ously overstretched by his predecessor Trajan, within defined, consoli-
dated limits; this barrier would be the spine of its northernmost frontier
zone. The wall extends eighty Roman miles (seventy-four of ours) from
the Solway Firth in the west to the Tyne in the east, punctually marked
by eighty-one milecastles, or fortified gatehouses, allowing (or rather
controlling) access to the north or south. Between each milecastle came
two turrets; and at times the line of the wall suddenly opens out into
a large rectangular enclosure where a fort once stood.

Sometimes the wall rises and falls in graceful increments, working
in discreet harmony with the landscape; but at others, particularly
just a little further west from here, around the famous spot known
as Sycamore Gap, it seems to compete directly with the terrain, making
swooping dives and wild climbs, describing curly U's and precipitous
W's. Sycamore Gap itself is a much-photographed spot: here the wall
performs a perfect acrobatic parabola, and at its very bottom grows
the lonely tree for which it is named. You can discern the Roman love
of regularity and order here: even though the milecastle at Cawfields,
for example, is built on a ludicrously steep slope, it still has a northern
gate opening out on to thin air at the escarpment's edge. (The line is
drawn at Sewingshields Crags, where no northern gate seemed to be
deemed necessary, since it would have opened straight on to a plunging
cliff, like a trapdoor.)

The traditional idea of the wall – that it must have been built purely
to keep the aggressive northern peoples out of Roman territory –
should be set aside, according to current theories. It is now thought
that it was much more porous and provisional than that. The very
fact of its thickly spaced exit and entry points suggests plenty of traffic
through the checkpoints. Just east of Housesteads, at Knag Burn, an
extra gateway with a pair of guard chambers was built into the wall
in the fourth century: perhaps this was a convenient point for traders
and farmers taking sheep to their seasonal grazing.

What can have been the effect on the Britons of this astonishing
structure? This wall in the wilds of northern Britannia divides nowhere

from nowhere. Visually, it makes about as much sense as René Magritte's open door suspended in a cloudscape. The effect of all this insistence on uniformity and precision despite the terrain must have been impressive, if not cowing; part of its purpose, surely, was to intimidate. It is now thought that its value as a symbol of Roman might was at least as great as any practical, defensive purpose.

I was walking the wall with my friends Joshua and Damian, as a few days' respite from work and London. West of Knag Burn, at the visitors' centre at the delightfully named Once Brewed, we paused to eat a picnic, safely out of the high wind that was buffeting the tops. Nearby was an improvised pavilion supported on fake Roman standards. Under it, a woman deep in a book of sudoku puzzles sat on a folding chair next to a table laden with reproduction swords, strigils (the curved metal instruments Romans used to scrape oil from their limbs in the baths), and some sponges on sticks, the reputed Roman equivalent of lavatory paper. A little apart, as still as a statue as we approached, his red cloak flapping in the breeze and his breastplate glinting, stood a tall, thickset man, his height made more formidable by his crested helmet. Occasionally a family came up, hesitated shyly for a moment before starting to chat, and then a boy would put on a spare helmet and have his photograph taken with this imposing figure.

He introduced himself as Marcus Aufidius Maximus, of the 6th Legion. He had borrowed the name of a real Roman, who had dedicated altars at Bath. When in civvies he was Steve Richardson, from Newcastle; he was, he said, 'a full-time Roman centurion'. The souvenir stall was just for the summer; usually, he said, his work was school visits and events at archaeological sites and museums. At primary schools, he and his wife Lesley kitted out the children in uniforms and then 'I take them out on drills.' He had the six- to eight-year-olds doing the '*testudo*', the famous 'tortoise' infantry formation in which the soldiers locked their rectangular shields together to form a carapace against arrow showers.

How did he come to be a Roman centurion? 'I got fed up with selling kitchens and bathrooms,' he said. An interest in archaeology led to his getting a job working front-of-house at the Roman fort and museum of Segedunum, in Newcastle. One day a bakery wanted to photograph someone dressed as a Roman soldier for an advert. Richardson volunteered, and on his way back from the shoot to the fort he was, he said, 'mobbed by excited kids'. The museum management realised it could do something with a Roman soldier, so he started appearing at events at the fort and eventually went freelance as a centurion. After meeting him, I began to spot his good-natured face in all kinds of places: on a poster for a museum in Newcastle; even advertising the 'Roman Britain' ice cream produced by Doddington's, a local dairy. (The flavour is honey, cherry, apple and cinnamon.) 'I get paid for playing soldiers,' he said. 'What more could I want?'

Each night of our walk, Joshua, Damian and I put up in B&Bs. At Greencarts Farm, through which the wall runs, Sandra Maughan was struggling with her faulty Victorian pipes, fielding complaints, she said, from city folk expecting urban levels of water pressure, though she was not on the mains supply. Framed in her hallway were some humorous verses about the 'types' who walk the wall, with their unsuitable footwear, short shorts and dangly earrings. When we came down for our hearty walkers' breakfast, Maughan – an energetic redhead in late middle age, with a rich north-eastern accent – dropped us a conspiratorial wink as we shot a glance at the other guests, who were discussing Roman military matters with single-minded commitment over bacon and eggs. When the journalist Hunter Davies came here in the 1970s to write his book *A Walk on the Wall*, the farmers he spoke to didn't want tourists coming, leaving gates open, damaging fences. 'The most important thing in this area is farming. The wall comes second. It must never be allowed to take over,' he quoted one as saying. This now sounds like the dead rhetoric of a bygone age. Hill farms are less and less economically viable. In 2001, the last really serious British outbreak of foot-and-mouth disease started a few miles east of here at Heddon-on-the-Wall, with terrible consequences for the local economy. 'We were one of the last farms to lose all our animals,' Maughan told me. 'Foot and mouth came straight down the wall. Your farm got wiped out.' A neighbouring farm had one suspect animal – and then that was that. The slaughter began. 'It was spring; there were little lambs jumping around. And then your whole life was wiped out in two days,' she said. When the Hadrian's Wall path opened as an official tourist attraction in 2003, the farms were still in a bad state; the natural thing to do was to branch out into offering accommodation, and there was certainly the demand. Maughan started

putting people up in a couple of spare bedrooms; these days, at peak
times, she has had as many as 600 staying, what with the campsite
and the bunk house. The farm now makes 50 per cent of its income
from accommodation. Some of her friends, she said, 'don't like people
looking in your windows, knocking on your door'. The path has
certainly 'changed life dramatically'. But on the whole, Maughan
seemed to have found the experience enriching – a far cry from the
lonely farming existence of previous generations. 'You get English
people, foreign people. You get used to different cultures and expectations. You get politicians, actors, famous people stopping. There's only
the odd one you'd like to strangle.'

I spoke to one of the local MPs, who was trying to find ways to
dramatically increase the number of visitors. At the moment, a million
a year come to visit museums and sites on the wall; 200,000 walk part
of the trail; and around 11,000 walk it end to end. He'd like there to
be more than that. 'We need people to come away from the Lake
District and visit here instead,' he said. 'There's nothing here that can
make the farmers any money. Except the landscape.' There was debate,
he said, about how to make the wall more attractive, more vivid. He
thought that rebuilding a section, so that tourists could get a sense of
how colossal and imposing it had once been, might help. Linda Tuttiett,
who runs the organisation that oversees what is known as 'the
Hadrian's Wall corridor', told me that the wall brings in about £880m
a year to Cumbria and Northumberland – but she'd like to see that
go up by £300m over the next twenty years. She too wanted tourists
to the Lake District to come to the wall: 'We can have two international brands working really hard for Cumbria,' she told me. 'Hadrian's
Wall is one of the most iconic World Heritage Sites. The opportunity
for it to underpin the economy of the north is vast.' It is not just a
matter of the farming economy. When Hunter Davies stopped at
Segedunum fort in Newcastle, he tried to visit Swan Hunter, the
shipyard not far from there along the A187 (or Hadrian Road, as it is
named locally), but found the workers on strike: 'The boilermakers
were wanting an increase of £4 a week on their average wage of £34,'
he wrote. At the time, the yard was building the *Ark Royal*. Today
Swan Hunter is stilled: the cranes and floating dock have been sold
to India. The company still operates, but with a staff of 200, concen-
trating on engineering and design services.

Once Brewed is within spitting distance of Housesteads and Vindolanda, two of the most important forts in the area. Housesteads was built on to the wall; Vindolanda pre-dates it. Around the military forts tended to spring up a *'vicus'*, or civilian settlement. The forts were built to a more or less uniform plan: a rectangular stone perimeter with rounded-off corners; a gate in the centre of each wall; an HQ building often with a basilica; a commanding officer's quarters with a suite of baths; and barracks for the troops. You could walk into a fort anywhere in the empire from Egypt to Spain to Romania, and still find your way around. Seeing fort after fort along the wall, we soon began to grasp the grammar of them, to find their layouts familiar. At Housesteads, the troops were Tungrians from modern Belgium, who set up a temple with magnificent sculptures to Mithras. The god's men-only mystery cult, beloved of the military, seems to have developed in the west of the empire (the earliest known Mithraeum is in the outskirts of Frankfurt), but it was marinated in the mysticism of the east, of Persia. Great Chesters, further west, was manned by Belgians, then Raetians from the German–Austrian border, then Astures from north-west Spain. At Carvoran fort, there was, in the second century AD, a cohort of soldiers from the modern Syrian city of Hama, who set up an altar to their goddess, Hammia. Eventually they were replaced by Dalmatians, from Croatia. At Arbeia, Iraqis from the Tigris plied the mouth of the Tyne. At Carlisle, there were Algerians. In the Great North Museum in Newcastle (where you can also see the sculptures from the Housesteads Mithraeum), there is a little azure-blue glass bottle, in the shape of a smiling African face, found at South Shields; it probably came from Egypt. And in the late second century, one Tineius Longus, a prefect in command of a cavalry regiment of the 20th Legion, dedicated an altar to an otherwise obscure local British god, Antenociticus. Tineius Longus was fulfilling his vow on his promotion to *quaestor* – a junior magistrate's role that would have put him on the path to a senatorial career, high political office in Rome.

As we walked the wall, the days were filled with genial chat; each night, after we found our B&B, we gratefully removed our boots, ate a hearty pub supper and slept off the day's hard walking. There was a comforting rhythm to it: a tremendous simplicity about doing nothing but walking east. The wall was like another companion. On the penultimate day of our journey, we arrived at Heddon-on-the-Wall, nine miles west of Newcastle. The post-war housing estate we walked through had grandly classicising street names. 'Marius Avenue, leading to Calvus Drive, Camilla Road, Valerian Avenue and Antonine Avenue', read one sign. Here was the easternmost surviving stretch of the wall, running 100 metres or so, between a busy B road and a paddock fringed with ash trees. Behind it, the sunlight glinted off someone's greenhouse and washing flapped on a line. An ice-cream van played a tune somewhere a few streets away; as melancholy a sound as you could imagine. We said farewell to the wall, and began to descend to Newcastle.

Walking the wall was not always such a gregarious activity. William Camden came in 1599, and wrote, 'Verily I have seene the tract of it over the high pitches and steepe descents of hilles, wonderfully rising and falling.' But the wall was then part of what Camden called the 'batable ground' – disputed, lawless territory between England and Scotland, inhabited by cattle-rustling reivers 'infamous for theeving and robbing'. Describing his foray to the central section of the wall, near the notorious crime spot of Busy-Gap, Camden wrote that he 'could not with safety take the full survey of it for the ranke robbers there about'. He was able, though, to study numerous sculptures, including an altar dedicated to the deity whom the Romans called 'the Syrian goddess', Atargatis – which was being used as a laundry stone by the local women.

It was many years later that visiting the wall was regarded as anything approaching a pleasure trip. The antiquary John Warburton published an account of it in 1753, noting that the country was 'wild and baron', and few 'searchers after Roman ruins' had ventured here. Warburton is today best remembered for having dimwittedly entrusted some fifty Elizabethan and Jacobean plays in manuscript, some of them the sole surviving copies, to his cook, who 'unluckily burnd or put under pye bottoms' all but three. His survey of the wall was dedicated to the Duke of Cumberland, the 'Butcher' Cumberland who had quashed the Jacobite rebellion in 1745. The work began with a pointed 'I-told-you-so', informing readers that as far back as 1715 Warburton had attempted to persuade the government of the necessity of renewing the Roman military road, running south of the wall, for modern use, making it 'passable for troops and artillery' between Carlisle and Newcastle. An Act of Parliament of 1751 had finally brought this about, and much of this military way, now the B6318, was built over the wall's remains, which were ruthlessly flattened for miles.

Change was gradually on its way. In 1801, William Hutton, a native of Birmingham, walked from his home city to the wall. He tramped along it twice, there and back, and then took himself back to the Midlands. At the end of his account of the walk, published in 1802, he reported his 'loss, by perspiration, of one stone of animal weight; an expenditure of forty guineas, a lapse of thirty-five days, and a walk of six hundred and one miles'. That was an average of seventeen miles a day. He was seventy-eight years old. 'Perhaps,' he wrote, 'I am the first man that ever travelled the whole length of the Wall, and probably the last that ever will attempt it.'

Hutton's *History of the Roman Wall* was not intended for antiquaries, but for the amusement and edification of an interested but less expert public, who would, he hoped, travel 'with me, though by your own fire-side'. It began with a cheerful denunciation of antiquarian prose style. '[The antiquary] feeds upon withered husks, which none can relish but himself; nor does he seem to possess the art of dressing up his dried morsel to suit the palate of a reader.' Accounts of ruins, he said, were 'the dullest of all descriptions'. His approach would be different. He would 'enliven truth with a smile; with the anecdote'. Needless to say, he was not the last to walk the wall. Rather, perhaps, he was the first example of a new breed of visitor: the tourist.

For his walking tour, Hutton dressed entirely in black ('a kind of religious travelling warrant'), and carried a bag, 'much like a postman's letter pouch', filled with maps, including Warburton's plan of the wall. To that was strapped 'an umbrella in a green case, for I was not likely to have a six weeks tour without wet'. He clearly cut a remarkable figure as he strode through the villages of Staffordshire, Cheshire and Lancashire. 'The crowds I met in my whole journey viewed me with an eye of wonder and inquiry, as if ready to cry out "In the name of the Father, &c, What ar't!"'

The second edition of Hutton's book, published in 1813, included a contribution from his daughter, who accompanied her father on horseback as far as the Lakes, already an established tourist destination. Catherine Hutton was a fascinating character: a novelist, she lived to be ninety, amassing a correspondence of more than 2,000 letters with figures such as Charles Dickens. She described the shape of their days as they journeyed north: 'He rose at four o'clock, walked to the end of the next stage, breakfasted, and waited for me. I set out at seven; and, when I arrived at the same inn, breakfasted also. When my horse had fed properly, I followed; passed my Father on the road, arrived before him at the next inn, and bespoke dinner and beds.' She added: 'My Father was such an enthusiast with regard to the Wall, that he turned neither to the right or the left, except to gratify me with a sight of Liverpool.' She recalled how he had ignored her pleas ('with tears') that he should do at least some of the journey by carriage; and noted that he insisted on walking entirely on his own so as 'not to be put out of his regular pace'.

Hutton was, indeed, an ardent admirer of the wall: 'Men have been deified,' he wrote, 'for trifles compared to this admirable structure.' During his walk, he grew as fond of it as we did in ours, nicknaming it 'Severus', after the emperor who was then thought to have built its stone central section (it was not attributed to Hadrian until the mid nineteenth century). His horror at the wall's rapid demolition, in this era of urban expansion, was in proportion to his admiration. 'From the destruction of so large a part of these magnificent works, I fear, I shall be the last Author who shall describe them. Plunder is the order of the day.' At Byker's Hill (now part of Newcastle) he denounced the levelling of the Roman ditch and its conversion into potato beds, and at St Oswald's he noted a recent calamity. 'Had I been some months sooner, I should have been favoured with a noble treat; but now that treat was miserably soured. At the twentieth-mile stone, I should have seen a piece of Severus's Wall seven feet and a half high, and two hundred and twenty-four yards long: a sight not to be found in the whole line. But the proprietor, Henry Tulip, Esq. is now taking it down, to erect a farm-house with the materials.' He conveyed, via a servant, his remonstrations to Tulip for 'putting an end to the most noble monument of Antiquity in the whole Island'.

While the countryside around Hadrian's Wall was no longer the lawless territory it had been when Camden visited, Hutton's struggles to find a bed each night made our own intricate advance booking of B&Bs look easy. He was consistently, he wrote, regarded with bitter suspicion by the locals – at Birdoswald mistaken for a tax inspector; at Harlow Hill for a 'spy employed by the Government'. At one pub he caused conversation to dry up entirely because the drinkers assumed he was a disapproving Methodist preacher. At the Twice Brewed Inn on the military road, which still serves pints to thirsty wall walkers, he dined magnificently on a 'piece of beef out of the copper, perhaps equal to half a calf', but was offered a room sharing with 'a poor sick traveller who had fallen ill upon the road'. At Stanwix, he was reduced to knocking on doors to find a billet. One was opened by a woman, once clearly a beauty, who 'yet shewed as much of that valuable commodity as could be expected from forty-five'. She refused to put him up on grounds of propriety, to his disbelief: 'Did you ever hear of a woman losing her character by a man of seventy-eight!' He eventually found a place to sleep, only to be plagued by fleas, 'the dancing gentry of the night'.

What is striking about Hutton's account, aside from his wit and charm, is the force of meaning he ascribes to the wall: its moral content. 'This Wall,' he wrote, 'is also a clear proof, that every species of cruelty that one man can practise to another was here, and pronounces the human being as much a savage as the brute. This Place has been the scene of more plunder and murder, than any part of the Island, of equal extent.' For him the wall provided a bleak commentary on human affairs. The world is not 'advancing towards perfection', he argued. Man may be 'better informed' than he was in previous centuries, but he is 'not mended'. The Romans were as much barbarians as the Scots who marauded against the wall – worse, for they 'surprised, murdered, plundered, and kept possession'. So did the Saxons, Danes and Normans. They were all barbarians. 'Whoever deprives an unoffending man of his right, comes under this word,' he wrote.

It was still some time before visiting the wall was regarded as an excursion for pleasure-seekers rather than an eccentric escapade. In 1849, however, came another change, when the Newcastle antiquary and schoolteacher John Collingwood Bruce led the first 'pilgrimage' to the wall. It came about after he was compelled to abort his plan to visit Rome in the summer of 1848 because of the revolutionary upheavals in Europe. He went to the wall instead, and that winter gave a series of lectures on his trip at the Newcastle Literary and Philosophical Society. He remembered, nearly forty years later, 'I was impressed during the delivery of them with the idea that some of my hearers thought that I was describing the structure in too glowing terms, and that the Wall in reality was not as grand an object as I represented it.' And so he offered to lead a party the following summer to travel along it 'from end to end – forming a pilgrimage like that described by Chaucer, consisting of both ladies and gentlemen'. In due course he 'issued a programme of the intended pilgrimage, prefacing it with some remarks upon the beauty of the country to be traversed and the attractive features which it presented to the botanist and geologist as well as the antiquary'. Hutton had been less enamoured of the surrounding landscape. 'A more dreary country than this in which I now am, can scarcely be conceived,' he complained, when walking just that section of the wall that is now regarded as the most picturesque.

Twenty 'pilgrims' set forth on foot, their luggage following on the road in a 'wheeled conveyance' that was roomy enough to accommodate the travellers when they felt footsore. On several occasions their numbers were substantially swelled by locals – enthusiasts from Hexham causing their cavalcade to extend 'a mile upon the road'. At the temple at Brocolitia, they found men quarrying for Roman stone. 'A general rush was made to the newly upturned earth, and beyond the expectations of most, one article of interest after another was produced, Samian ware and a few coins.' Crowds formed at Housesteads. 'Never probably since the departure of the Romans was the city so numerously tenanted. Many of the neighbouring gentry . . .

had there assembled in holiday attire.' After Collingwood Bruce gave a lecture, the pilgrims 'showed our loyalty. In my address I . . . stated that now in Windsor's princely halls was seated a lady who ruled over "Regions Caesar never knew" and who wielded a sceptre which was lovingly obeyed by four times the number of subjects great Julius ever swayed. Mr Falconer, one of the pilgrims, proposed three cheers for Queen Victoria, which were given with thrilling effect.' A crucial link between tourism and preservation was made: 'I am impressed with the idea that such expeditions are valuable as a means of exciting, in the minds of the people inhabiting the district through which we pass, a sense of the importance of the remains . . . When they see that gentlemen of education, and especially cultivated ladies, regard it with something like veneration, they will learn to respect it too.'

Nearly a century later, tales of the pilgrimage, and of Hutton's walk, were reworked into W. H. Auden's radio play *Hadrian's Wall*. Auden had antiquarianism in his blood: his uncle, the Revd John Auden, was one of those who gave financial support to the excavations at Wroxeter that the youthful Wilfred Owen had visited in 1913, and he was named Wystan for an Anglo-Saxon saint commemorated at the parish church of Repton in Derbyshire. As significant, though, was his abiding love of the landscape of northern England. In a letter of 17 January 1950, he was to write: 'My great good place is the part of the Pennines bounded on the S by Swaledale, on the N by the Roman wall and on the W by the Eden Valley.' When he lived in America, he had a map of this territory on his wall: it was for him an internal landscape, a trigger to the imagination. The script of the *Hadrian's Wall* broadcast, which was aired live from Newcastle on 25 November 1937, survives. It is a delightfully and unashamedly educational play about the history of the wall, framed by the device of a family's day trip to Housesteads, incorporating what would now be called 'found texts'. Some of the words of Catherine Hutton were woven in, as well as those of her father. Auden invented voices, too, for the Romans who once manned the wall. Benjamin Britten wrote and conducted the incidental music, which included a setting of a poem written for the occasion, 'Roman Wall Blues'. The broadcast went, reported Britten in his diary entry for the day, 'fearfully badly'. But, he added: 'There's good stuff in it I know.' The critic of the *Listener* agreed, admiring the 'terrific vitality' of the music. She also noted – the broadcast was of course live – 'an uncomfortable pause during which an actor was told in several very audible whispers to turn to page three'.

Britten's music for 'Roman Wall Blues' was thought lost, until 2005, when a hand-written copy of the vocal line turned up in the possession of a ninety-nine-year-old former employee of the Bank of England, who had been part of the local choir brought in to sing it. In the end, the choir wasn't used – at the last minute, a crooner from a Newcastle dance hall, whose voice was felt to be more appropriate to the material, was roped in. The music is very bluesy indeed: mournful, bittersweet, with shades of Gershwin's 'It Ain't Necessarily So' (*Porgy and Bess* hadn't yet had its British premiere, but Britten may have heard some of the songs on a 1935 RCA Victor recording). After I told composer Colin Matthews, who was Britten's assistant in the 1970s, of my interest in 'Roman Wall Blues', he kindly offered to write a piano accompaniment to complete the song:

Roman Wall Blues

Over the heather the wet wind blows
I've lice in my tunic and a cold in my nose.

The rain comes pattering out of the sky
I'm a Wall soldier; I don't know why.

The mist sweeps over the hard grey stone
My girl's in Tungria; I sleep alone.

Aulus goes hanging around her place
I don't like his manners; I don't like his face.

Piso's a Christian; he worships a fish;
There'd be no kissing if he had his wish.

She gave me a ring but I diced it away;
I want my girl and I want my pay.

When I'm a veteran with only one eye
I shall do nothing but gaze at the sky.

Roman Wall Blues

W H AUDEN

BENJAMIN BRITTEN (1937)
Piano part by Colin Matthews

O - ver the hea-ther the wet wind blows I've lice

— in my tu - nic and a cold in my nose. The rain comes pat-ter-ing

out of the sky I'm a Wall sol - dier; I don't know why. The mist

— sweeps o - ver the hard grey stone My girl's— in— Tun - gria; I

sleep a - lone. Au - lus goes hang-ing a - round her place I don't like his man-ners I

don't like his face._____ Pi-so's a Christ-ian; he wor-ships a fish;

There'd be no kiss-ing if he had his wish. She gave me a ring but I diced it a-way; I

want my girl and I want my pay._____ When I'm a ve-te-ran with on - ly one

eye I_____ shall do no-thing but gaze at the sky.

The words shiver with the chill of loneliness and isolation. The music vibrates not with the triumphal chords of the conqueror, but with the Southern cadences of the dispossessed: a black American musical form given to the imperial master. Auden's drama feels very much like a pre-war creation, bristling with the threat of violence. 'No war can be justified but that of defence,' Hutton had written, but Auden edited the line from his play text. Perhaps the sentiment felt out of tune with the times.

'Roman Wall Blues' brought into poetic form the life of a wall soldier as many still imagine it: a hardship posting on a cold, desperate, lonely edge of the empire. (Though can it have been any worse than a posting on the violent fringes of Parthia? Can its climate have been more uncomfortable than the chill of a German winter, or the relentless heat of an African summer?) If the poem has become less popular than it once was, that may be because since its composition we have gained something extraordinary: the Vindolanda writing tablets. These are a vast cache of real words written in the first century AD by Romans living and working a few miles south of where the wall would, some decades later, be built. Had Auden been writing his radio drama today, it is surely the Vindolanda tablets that he would have harvested.

The first of these objects – the word 'tablet' lends a deceptively sturdy, lapidary air to these delicate fragments – was discovered by the historian and archaeologist Robin Birley in 1973, digging at the Roman fort of Vindolanda, which stood on land at Chesterholm that had been purchased by his father, the eminent archaeologist Eric Birley. 'If I have to spend the rest of my life working in dirty, wet trenches, I doubt whether I shall ever again experience the shock and excitement I felt at my first glimpse of ink hieroglyphics on tiny scraps of wood,' he later recalled. He had unearthed two thin fragments of wood, 'which looked rather like oily plane shavings'. He passed one to his assistant, who observed that it seemed to have some odd marks on it. 'I had another look and thought I must have been dreaming, for the marks appeared to be ink writing. We took the piece over to the excavation hut and gently cleaned it, discovering that there were in fact two slivers of wood adhering to each other. After gently prising them apart with a knife, we stared at the tiny writing in utter disbelief.' The tablets, as they gradually emerged, were so friable that even the faintest pressure – such as removing a bracken frond from their surface – could fracture them, he wrote. Their remarkable survival was down to the anaerobic conditions of the waterlogged ground in which they had been trapped for nearly 2,000 years. When they emerged, delicate and with the consistency of wet blotting paper, they could not be allowed to dry out, or they would fast disintegrate. Complete, they were about the size of postcards. Postcards from the past.

A year later, on a hot spring day in 1974, a papyrology expert called Alan Bowman set out with colleagues and students from the University of Manchester, where he was then a lecturer, for a field trip to Vindolanda. Bowman spent the sunny afternoon getting a headache indoors, having been handed a tablet to decipher. 'Robin at first thought they might be in Greek,' he said. They were, rather, in Roman cursive handwriting, notoriously difficult for the untrained eye to read. The tablet 'was a letter about barley and beer', he told me, drily. At about the same time, unbeknown to him, Professor David Thomas, a papyrologist based at the University of Durham, was also being consulted about the new discoveries; eventually the two joined forces and worked together for more than thirty years. That excavation, which ran from 1973 to 1975, yielded tablets in dribs and drabs. Later, in the 1980s, came a glut. The material constituted 'a massive percentage of Roman letters as a whole', Bowman said. It meant that, from nowhere, suddenly 'Roman Britain was providing the most important information on the development of Latin in the first century'. Bowman, now a professor at the University of Oxford, has since worked with Thomas on deciphering around 1,500 Vindolanda tablets, dating from circa AD 85–130.

From these discarded shards – drafts, scraps, lists, memoranda, letters received and thrown away – came a picture of a community. Characters, real people, emerged from the soil: the fort commander at the turn of the first and second centuries was Flavius Cerealis, prefect of the ninth cohort of Batavians, from the mouth of the Rhine in what is now the Netherlands. His wife Lepidina and their children were with him. The tablets contained inventories and shopping lists ('chickens, 20; 100 apples, if you can find nice ones, 100 or 200 eggs, if they are for sale there at a fair price'). There was a soldier's note requesting leave; letters about buying items such as hides and corn;

and mentions of booze (the word usually translated as 'Celtic beer' is *'cervesa'*, which is surely the ancestor of the Spanish *cerveza*). There was a scrap of a military report referring to the fighting capabilities of the Britons, who were referred to by the diminutive 'Brittunculi', meaning 'little Britons', or, perhaps more dismissively, 'wretched Britons' – though it is hard safely to extract the word's tone. The whole fragment reads: '. . . the Britons are unprotected by armour (?). There are very many cavalry. The cavalry do not use swords nor do the wretched Britons mount in order to throw javelins.'

One correspondent, Octavius, grumbled to Candidus that he had not been sent the promised cash for a planned purchase of corn, and then mentioned he would not be using his wagon *'dum viae male sunt'*, while the roads were bad. Flavius Cerialis wrote to somebody called Brocchus: 'If you love me, brother, I ask that you send me some hunting-nets . . .' Brocchus wrote to Flavius Cerealis too, assuring him that he would soon meet the provincial governor. According to Bowman, 'They didn't go into their feelings too deeply. It's mostly "send me two more cabbages", not great outpourings.' He added, opaquely: 'It's probably just as well,' as if cabbages were, after all, more his thing than emotions. What this wasn't was Auden's vision of chilly isolation. The tablets conveyed a picture of a busy, connected community.

The big surprise, perhaps, was the extent and the depth of literacy among the soldiering men of Vindolanda. Indeed, some of them were clearly also literary. In 2010, Bowman, Thomas and Dr Roger Tomlin, who had joined the collaboration in the later stages of the work, published their interpretations of a set of tablets that had been excavated in the years 2001–3. One of them contained a run of indistinct letters (and bear in mind that the Romans did not put gaps between words) that the scholars read as *'certalate'*. The particular quality of the handwriting (a neat copybook style) told them, from experience, to expect a literary quotation. They ran the letters through a database of the whole corpus of surviving Latin literature, and found that this particular combination occurs in just one place – in the line *'nunc varia in gelida sede lacerta latet'*, or 'the spotted lizard now lurks in its chilly home'. The poem from which it comes, known as 'The Hostess', is a paean to the virtues of drinking. It's a hot day, says the seductive Syrian hostess of the poem. The cicadas are bursting the trees with

their song; even the lizards have sought the shade. Lie down, garland
your head with roses, kiss a pretty girl, drink from a crystal glass. It
is a vision of summertime heat and sexy Mediterranean luxury. It was,
and is, also a pretty obscure poem, handed down to us as part of a
group of works known as the *Appendix Vergiliana*, once (but no longer)
attributed to Virgil. 'Think of it: the bloody Batavians sitting on the
northern frontier reading the *Appendix Vergiliana*!' exclaimed Bowman
in his rich Mancunian accent. Another fragment in the same set of
tablets contained the sentence *'ante iovem nulli subigeba(nt) arva coloni'*
– from Virgil's poem on farming, the *Georgios*. 'Before Jove's time,' it
means, 'no settlers brought the land under subjection.' The line comes
from a passage on a lost golden age, a time, impossible aeons ago,
when the earth brought forth her Edenic bounty spontaneously, before
man had learnt to till the soil.

When I visited him in late 2010, Alan Bowman had just been elected
principal of Brasenose College, though his bluff, straightforward
manner hardly marked him out as a typical Oxford head of house.
His office had a feel of not having quite been settled into. The spine
of one A4 file was marked, facetiously, 'bureaucratic crap'. The task
of interpreting the Vindolanda tablets, and other texts that have
emerged from the British sod, is one of extraordinary complexity, he
told me. It is not just a matter of translating Latin; it is translating
eccentric Latin that is often so fragmentary that it contains more gaps
than surviving words, written in a script that is faded beyond recognition to any but the most practised eye. He and Thomas are, he told
me, cruciverbalists by temperament. 'I used to do the *Guardian* cross-
word,' he said. 'Now it's too much like bloody work.' Tomlin has a
slightly different, and complementary, approach: 'Roger's much more
artistic than me; he sees the work more in terms of images and shapes,'
said Bowman. When I visited Tomlin in his office at Wolfson College,
Oxford, half the floor space was occupied by stacks of oriental carpets,
the object of another of his scholarly passions. He was about to give
a talk titled 'Knotted Feathers: Birds in Small Persian Rugs'. On a table
lay some rolls of paper: Tomlin's own line drawings. When I half
jokingly asked whether he thought he would have been drafted to
Bletchley Park during the Second World War, he agreed unhesitatingly.
'I am sure there are a lot of analogies between what we do and
wartime code-breaking,' he said. (In fact, the don who interviewed

him for a place at Cambridge had been a Bletchley code-breaker who managed to turn out a book on Horace while he was there.)

Before the deciphering begins in earnest, the tablets are subjected to electronic imaging processes and infrared photography to make the ink more visible. 'One ideally also checks the original to see whether a mark is a flaw or a letter,' said Tomlin: blemishes on the ancient strips of wood can easily be confused with ink marks, working all kinds of mischief on the interpretation. A first look will give the sense of 'what the document is likely to be', he added. Tablets written across the grain (that is, in a portrait format) often turn out to be military memoranda. Those written along the grain (landscape) are more likely to be letters. Then, he said, it is a question of 'getting to know the letter forms and how they are made', and 'identifying legible letters'. Many of the individual letters are 'maddeningly similar to each other': A's blur into R's; C's, P's and even T's can be almost indistinguishable. He often copies out the text himself on to a large sheet of paper. This process of inhabiting the original writer's physical movements can help him resolve the tangle into individual characters. But you can't just transcribe a text letter for letter, he said: 'It is not just a visual code.' Rather, the work involves a slow, iterative process of holding several hypotheses in mind simultaneously and discarding them where necessary, bringing to bear not just palaeographical knowledge but literary, historical and linguistic insight, as well as common sense, experience and intuition.

Tomlin told me how he once translated a curse tablet found in Bath from which the top right-hand corner was missing. He supplied what he believed were the likely missing words and letters. Later, the real missing piece turned up in a box of miscellaneous fragments. His original interpretation was found to be slightly inaccurate because the writer had made a number of small mistakes, including not accurately 'centring' his text – he had squashed in a long word where Tomlin, applying the reasonable logic of an Oxford don, reckoned only a shorter one would fit. If the papyrologists are solvers of crosswords, then they are dealing with setters who break the rules of the game. 'You've got to have a good eye for the thing, and be prepared to believe you've got it wrong,' says Bowman. 'There's no flash of light, just a slow realisation.' Bowman admits that the longer he has gone on deciphering Vindolanda texts, the more mistakes he realises he has made over the years. Scholars such as these work in the shadowy realm of the provisional, never the blinding light of the definitive.

You can see some of the Vindolanda tablets in the Roman Britain gallery of the British Museum, and they look deeply unimpressive. They are thin, small, brownish rectangles covered with thin, small, brownish writing. And yet, craning my neck at an uncomfortable angle to try to read the indistinct strokes, I found myself with a catch in my throat when I came face to face, for the first time, with a tablet whose text I knew already:

> Claudia Severa to her Lepidina greetings. On 11 September, sister, for the day of the celebration of my birthday, I give you a warm invitation to make sure that you come to us, to make the day more enjoyable for me by your arrival, if you are present (?). Give my greetings to your Cerialis. My Aelius and my little son send him (?) their greetings.
>
> I shall expect you, sister. Farewell, sister, my dearest soul, as I hope to prosper, and hail.

Sulpicia Lepidina was the wife of Flavius Cerialis, the camp commandant. Claudia Severa was the wife of Brocchus, he of the hunting nets. The letter is written in two hands. The body of the note is in a clear, competent script that has been identified on other tablets – perhaps that of a scribe. The sign-off – warm, personal, urgent – is in another hand. It is probably, according to the papyrologists, Severa's own. If it is, it means these are the first words to have survived, from anywhere in the empire, in a Roman woman's own handwriting. 'Sperabo te soror, vale soror, anima mea, ita valeam karissima et have,' reads the Latin. The words 'anima mea karissima', my dearest soul, may have been a bland formula ('lots of love'?), but I none the less felt ambushed by the affection and sweetness in them. The fragment contained an atavistic magic that scepticism could not entirely blot out. The years seemed to collapse as I read it, picking out the faint, spidery Latin on the dull wood. I read the words over and over again, and thought of the lost life of the woman who wrote them.

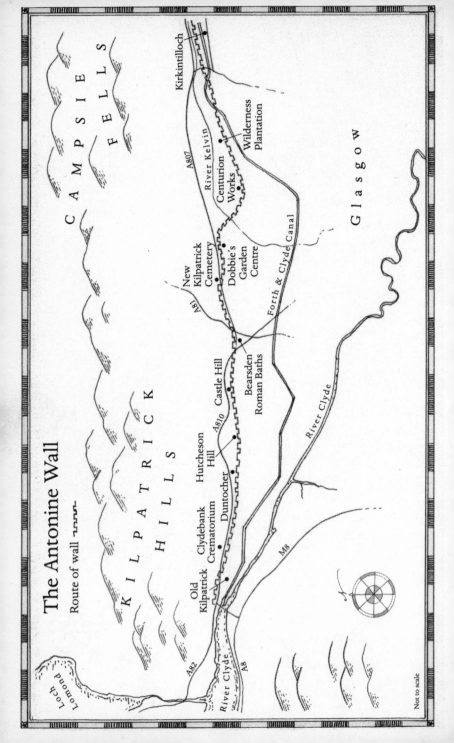

The Antonine Wall

Route of wall ⌐⌐⌐⌐

Loch Lomond

CAMPSIE FELLS

KILPATRICK HILLS

Kirkintilloch

River Kelvin

A807

Wilderness Plantation

Centurion Works

Forth & Clyde Canal

Glasgow

New Kilpatrick Cemetery

Dobbie's Garden Centre

A81

Castle Hill

A810

Bearsden Roman Baths

Hutcheson Hill

Clydebank Crematorium

Duntocher

Old Kilpatrick

River Clyde

A82

A8

River Clyde

M8

Not to scale

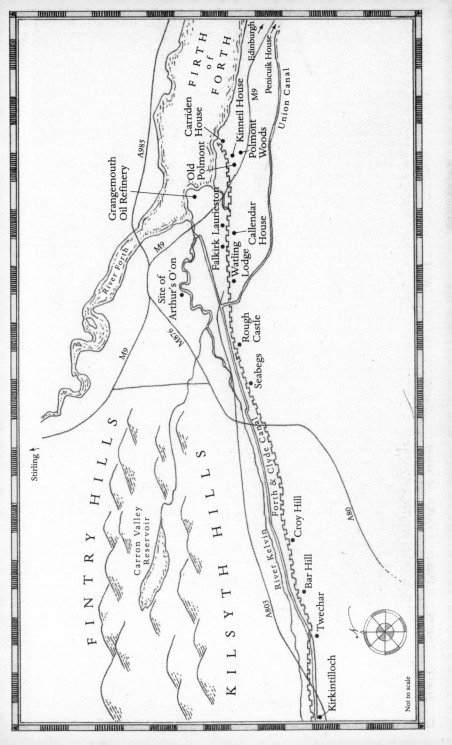

8

Scotland

Of this dyke, or wall, there are evident signs and genuine traces to be seen to this day.

John of Fordun, fourteenth century

I have lost count of how many people have said to me, 'But the Romans didn't get beyond Hadrian's Wall, did they?' What is certainly true is that the Romans never secured the Highlands, though Agricola fought through to the Grampians in the far north-east and briefly conquered – at least according to Tacitus – the whole island. It is also true that there is no evidence of Roman civilian settlements: no villas, no towns. But there are over 200 sites north of Hadrian's Wall that have produced Roman archaeological finds. The Romans had persistent contact with, and at times power over, parts of Scotland. Twenty years after the building of Hadrian's Wall, a second barrier, the Antonine Wall, was built between the firths of Forth and Clyde and held for a generation: it was thickly dotted with forts. There is also a line of signal stations north of Dundee, along the Gask Ridge – the most northerly of a great mass of information-gathering systems that extended beyond the main garrisons, ready to send news of trouble south. The wild territories of Scotland are sprinkled with the traces of marching camps as far north as the Moray Firth. Septimius Severus, in the early third century, campaigned brutally in Perthshire and Angus, beyond the walls. A military base at Cramond, near Edinburgh, left an extraordinary monument in the form of the Cramond Lion, a sculpture of a great feline devouring a man, its sharp teeth sinking into the man's head, its huge claws clutching his shoulders.

A walk around the galleries of the Museum of Scotland in Edinburgh is instructive. Here are fragments of Samian ware, the bases of the dishes inscribed with their owners' – the soldiers' – names. So that we know that at Newstead, in the borders, a man called Domitius took his rations; and in Inveresk, in East Lothian, Victor had his mess-pot. Also at Newstead, we know from an amphora scratched with the letters '*VIN*', the troops, or at least officers, were drinking wine with their rations. Through various kinds of contact – trade, diplomacy and, no doubt, looting – Roman things ended up scattered throughout Scotland. At Trapain Law in East Lothian, an extraordinary cache of late Roman silverware was discovered in 1919. Here were fifty-three pieces, including wine cups, dishes with beaded rims, strainers, spoons: the impedimenta of an elegant Roman feast. Perhaps the hoard was a diplomatic payment, or subsidy, or bribe, to a local tribe. At Carlungie, far to the north in Angus, a French wine amphora was discovered, its contents perhaps enjoyed by the local grandees. A glass Roman dish was found on Westray, one of the northernmost of the Orkneys; a fragment of Samian in Berie in the Outer Hebrides. On a dig that ran between 1998 and 2011 at Birnie, just south of Elgin near the Moray Firth, archaeologist Dr Fraser Hunter and his colleagues found, on an Iron Age site, two hoards. One contained 320 Roman coins, the other 310. The coins, the latest of which dated from the early third century, had been wrapped in leather pouches and buried in ceramic pots lined with bracken. The peoples of the far north were not becoming Roman, but they were taking Roman things and making them their own. Scotland has a Roman past. And that Roman past comes into sharp focus at another period in Scotland's history: the eighteenth century and the fault line running through it, the Jacobite rebellion of 1745.

When George II's troops marched north to fight off Charles James Stuart's attempt on the British throne, they were hampered by their imperfect knowledge of the Highlands. Of the infinitely complex contours of the northern mountains, the ragged outline of the coast, the watery interplay of the lochs and burns and bogs, there existed no accurate maps. To many Lowland Scots, leave alone the English, the Highlands were terra incognita, a desolate, remote, even primally savage land, culturally and linguistically distant from the intellectual ferment of Enlightenment Edinburgh. There were few roads that afforded efficient transportation of troops; meanwhile, the Jacobites

had the advantage of knowing the territory. So it was that the Young
Pretender, Bonnie Prince Charlie, was successfully spirited away from
the bloodbath of Culloden to safety on Skye, and thence to Rome.

The redcoats were not the first invading army to attempt the
subjugation of the Highlands. In AD 79 or 80, the governor, Agricola,
according to the biography by his son-in-law, Tacitus, advanced into
what is now Scotland. He garrisoned the Forth–Clyde line; and contemplated the invasion of Ireland, which he later claimed (idle boast!) he
could have reduced with a single legion and a force of auxiliaries.
Beyond the narrow stretch between the firths the territory broadened
out again into what Tacitus described as 'almost another island'. Here
Agricola now ventured, his infantry shadowed by his fleet and marines.
They came under attack from the Caledonian tribes, and some of
Agricola's officers advised a strategic retreat; but the general was
determined to press on. When the Caledonians learned of his intention to advance further, they massed together for a terrifying night
attack on the encamped 9th Legion. The Romans successfully fought
them off, but the Caledonians melted away into *paludes et silvae*,
marshes and forests. This hard-won victory filled the Roman troops,
reported Tacitus, with an appetite to drive yet deeper into Caledonia
and reach the 'farthest limits of Britain'. The next summer, 83 or 84,
they came to Mons Graupius – where, said Tacitus, more than 30,000
men rallied to fight them. The location of this battlefield has never
been satisfactorily identified, though there are reasonable grounds for
suggesting that it may have been Mount Bennachie, north-west of
Aberdeen, near to which a large Roman marching camp was discovered
in the 1970s. At any rate, it was the untraceable Mons Graupius, courtesy of the fifteenth- to sixteenth-century Scottish historian Hector
Boece, that gave its name to the Grampian mountain range. The shift
from Graupius to Grampius is thanks to a typesetting error in the
earliest printed edition of Tacitus's *Agricola*.

At this point in his narrative, Tacitus gives us one of his most
remarkable passages: a speech delivered to the Caledonian troops by
the war leader Calgacus. Of this Calgacus, nothing further is known:
but the speech that Tacitus invents for him is one of the historian's
greatest, and most moving, acts of rhetorical ventriloquism. Today
will be the birth of liberty for Britain, he declares. We will fight well
because we are free. Here in the remote north, far away from the

grasp of tyranny, have been born the best of men. The Romans are
'*raptores orbis*', the pillagers of the world. Neither east nor west has
sated them. To theft, murder and rapine they give the false name of
power. They make a desert, and call it peace. Look at their troops: a
motley crew of Germans, Gauls – even, it shames me to say, Britons.
These people were Rome's enemies for far longer than they have been
her slaves. Here, on the battlefield, the Britons will remember their
true cause; the Gauls will recall their former liberty; the Germans will
desert them.

The speech is both a bitter critique of the moral vacuum at the
heart of the imperial project, and an expression of a deep anxiety
about its potential for collapse. What if the provincials really were to
throw off those habits of mind and manners that made one Roman?
Romanitas could be acquired; and so, perhaps, it could also be jetti-
soned. (Indeed, only a few chapters earlier in his narrative, Tacitus
had described the mutiny of a cohort of German troops, who
murdered their centurions, seized three warships and sailed around
north Britain before being captured in the Low Countries and sold as
slaves.) But perhaps the idea of such disasters could be safely enter-
tained precisely because they did not come about. The battle was, like
Culloden, a rout. The Caledonians scattered to the forests, where they
were pursued by the relentless Romans. Arms, bodies, limbs lay on
the blood-soaked earth. The day after the battle, an unsettling silence
hung in the air: the hills were deserted; torched buildings smouldered
and smoked in the distance.

As it turned out, Agricola did not get the opportunity to capitalise
on the victory, or to turn conquest into the deadening slog of provincial peacekeeping. He was recalled to Rome by the emperor Domitian,
whom Tacitus characterised as jealous of Agricola's military success.
'*Perdomita Britannia et statim omissa*' – Britannia was completely subjugated and immediately let go – wrote Tacitus in his *Histories*. As far
as Agricola's biography was concerned, Tacitus made Britain perform
the role he required of it. These remote and primitive lands, so far
from the dissolute centre of empire, provided the writer with a stage
on which his subject could be the Roman he needed to be: a virtuous
warrior, destroying enemies themselves untainted by the rottenness
of Rome. As a by-product of his need to heroise Agricola, he created
the idea of the redoubtable, freedom-loving Highlander, just faintly

perfumed with a whiff of savagery – an image that still endures. In William Hole's great Victorian frieze of notable Scots that circles the entrance hall of the Scottish National Portrait Gallery in Edinburgh, Calgacus is the first named character, closely followed by those honorary Scots Tacitus (who was probably Gaulish) and Hadrian (who was Spanish).

That there were parallels between Romans and Hanoverians in Scotland was not lost on at least some of those in George II's army. One bitingly cold winter day, Matthew and I drove north-east from Glasgow, stopping at the Perthshire village of Braco to admire the fort of Ardoch, which was probably built in the Agricolan period. It is the best-preserved Roman fort in Scotland, surrounded by quintuple earth ramparts that rise up to two metres tall, and then drop into ditches the same depth, as if the land had been ploughed into furrows by the giants that Geoffrey of Monmouth said once roamed Britain. We crunched over the frosted ground to look at the traces of two larger temporary camps from later centuries, whose geometries bafflingly criss-crossed each other through the sheep-grazed fields. From there we drove on to the little town of Aberfeldy, north-west of Perth, not to look at Roman remains, but to see the bridge built here over the Tay by General Wade, part of the network of forts and military roads (like Roman roads, made as straight as the territory would allow) constructed after the first Jacobite uprisings of 1715 and 1719.

The bridge is a grand and lovely thing, designed by William Adam, father of the better-known Robert. Five arches span the river; four obelisks ascend from its central parapet, and the river flows silver and supple beneath. When it was built, it was the only bridge across the Tay. As we crossed it, we saw two inscriptions. Facing south was one in English, recording that the bridge had been erected in order to secure 'a safe and easy communication between the Highlands and the lowland trading towns'. The other, facing north, was in Latin, crusted over with lichen and largely obscured. We scraped away at the scales of grey-green growth, piecing together the words as the traffic bowled past us. It was composed by Robert Freind, an eighteenth-century headmaster of Westminster School. Translated, it read:

Marvel at this military road, stretched out on both sides of the river for 250 miles beyond the Roman frontier, mocking wildernesses and swamps, opening up through rocks and mountains and, as you see, laid over the indignant Tay. George Wade, commander of the forces in Scotland, completed this work in the year of our Lord 1733 through his own ingenuity and his soldiers' 10 years' labour. Behold how mighty is the royal will of George II.

It is a knowing echo of the speech to the Roman troops that Tacitus put into the mouth of Agricola at Mons Graupius, the rhetorical counterbalance to Calgacus's rousing words. In that flight of oratory, Agricola cries: 'Britain is discovered and subdued. How often on a march, when you have been struggling over bogs, mountains and rivers [*paludes montesve et flumina*], have I heard the bravest among you exclaim, "When shall we meet the enemy? When will they come and fight us?"' General Wade's inscription claims that he has subdued these same '*tesquis et paludibus . . . rupes montesque*' – wildernesses and bogs, rocks and mountains. His boast is that he has achieved what the Romans did not – he has built roads beyond their frontier; he has tamed the landscape that eluded his ancient predecessors.

Wade's subjugation of the Highlands was, at best, partial; and after the traumas of the 1745 Jacobite rebellion, the urgent necessity for accurate maps of the north was recognised. It was William Roy – a factor's son from Lanarkshire, nineteen at the time of Charles Edward Stuart's uprising – who was put in charge of the small group of men who were to undertake the physically exhausting, technically demanding work of surveying Scotland, under the supervision of the Board of Ordnance. Roy began his labours in 1747. It took him and his band eight and a half years to complete the work, spending the springs and summers enduring the vicissitudes of the Scottish landscape and climate, and the winters working on the maps in Edinburgh. The result of their labours was the *Military Survey of Scotland*, 'undertaken by order of William Augustus, Duke of Cumberland'. It was this achievement that laid the foundations for the Ordnance Survey, the comprehensive mapping of the British Isles that began in 1791. 'The Duke of Cumberland's map', as it is known, is magnificent: thirty-eight large sheets, backed with linen, that present a sweeping picture of a country in ink and watercolour. As I unloosed them from their box, on the largest table in the British Library's map room, I could barely believe that I had been allowed to touch them. Mountains loomed as daunting grey whorls. The coastline was a snake of delicate turquoise; the burgeoning towns were picked out in grids of crimson; the parks and estates of the Lowland gentry were domesticated geometries of grass-green. And in a clear, confident red line, like a vein between the seas, ran the Antonine Wall.

The wall was built in AD 142 by Hadrian's immediate successor, Antoninus Pius. In pushing the boundary of Roman Britain north from Hadrian's Wall to the Forth–Clyde line, this essentially unmilitary emperor provided himself with a victory that, however meaningless in reality, could be made to bolster his martial credentials back in Rome. The barrier was held for a mere twenty years before the Romans withdrew south to the Hadrianic frontier.

There was no strategic need for the Roman wall to be marked on the Duke of Cumberland's map; its appearance is, rather, a conscious salute by Roy to his Roman predecessors. While working on the *Survey of Scotland*, he took detailed plans of the Antonine Wall and the surrounding Roman forts and camps. Forty years later, his maps and descriptions of the *Military Antiquities of Britain* were published posthumously by the Society of Antiquaries, in an imposing elephant folio volume. In his preface, he wrote of his peculiar suitability for the task of researching the past. 'Military men . . . in reasoning on the various revolutions they have already undergone, or on those which, in certain cases, they might possibly suffer hereafter, are naturally led to compare present things with the past; and being thus insensibly carried back to former ages, they place themselves among the ancients, and do, as it were, converse with the people of those remote times.' I like to think of the young William Roy – later the eminent Major General Roy – 'conversing' with the Roman military engineers whose work he admired so much, and reflecting, via the rugged geography of central Scotland, on the abundant reversals of life and war.

At the heart of the book is Roy's fold-out map of the whole line of the Antonine Wall, showing it in exquisite detail as it runs past the villages of Grange and Grange Pans, where the oil refinery of Grangemouth now stands, through the little town of Falkirk and over the steep slopes of Croy Hill and Bar Hill, through Kirkintilloch and thence to the open countryside that would later be swallowed up by the Glasgow suburb of Bearsden, out to Old Kilpatrick (or Kirkpatrick, as Roy calls it), where the A82 now thunders, and finally the broad sweep of the Clyde. When I spread out its pages for the first time I experienced a curious sense of both familiarity and estrangement: I had just walked the line of the Antonine Wall and knew, I felt, this land well; but how changed it was. Examining Roy's map was unexpectedly poignant – rather like looking at the childhood photograph of a familiar, elderly face, in which we can recognise the essential features, once we have mentally stripped away the accretions of old age. Roy's map stands at a junction in the history of Scotland, created as this tract of land between Edinburgh and Glasgow stood poised on the brink of industrialisation. What does not appear on his map is the Forth–Clyde canal, which now shadows, and at time obliterates, the Antonine Wall: it was begun in 1768. The territory was changing fast. By the time it was published in 1793, the map was already commemorating a lost landscape.

The Antonine Wall is not to be walked for pleasure, at least in any straightforward sense. It is quite unlike Hadrian's Wall, with its friendly wooden fingerposts, its reassuringly solid mass sweeping for miles over crag and pasture, its visitor centres and youth hostels and B&Bs. The Antonine Wall, by contrast, is cussed and shy and recalcitrant. Its traces are hard to discern and often inaccessible; even when they are not tangled in suburban sprawl or devoured by trunk road or canal, as they often are. Now, where the wall can be made out at all, it is most often glimpsed as a ghost of the deep ditch dug to its immediate south: a dip, a depression in the soil. Sometimes – at Bar Hill, or in the woods at Seabegs, or around the tower blocks of Falkirk – the ditch is a mighty trench that gives a corresponding impression, in the imagination, of the hefty proportions of the wall. More often, though, it is a shadow of a faint contour seen in low light across a hillside; or a watery channel running at a field boundary. On foot the route is circuitous and fractured. To walk its thirty-five-mile length, you must often divert and take a parallel path, or stride grimly ahead into A-road traffic. Nor will one find companions on the road: this is a route that lends itself to solitude and introspection.

It must once, though, have been a grimly impressive thing. The wall itself was a turf rampart laid on a stone base, rising to 3.5 metres. Alongside it was a ditch that sank as deep. Imagine the whole apparatus as a cross-section: there was the military way running at the extreme south, then to its north a rampart, then a flat piece of ground known as the berm, then the ditch, and finally a mound created by the spoil from the ditch. It was the soldiers of the 2nd, 6th and 20th Legions who built it, carving elaborate 'distance slabs' to commemorate the sections they had constructed. Sixteen of these sculptures can be seen in the Hunterian Museum in Glasgow; one is in the National Museum of Scotland. (One perished in the Chicago fire of 1871, but a cast can be seen in the Hunterian.) They are richly carved things, featuring such scenes as Victory placing a laurel wreath on a Roman legionary standard, and Caledonians being trampled by Roman cavalry or else crouching in submission, bound and naked. Several are decorated with the distinctive mascots of the soldiers' legions: a running boar for the 20th; a Pegasus and a Capricorn (after the Emperor Augustus's star sign) for the 6th. The last to be discovered – so far – was ploughed up in a farmer's field at Hutcheson's Hill in 1969. Lawrence Keppie, professor emeritus of Roman history and archaeology at the University of Glasgow, remembers its circuitous route to the museum: the slab was spotted by a company rep in the farmyard, who told his doctor, who told the Royal Commission on the Ancient and Historical Monuments of Scotland. One of Keppie's first jobs when he started at the museum, he told me, was to clean it of the whitewash with which it had been spattered while it lay in the farmyard. In the Hunterian can also be seen an elaborate mauso-leum carved with images of togaed figures reclining on couches, found near Kirkintilloch; and the tombstone, erected by his father, of a boy called Salamenes – to judge by his name, he must have come from Greece or the Middle East. Also: fragments of precious glass, delicate intaglios, red Samian ware for dining, and, spine-tinglingly well-preserved, adults' and children's leather sandals. The Mediterranean had been brought to the Central Belt.

My way started by Carriden House, near the muddy banks of the Forth, and took me through the park of the seventeenth-century Kinneil House, where stood not only the traces of a Roman fortlet, but also the ruins of a workshop in which once toiled the Scottish inventor James Watt. He was brought here in 1769 to design an engine that could pump water out of the Bo'ness colliery, owned by John Roebuck, the tenant of Kinneil. The route then climbed high above the Firth; I could see the glum mountains of Fife across the water,

while above me larks sang their trickling song and the air was thick
with the perfume of honeysuckle. But at the bottom of the hill, on
the estuarine shore, was the Grangemouth oil refinery. Even from far
above, I could hear the chthonic industrial hum of this vast installation. Steam choked from great chimneys and fiery tongues flew from
towers. Monstrous pipes vermiculated their way around structures
made on no human scale. This is the terminus of another route
crossing this slender neck of Scotland: that of the pipeline that pumps
crude oil fifty-eight miles from Loch Long on the west coast.

I walked through Old Polmont, where the wall is lost in the
hummock of a dry ski slope, and through Polmont Woods, where I
encountered a roving group of shirtless teenage boys and then a little
band of girls, all clutching bottles in plastic bags. Through Laurieston,
the route of the wall ran straight along Grahamsdyke Street. Graham's
Dyke, or Grym's Dyke, or Grim's Dyke, is the old name for the wall,
hinting at a long-lost belief that such mighty earthworks must have
been built by the Devil. The fourteenth-century chronicler John of
Fordun, on the other hand, had another tale to explain the name: he
tells that the hero Gryme – grandfather of the legendary Scottish king
Eugenius – broke through the wall, which was then named after him.

It was only when I reached the Callendar estate that there was
anything very much to see: here the ditch was deep and deliberate,
running through the stately gardens of Callendar House (besieged by
General Monck in 1651), and then between a cluster of tower blocks,
before being stamped out by the streets of modern Falkirk. Beyond
the town, at the open ground of Watling Lodge, the ditch emerged
again, canopied with dripping oaks and garnished with litter. At Rough
Castle, one of the most famous sites on the wall, the rampart stood
a metre tall; and here were the traces of a fort, with its granaries,
commanding officer's house and baths; and the curious series of deep
pits, interpreted as defensive devices called 'lilia', or 'lilies', in which
stakes might have been buried as a deadly trap against enemy
incursions.

At Croy Hill, the ditch had been cut through the hard dolerite itself;
even solid stone was not to stand in the implacable way of the wall.
As Alexander Gordon, the Scottish antiquary, wrote in his 1726
Itinerarium Septentrionale, the wall entered along 'a continued Track
of Rocks and frightful Precipices, the Ditch all along being cut thro''

the said Rocks, running on the Sides of these Precipices, where I think there is more of the Roman Resolution and Grandeur to be seen than on its whole Track; for it is scarcely conceivable what Pains and Expence must have been used, in cutting thro' such an amazing and rough Scene of Nature'. At the next eminence, Bar Hill, I lost my bearings and wandered about among the trees and scrub, speculating whether this dip or that mound was ditch or fort, until at last I came upon the most magnificent sight of the whole route: the deep ditch soaring up the hill, steep and smooth, and then plunging down to the west again, through the remains of another fort and bathhouse. From here, as Gordon noted, there was an 'extended Prospect of a vast Country on all Hands'. Through Twechar, through Kirkintilloch, through the aptly named Wilderness Plantation I walked, eluding curious cattle, sighting the ditch as the merest wrinkle in the smooth skin of fields. On a long, dead-straight length of canal, a man tried to find out where I was walking to, and why, and whether I was alone, and I felt unreasonably panicked and vulnerable. On the Balmuidy Road I paused outside the gates of the Centurion Works, an outpost of an industrial demolition firm, enjoying the notion that someone had named the premises as a nod to this Roman route, but as I stopped to sit on the soft grassy verge awhile, a security guard drew up in his car and moved me on. I followed the ditch up nettled banks and over barbed-wire fences, and crossed the Kelvin, having no choice, over a bridge marked 'No unauthorised access; danger of falling'. Cutting through a final stubbled field, I reached Dobbie's Garden Centre, through whose grounds the wall runs. After a morning of cross-country solitude and bovine adventure, it felt peculiar to have emerged, somehow illicitly, into a busy world of petunias, hanging baskets and plastic furniture.

At the New Kilpatrick cemetery, among graves of Curries, Gillespies and Capaldis, I looked at two stretches of the wall's stony foundations, exposed during landscaping of the cemetery in the early twentieth century. I followed it on through the generous gardens of the respectable Glasgow suburb of Bearsden, where a set of bathhouses from the fort was hemmed in among a 1970s block of flats. When the archaeologists analysed sewage deposits from the Roman latrines, they found that the soldiers had been eating raspberries, strawberries and figs, and poppy- and coriander-seed bread. As were, I suspected, the middle classes of today's Bearsden. West again, and the wall – aside from a tiny, rather sad stretch preserved in a narrow park between streets of bungalows – was lost in a maze of crescents, avenues and drives. I chatted to a retired schoolteacher on Iain Road, who was watering delphiniums and Canterbury bells in her front garden, and realised she was the only person with whom I had had a conversation for three days. She walked with me to Castle Hill, a magical spot circled by beeches and sycamores, with views sweeping south to the tip of Glasgow and its tower blocks, east back to Bar Hill and south-west to Hutcheson Hill, marking out my onward route. Optimistically I set forth cross-country, but, tired, and finding myself drowning in a field of chest-high grass and thistles, gave in, and put myself on to a bus to Duntocher.

This was the last lap of my journey. In Duntocher, I followed the course of the wall along Beeches Road, lined with pebble-dashed terraces. It was early evening, and families were queuing for fish and chips. In the distance I could hear the melancholy, distorted notes of 'Greensleeves' playing from an ice-cream van. As Duntocher petered out, I pressed on through wasteground, and a group of lads clambered out of a car, regarding me with elaborate casualness. At the Clydebank Crematorium, among the dead, I stopped, exhausted, my way barred by the pulsing rush of the A82. Ahead snaked the Clyde, spanned by the Erskine Bridge, and below was Old Kilpatrick, the terminus of the Antonine Wall.

On Roy's map of the wall, north of Falkirk on the banks of the river Carron is neatly inscribed the following words: 'Here stood Arthur's Oon'. Arthur's O'on, or Oven, was one of Scotland's most impressive ancient monuments: a beehive-shaped stone building that had attracted a certain amount of Arthurian legend in the Middle Ages, not least because of its proximity to the village of Camelon, which some identified with Camelot. By Roy's lifetime, however, it was confidently ascribed to the Romans, and indeed had been so as long ago as the fourteenth century, when John of Fordun had described it as a *'rotundam casulam'*, a round chamber, *'columbaris ad instar'*, in the form of a dovecote. (Less convincingly, he argued that it had been built by Julius Caesar either to mark the northernmost boundary of his military endeavours; or else as a kind of mobile home that he had 'built up again from day to day, wherever they halted, that he might rest therein more safely than in a tent; but that, when he was in a hurry to return to Gaul, he left it behind'.)

William Stukeley published a tract on Arthur's O'on in 1720, without, let it be said, having made the journey to Scotland to study it in person. Conjecturing that it was a temple 'dedicated to Romulus the parent and primitive Deity of the Romans', he compared it lavishly to Rome's Pantheon, which he had also never seen. (He included just the faintest pre-emptive acknowledgement that 'some may think we have done the Caledonian Temple too much Honour in drawing such a Parallel'.) Gordon included a description of it in his *Itinerarium*, arguing that it was 'not a Roman Temple for publick Worship' but, rather, 'a Place for holding the Roman Insignia', or legionary standards. However, the two men agreed about its appearance, describing an imposing dome of a building, constructed from large blocks of masonry, some six metres tall. For Stukeley, it was 'the most genuine and curious Antiquity of the Romans in this Kind, now to be seen in our Island or elsewhere'. It gave its name to the nearby village of Stonehouse, as it is marked on Roy's map – now the town of Stenhousemuir. (Thus Arthur's O'on has the distinction of being the only Romano-British monument to have a football team named after it.)

In 1743, however, came disaster. The landowner, Sir Michael Bruce of Stenhouse, decided to build a dam on the Carron, part of the creeping industrialisation of the river that would, a few years later, see the opening of the Carron Ironworks. (These are marked on Roy's map; by 1814 they would be the biggest ironworks in Europe, producing cannon for the Napoleonic wars under contract to Roy's employer, the Board of Ordnance.) To build his dam, Bruce needed stone: so he simply demolished the Roman building on the riverbank and used its masonry.

The destruction of what was surely – even without recourse to the hyperbole of Stukeley et al. – one of Scotland's most important ancient monuments provoked a furious reaction from antiquaries. Chief among them was Sir John Clerk of Penicuik, a Baron of the Exchequer in Edinburgh, whose eventful life had seen him, as a young man, taking violin lessons in Rome with Arcangelo Corelli before being appointed a commissioner for the Act of Union between England and Scotland. He communicated news of the loss in a despairing letter to his friend and fellow antiquary Roger Gale, who had it transcribed into the minute book of the Society of Antiquaries in London: 'No other motive induced this Gothic knight to commit such a peice [sic] of barbarity but the procuring of as many stones as he could have raised out of his Quarrys there for five shillings . . . We all curse him here with Bell, Book and Candle.' Gale wrote to Clerk: 'I like well your project of exposing your stupid Goth by publishing a good print of Arthur's Oven with a short account at the bottom of this curious fabrick when intire, and of its destruction . . . to be done without mentioning any name but the Brutes.' Five years later, Clerk was still fulminating in a letter to Stukeley about the 'barbarous demolition of the ancient Roman temple called Arthurs Oven' and gleefully communicating that 'some weeks ago the mill and mill dam which had been raised from the stones of Arthur's Oven, were destroyed by thunder and lightning'. It is almost as if Arthur's O'on were some kind of ritual sacrifice to the Industrial Revolution, though the great manufacturing plants its destruction ushered in are themselves now stilled. The Carron works finally went into receivership in 1982. Now owned by a Swiss company, its successor, Carron Phoenix, makes sinks, and lacks its old, bold Latin motto: *'Esto perpetuo'* – May it last for ever.

Arthur's O'on had a curious afterlife. Sir John Clerk died in 1755, after composing a richly enjoyable set of memoirs, based on his journals, which peter out in 1754 after his taking ill of a flux 'occasioned by eating too much cabage broth. NB – All Greens affect me in the same way, and for the future must be avoided.' (That said, both he and his wife were sufficiently doughty to produce a child when aged, respectively, sixty-two and fifty-one.) Riches were flowing into the family from their coal mines at nearby Loanhead, which enabled Sir John's successor, Sir James, to build a fine new Palladian mansion on the site of the family's old house at Penicuik. Sir James also erected a handsome stable block. It was a suite of buildings surrounding a quadrangle; on one side, they were topped by a rather fanciful clock tower, giving them an ecclesiastical air; and on the other, by a dome. The dome was a reconstruction, as accurate as possible according to the extant accounts and drawings, of Arthur's O'on. It still stands. The new Arthur's O'on was built to serve as a dovecote. That was appropriate, since the doomed domed original had often been compared to one by observers from Fordun onwards: Stukeley once wrote in a letter to Sir John that after 'my publication of Arthurs Oon people laughed at me for adoring a dovecoat as they called it'.

The current baronet, Sir Robert, showed the new Arthur's O'on to me: we climbed up a dark, narrow stone staircase into the interior of the dome, which was lined with little stone compartments – the pigeonholes. He and his family live in quarters converted from the stables by his indomitable-sounding great-grandmother, after a fire in 1899 damaged the main house so seriously that the then baronet – harder up than his ancestors – could not afford to make it habitable. Penicuik House, with its pedimented front and grand classicising features, is now itself a picturesque ruin that Sir Robert is fighting to preserve.

William Roy's *Military Antiquities* is a joyous book. Aside from his beautiful map of the Antonine Wall, there is page after page of meticulously drawn plans of Scotland's Roman forts and camps, each as if seen by a bird's eye, with the slope of hills shaded in tones of graphite, and woodland indicated by delicately drawn individual trees, each with its own shadow. The combination of the Roman geometries and the swollen contours of the landscape make these images sometimes resemble abstract works of art rather than functional maps. Of Roy's copious text, though, much less can be said; for the writings of this scrupulously empirical, careful mapper of the land were fatally infected. In common with his great-and-good antiquarian peers, he had fallen for one of British historiography's most successful, and most damaging, forgeries.

It began when William Stukeley received a letter, on 11 June 1747, from one Charles Julius Bertram, a teacher of English language in the Royal Marine Academy of Copenhagen. The letter was, Stukeley later wrote, 'full of compliments, as usual with foreigners' (Bertram was in fact an émigré to Denmark from Britain). It also mentioned a medieval manuscript that Bertram said he had seen, composed by one Richard of Westminster. The text was a history of Roman Britain, along with an 'antient map'. Stukeley recalled: 'I press'd Mr Bertram to get the manuscript into his hands, if possible. Which at length, with some difficulty, he accomplished: and on sollicitation, sent to me in letters a transcript of the whole; and at last a copy of the map.'

On studying the transcript, Stukeley identified Richard of Westminster with Richard of Cirencester, a known fourteenth-century chronicler. Richard's work, titled *De Situ Britanniae* (*On the Situation of Britain*), drew on known texts about Roman Britain, such as Caesar, Tacitus, the *Antonine Itineraries* and Solinus. (The *Antonine Itineraries* were ancient route planners: of uncertain imperial date, they describe journeys through various parts of the Roman empire by listing the places through which a traveller would pass to get from one point to another. Several deal with routes through Britain – giving, for example, directions from Caerwent to Silchester.) But the revelation was that he appeared to have had access to a host of lost original sources, as well as an entirely fresh crop of Antonine Itineraries – indeed, a great deal of significant geographical knowledge that had allowed him to come up with a comprehensive map of the British Isles under the Roman empire. Among this wealth of fresh material came evidence of a previously unknown province of Britain. Scholars already knew of the division, in the last years of the third century or early years of the fourth, of Britain into four provinces – Prima, Secunda, Flavia and Maxima – which between them made up the 'diocese' of Britain. They also knew of the disputed, possibly non-existent or only briefly existent Valentia, somewhere in the north of Britain. Richard of Cirencester's map fixed the location of Valentia between Hadrian's Wall and the Antonine Wall; and, most excitingly of all, introduced the notion of a further province of Vespasiana, in the Highlands of Scotland.

Stukeley revealed the manuscript's contents in a series of papers to the Society of Antiquaries, published in 1757 as *An Account of Richard of Cirencester, Monk of Westminster, and of his Works*. 'He gives us more than a hundred names of cities, roads, people and the like: which till now were absolutely unknown to us. The whole is wrote with great judgment, perspicuity, and conciseness, as by one that was altogether master of his subject,' he enthused. The 'highland part of Brittain', he added, was described 'very particularly'. The map and new *Antonine Itineraries* – one describing the mighty journey between Inverness and Exeter – gave Roman names to places that no one had imagined had had the slightest Roman contact. By applying the information

contained in Richard's map to known locations, Stukeley was able to
identify numerous Latin place names: Falkirk was Ad Vallum Antonini,
Inverness was Alata Castra, Aberdeen was Devana, and the Grampians
were Montes Grampium (which was a dead giveaway if anyone had
chosen to see it, given that the Grampians became the Grampians
only after that 1476 misprint of Mons Graupius). Some of the names
even had a Hellenic flavour: Dumbarton was identified as Theodosia
– Greek for 'God's gift', though perhaps it was primarily intended to
recall the general Theodosius, who put down a northern British insur-
gency in the fourth century.

In 1759, Charles Bertram published the Richard of Cirencester manuscript as part of his *Britannicarum Gentium Historiae Antiquae Scriptores
Tres (Three Ancient Writers on the History of the British People)*. Thanks
to Stukeley's passionate advocacy, its authenticity as a genuine medieval
document was not questioned – despite the fact that, as Stukeley
himself recorded, his requests to be shown the original manuscript
were, mysteriously, fruitless. The best he got was a copy of the handwriting of the first few lines, 'which I shewed to my late friend Mr
Casley, keeper in the Cotton library, who immediately pronounced it
to be 400 years old'. If there were any immediate doubts about the
discovery, they were confined to the truthfulness of Richard as a
historian rather than to the intentions of Charles Bertram; and Roy
was one of many antiquaries who wasted oceans of ink in trying to
square his own accurate on-the-ground observations with the document's fantasy geography. *De Situ Britanniae* had a new burst of life
when, in 1809, it was brought out in a new edition, with an English
translation by Henry Hatcher, whose preface defended Richard as
'scrupulously exact'.

Some of the document's spurious Roman names persist indelibly.
The hill range that runs like a spine through northern England from
the Derbyshire Peaks to the Northumberland Cheviots had no single
name by the early nineteenth century. However, when Daniel
Conybeare and William Phillips came to compose their pioneering
work of 1822, *Outlines of the Geology of England and Wales*, they decided
that it would 'be useful to distinguish this ridge of mountains by some
collective appellation'. They noted that 'Richard of Cirencester's
description of the Roman state in Britain' had 'denominated them the
PENINE ALPS'. (Bertram almost certainly had the idea from Camden,

who, in his *Britannia*, likened the range to that other mountainous backbone, the Apennines of Italy.) Conybeare and Phillips announced that as the hills had 'clearly a title to this, as their earliest known, if not their original designation, we shall therefore henceforth call them the PENINE CHAIN'.

It took until the mid nineteenth century for Charles Bertram's work to be definitively revealed as a forgery. Doubts grew in the 1850s; and then, between 1866 and 1867, the *Gentleman's Magazine* ran a series of splendidly acidulated articles by Bernard Bolingbroke Woodward, a fellow of the Society of Antiquaries and librarian-in-ordinary to the Queen, which finally demolished its claims to authenticity. His grounds were numerous: Richard's Latin was 'more or less good idiomatic English put into Latin words, and apparently by the help of a dictionary'; he had clearly been working from a dodgy edition of Tacitus – 'a very badly edited printed one of the 17th or 18th century'; indeed, in order to have consulted Tacitus at all, the putative Gloucestershire monk would have had to have read the works in manuscript, which in his day languished, unremarked, in continental European libraries. Some of the place names he had put forward were derived from medieval linguistic roots. He had repeated mistakes that Camden had introduced in the sixteenth century. In short, it had 'every mark of being the production of such a man as Bertram translating bad English into worse Latin'.

And yet it was a clever and stupendously successful deception; it wove its inventions seamlessly into the accounts of Britain by known classical authors, and lavishly fed the eighteenth-century antiquarian interest in the origin and etymology of place names. Its revelations were significant and surprising, but not so fanciful, at least to its immediate audience, to raise suspicion. In fact, the credulity of anti-quaries was sufficiently notorious to be pilloried, not least by Sir Walter Scott. In his 1816 novel *The Antiquary*, the title character Jonathan Oldbuck was – like the real Stukeley, Clerk, Gale and Gordon – engaged in a voluminous, committed correspondence with 'most of the virtuosi of his time, who, like himself, measured decayed entrenchments, made plans of ruined castles, read illegible inscriptions, and wrote essays on medals in the proportion of twelve pages to each letter of the legend'. A marvellous scene in the novel has Oldbuck showing his new young friend, Mr Lovel, an 'entrenchment' that lies upon his Scottish lands, and attempting to persuade him that it marks the site of Agricola's camp at the battle of Mons Graupius. This looks reasonably convincing, until a local beggar appears and announces that he himself 'minds the bigging' of the trench, some twenty years before; and the inscription 'A.D.L.L.' marked on a wall, tortuously interpreted by Oldbuck as referring to Agricola, in fact stands for 'Aiken Drum's Lang Ladle'. (The scene is surely a joke at Alexander Gordon's expense: he had made a similarly tendentious interpretation of a series of letters once said to have been inscribed on Arthur's O'on.)

As to Charles Bertram himself: he died, aged forty-two or forty-three, in 1765, his deception intact. Little is known of him: his silk-dyer father was one of a number of Britons who decamped to Copenhagen in the retinue of Princess Louise, George II's daughter, when she married Prince Frederick of Denmark. He himself was born in 1723, studied at the University of Copenhagen, and was the author of English-language grammars and textbooks for Danish speakers, as well as an *Essay on the Excellency and Style of the English Tongue*. Among his English-language aids is a collection of moralising maxims: sayings such as 'The World oftener rewards the Appearances of Merit, than Merit it self'; ''Tis a great Weakness to be credulous, nothing being more common than Lying'; and 'The too great Goodness of a virtuous Man exposes him to Tricks and Deceits.' Also: 'Patience is the surest Remedy against Calumnies: Time, soon or late, discovers the Truth.' His contribution to linguistics, one modern scholar has judged, was 'not inconsiderable'. His patron was the Danish royal librarian Hans Gramm, a figure known as a distinguished scholar to British antiquaries, and whose letter of introduction to Stukeley lent Bertram's correspondence a reassuring tint of respectability. (This correspondence with Stukeley, spanning nearly a decade, is, alas, lost.) Bertram's motivations for perpetrating the forgery can only be guessed at. Stukeley mentioned that he had havered for a year before sending his first letter, which perhaps suggests some doubt that the fake could be pulled off. Perhaps he wanted the attention and scholarly kudos; perhaps he was all the time laughing at the gullibility of Stukeley. His own words, from his Latin preface to his edition of *De Situ Britanniae* of 1759, are both revealing and oddly wistful. 'It contains,' he wrote of the document, 'excellent fragments of a much better age, which you would seek in vain to find elsewhere.'

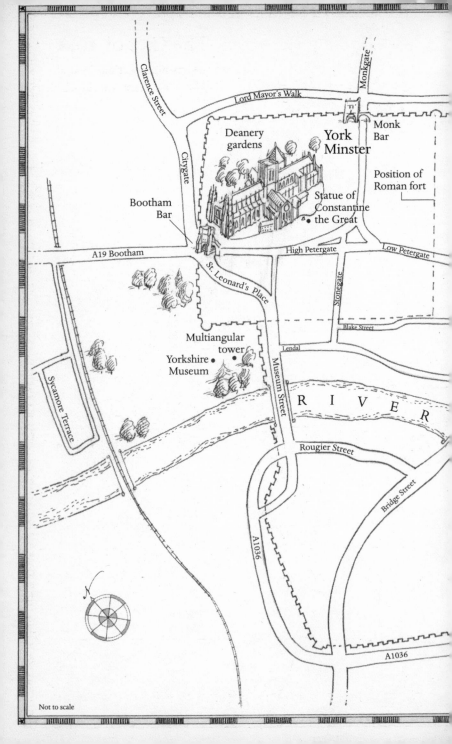

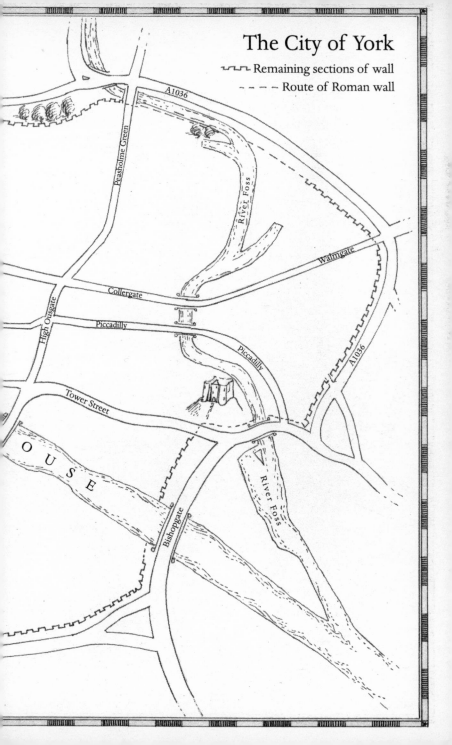

The City of York

∿∿ Remaining sections of wall
– – – – Route of Roman wall

A1036

Peasholme Green

River Foss

Walmgate

Collergate

High Ousgate

Piccadilly

Piccadilly

A1036

Tower Street

O U S E

River Foss

Bishopgate

9

York

Hence it may be gathered in what and how great estimation Yorke was .
in those daies, seeing the Roman Emperours Court was there held.

William Camden, 1607

'No city or town, in the united kingdoms, can present to the Author
so great a variety of wonderful events, for enriching the page of
history; or exhibit to the Antiquary so many mouldering relics of
former ages, as York, the ancient and venerable capital of the North.'
So began W. M. Hargrove's 1818 *History and Description of the Ancient
City of York*. Notwithstanding Hargrove's hyperbole, it is quite true
that the later history of York is inextricably bound up with its origins
as Roman Eboracum. The archbishopric here (the primate still signs
himself 'Ebor') sprang up because of York's past as a great Roman
centre. York was the springboard of invasion, the base of operations
for the legions as they advanced to Hadrian's Wall and beyond. When
the province of Britain was split into two administrative chunks in
the third century, the city became the capital of the northern portion,
Britannia Inferior, or Lower Britain. The first fortress was established
in AD 71 as the troops marched their way towards Caledonian conquest.
The emperor Septimius Severus settled his imperial court here between
AD 208 and 211 while he and his sons, Caracalla and Geta, waged war
against the northern tribes of the Caledonians and Maeatae. A century
later, in 306, the commander Constantius Chlorus died here; and it
was in this city that his son, Constantine the Great, was acclaimed
emperor by the legions. Six years afterwards, Constantine would
change the destiny of the empire by converting to Christianity at the
Battle of the Milvian Bridge, outside Rome. There are indeed moments
when York has been cast on to the great stage of world affairs.

When archaeologists were brought in to dig beneath the mighty Norman heights of York Minster in 1969, their aim was to discover the Anglo-Saxon church that the Venerable Bede had described as being the site of the baptism of King Edwyn of Northumbria in 627. What they actually found was a corner of the Roman *principia*, or fort headquarters, the elaborately frescoed walls of which are now displayed *in situ* in the minster's undercroft. Also here was a roughly bullish sculpted head that may, or may not, have been meant to represent Constantine the Great himself. By way of Christian aetiology for the spot, the minster authorities had to make do with a rather grubby terracotta tile fragment with XP – chi-rho, the first two letters of 'Christ' in Greek lettering – very faintly marked on it. This too is on show, with some flourish, its label making the suggestion that late Roman York had a 'considerable Christian community'. (In fact there are only the faintest traces of Christianity in the archaeology of Roman York, though the city is known to have sent a bishop to the Council of Arles in 314.) As I wandered through the dark spaces under the minster, it seemed to me that there was something appropriate in the Roman fortress's having asserted itself in this way, beneath the soaring spaces of York's most famous monument. The Norman minster, and no doubt its elusive Anglo-Saxon predecessor, were built here precisely because the fort headquarters represented the ancient seat of power. This was a potent spot; the place from which authority had to be wrested away and repurposed for a new Christian age. There is a beautifully preserved eighth-century Anglo-Saxon helmet in the Yorkshire Museum, which was found by a JCB operator in the city in 1982. The inscription that runs along the metal band on its crest tells us that its owner was Oshere, and that he was a Christian. The words themselves are in Latin – as if Oshere was borrowing the old rulers' power, as well as their language.

All this seems very far away from York's present, with its cafés, its tourist shops, its air of genial backwaterishness in its winding medieval streets. After my visit to the minster's crypt, I emerged blinking into the hot June day and wandered across the road to admire the huge modern bronze sculpture of Constantine enthroned; and nearby, a column from the collapsed Roman basilica, found during the 1969 excavations, which had been erected in the street to commemorate 1,900 years since the founding of the city. I walked on to the Yorkshire

Museum, where I met Patrick Ottaway, an expert on the city's Roman archaeology. He took me to the landscaped gardens of the museum, where together we surveyed the heft of the Roman walls and the 'multiangular tower' – a giant projecting polygonal mass, forward of the line of the town wall. 'As impressive a piece of military architecture as you will see in Britain,' said Ottaway. The tower's base is Roman; it is topped off by medieval stonework. Ottaway believes it may have been built when Septimius Severus was in York, with all the pomp of his retinue.

Septimius Severus was the child of a wealthy family of Lepcis Magna whose members had received Roman citizenship in the late first century AD; he was granted senatorial status under Marcus Aurelius. He studied in Rome, and served in Africa, in Syria and on the Danube. He won imperial power in 193, 'the year of the five emperors', by destroying all other claimants during the chaos that followed the murders of both the emperor Commodus, son of Marcus Aurelius, and his successor, Pertinax. Severus's final adversary was his erstwhile ally Clodius Albinus, who had been proclaimed emperor by his troops while governor of Britain and whom he defeated in battle at Lyon. A restless warrior, Severus campaigned in Parthia, sacking that empire's capital, Ctesiphon. Finally, he conducted two punitive expeditions in north Britain, whose tribes may have grasped the opportunity to rebel after Clodius Albinus led the British legions out to Gaul to pursue his imperial claim. Cassius Dio describes these two Severan expeditions vividly. The ailing emperor himself was carried in a litter into Caledonian territory, probably Perthshire and Angus (the Maeatae were said to occupy the lowland regions further south, around the Antonine Wall). The enemy never revealed themselves by way of meeting the Romans in battle, but instead picked off stragglers as the legions struggled with that more serious combatant, the highland terrain and climate. The Romans took to killing their own wounded to stop them falling into enemy hands. The following summer, Severus ordered genocide. Let no one escape sheer destruction, not even the babe in the womb of the mother, he commanded, according to Dio. Severus appears to have been grotesquely successful: there is no evidence of trouble from the north for over a century afterwards. Of Severus's wife Julia Domna – the stupendously wealthy Syrian empress – Cassius Dio wrote that she had discussed sexual mores with the wife of the Caledonian chief Argentocoxus. When the empress joked with the Caledonian woman about the free-and-easy sexual habits of the Celts, the chief's wife replied: 'We fulfil the demands of nature in a much better way than you do: for we consort openly with the best men; whereas you allow yourselves to be debauched in secret by the vilest.' It is a good story: but surely more to do with Cassius Dio's own commentary on contemporary Roman morals than with any conversation that might, or might not, have taken place.

In February 211, Severus died, aged sixty-five, in York (not without a little help from Caracalla, or so Dio claimed – on one occasion, he had had to be restrained from stabbing his father in the back in full view of the Roman troops). On his deathbed, Severus supposedly instructed his sons: 'Be harmonious, enrich the soldiers and scorn all others.' After his funeral, his sons and widow rushed back to Rome to secure power there, taking his ashes with them. The brothers at once became distinctly unharmonious. According to Dio, Caracalla requested that he and Geta should have a private audience with their mother in order to be reconciled to each other. But Caracalla had organised a gang of centurions to storm the room and kill his brother – who staggered bloodily towards Julia Domna and died in her arms.

Geta's name was subject to *damnatio memoriae* – all mention of him to be wiped from the official record, expunged from every inscription the length and breadth of the empire. There is, for example, in existence a rare painted portrait of Severus, Julia Domna and the two sons, in the collection of the State Museums of Berlin. Probably Egyptian in origin, it shows the dark-skinned, bearded Severus with his imperial crown; his wife with her beautifully curled hair, and the two sons – except that Geta's face is quite rubbed out. 'If anyone so much as wrote the name Geta or even uttered it, he was immediately put to death,' recorded Dio, who was a senator at the time, and an eyewitness to many of the atrocities of the period. Caracalla's most significant legacy as emperor was to drastically widen the citizenship – a move that Dio ascribed not to motives of generosity, but rather to the need to raise more cash to pay the legions, since citizens were liable for more tax than non-citizens. None the less, from his reign onwards, every free man across the empire, including Britain, was a Roman, with the same rights and responsibilities as a man born in the shadow of the Palatine.

Ottaway led me up now to the walls of the city. We ascended them by way of the medieval gatehouse of Bootham Bar, where a men's public lavatory was furnished with a plaque noting that this was the spot where the north-west gate of the old Roman fort had once stood.

With a few medieval dips and wobbles, Petergate, which runs into the city from Bootham Bar, follows the main street of the ancient fort: Ottaway told me about excavating here, and 'the extraordinary experience of standing on the Roman *via principalis*, five metres below ground, and looking upwards at all the layers of York's history'. We turned and looked the other way and imagined the line of the old Roman road heading north-west towards Catterick and beyond to Hadrian's Wall, lined with mausolea and cemeteries rather than pubs and little shops. We wandered atop the walls; from here to Monk Bar, another medieval gatehouse, they follow the line of the Roman fortress's defences, angling round the minster and affording lovely views of the soaring Norman architecture. Ottaway looked down longingly on the land he would never get to dig. There would be lines of barracks, he reckoned, beneath the deanery gardens. 'In my mind's eye I see it excavated,' he said. 'Not in my lifetime, but one day, when they build a nuclear power station here.'

He also told me the story, well known locally, of the Roman ghosts of York. One day in 1953, an apprentice plumber named Harry Martindale looked up from his work in the basement of a building in Chapter House Street to see the ghosts of Roman soldiers marching past. They were invisible from the knee down. Ottaway added that two years later, excavations took place in the same spot, which established that the earliest Roman floor level was, indeed, a few feet below the basement where Martindale had been working, thus making a certain sense of his curious vision. 'But,' said Ottaway with a grin, 'his soldiers seemed to be walking at an angle to the line of the Roman road.'

I walked back to the Yorkshire Museum and wandered round its galleries of Roman treasures excavated from the city. Here was an inscription recording the construction of a temple to the Egyptian god Serapis by one Claudius Hieronymianus, a high-ranking officer of the 6th Legion. Here were the spaces left by the Roman dead. The impressions of three corpses, one of them a baby in swaddling clothes, had been captured in the hardened plaster that had been poured into their shared coffin before they were buried – it was like looking at the dent your head makes in a pillow. Here, too, was a fragment of an inscription raised by the 9th Legion. The surviving portion lists the emperor Trajan's official titles and the length of time he had held them, and so can be accurately dated to the years 107–8 – the last-known reference to the legion in Britain.

The galleries of the museum were filled with death. Corellia Optata had died at the age of thirteen. Her father, Quintus Corellis Fortis, who set up her tomb, wrote a long, heartfelt inscription for her, calling himself '*spe captus iniqua . . . miserandus*', 'the pitiable victim of unfair hope'. To me the words have a Virgilian ring, echoing another outpouring of grief for a young person dead before their time: in the *Aeneid*'s eleventh book, Aeneas mourns the death of the boy Pallas, imagining his unknowing father at home '*spe multum captus inani*', 'utterly deluded by false hope'. In York, sadness seemed to seep from the stone. The father wept not for his daughter's end, but rather, somehow appallingly, her 'final end' – '*supremum finem defleo*'. '*Supremum*' is a word that might more appropriately be used of a long life, of a child burying a father rather than the other way around. The tombstone is missing its top half, so it contains only the text and no funerary relief, except for Corellia's carved feet, which lend a certain absurdity to the otherwise poignant object. In a glass case nearby lies the skull of another young woman, and her funerary goods: yellow-glass earrings, ivory bracelets from Africa, jet bangles from Whitby, an elegant blue-glass perfume bottle from the Rhineland, a silver mirror. She also had a motto in openwork bone buried with her – '*Soror ave vivas in deo*', 'Sister farewell, may you live in God', which may imply she was a Christian; or else, perhaps, that she was a follower of the Egyptian cult of Serapis.

This woman is known as the 'ivory bangle lady' to those who have studied her. She was buried at what is now York's Sycamore Terrace, near the banks of the Ouse, and her grave was excavated in 1901. The things buried with her are exceptionally fine: she was rich. She was a little over five feet tall, and between nineteen and twenty-three years old when she died, sometime in the fourth century. Recently, her skeleton was re-examined as part of a project looking at the movement of populations around the Roman empire. Her remains were subject to a range of techniques that are in their infancy as archaeological tools: among them craniometric analysis, or 'ancestry assessment' based on the typology of her skull. The researchers found that it had traits pointing towards mixed-race ancestry, and they suggested that she might have come from north Africa, where

Phoenician, Berber, sub-Saharan African and Mediterranean influences mingled. At the same time, researchers conducted strontium and oxygen isotope analysis on one of her molars. The technique aims to trace where an individual may have lived, through the influence, via the water the person consumed, of geology on tissue formation. They found that she was unlikely to have grown up in York, but perhaps spent her childhood either in the west of Britain or in a warm climate in the Mediterranean. 'In cosmopolitan Eboracum, which had been home to Severus and his troops nearly 200 years earlier, perhaps her appearance was not that unusual,' suggested the research team in a paper. Indeed, in assessing human remains from sites in Gloucester, Winchester and York, they found that up to 20 per cent of the individuals were not local to their burial places, but had originated from elsewhere in Britain, or overseas.

Were the 'ivory bangle lady' to have come from north Africa, it would not, in fact, be altogether surprising. Britain, after all, had already been governed by an African – Clodius Albinus, whom the late Roman collection of imperial biographies known as the *Historia Augusta* notes as being from Hadrumetum in modern Tunisia. And, as the researchers observed, York had played host to the Libyan-Syrian family of Septimius Severus. Nevertheless, the researchers' conclusions provoked a tumultuous response. On 28 February 2010, the *Daily Mail* ran a news piece to tie in with the publication of the findings in the journal *Antiquity*. The *Mail*'s article was headlined 'Revealed: The African queen who called York home in the fourth century.' It began: 'Startling new forensic research has revealed that multicultural Britain is nothing new after discovering black Africans were living in high society in Roman York.' The article ran fairly dispassionately through the evidence, and quoted one of the researchers, Dr Hella Eckardt, of the University of Reading, as saying: 'We're looking at a population mix which is much closer to contemporary Britain than previous historians had suspected. In the case of York, the Roman population may have had more diverse origins than the city has now . . . [The bangle lady's] case contradicts assumptions that may derive from more recent historical experience, namely that immigrants are low status and male, and that African individuals are likely to have been slaves.'

An avalanche of outrage descended on the article's comments thread. 'More mult-cult propaganda and lies,' wrote Oppenheimer, of

Dartford. Derrick, from Nottingham, described the research as 'insidious, neo-Marxist, multicultist [sic] propaganda'. David, from Nottinghamshire, thought it was a 'desperate attempt to fool us into thinking we've always had a multi-racial society'. Sylvia, from Kent, warned feverishly that the ivory bangle lady would inevitably have been a slave owner and that 'in those days the native population were the slaves of the Romans . . . and had their blonde hair pulled out to make blonde wigs for the Romans'. John, in France, wondered whether the researchers were 'from the same university as the "climate change" mob'. Chillingly, Middlesbrough's Ste felt that one good thing had come out of the article: it showed that 'if we were multicultural once and managed to reverse it, we can do it again'.

Only a few voices dissented from the prevailing tone. Ali, from London, was cheerfully impressed that 'some of my ancestors were actually here (and as socialites) in the fourth century'. Maggie, from London, made an astute remark: 'She wouldn't be the first military wife to find herself somewhere random, and she won't be the last. We army wives have been doing this for centuries.' Reader comments on the article were disabled. 'But within a day or two,' according to Andrew Morrison, chief curator at the Yorkshire Museum, 'the piece seemed to have been picked up by right-wing organisations in America. Then we started getting email at the museum. I've never encountered a story about the interpretation of an archaeological object that's been reacted to like that. We were accused of promoting black culture; of making the research up; of rewriting history to lever black people into it.'

It was an unpleasant episode; but if nothing else, it threw up, and not for the first time, troubling questions about the significance of the Romans in Britain, and the place of Britain's Roman period in the sweep of its history. In the early twenty-first century, when immigration is a political flashpoint, when selective historical precedent is – naively or perniciously – sometimes drawn on to defend a specifically northern European identity for Britain, the suggestion that Roman Eboracum was more ethnically diverse than modern York was clearly deeply threatening to some people's sense of Britishness. At the same time, the idea of Roman Britain as ethnically diverse is precisely that aspect of the period that is being harnessed by museums, including the Yorkshire Museum, to lend this potentially dusty corner of history relevance to contemporary British life. In the Yorkshire Museum the skull and grave-goods of the 'ivory bangle lady' are accompanied by an artist's impression of her face that – dispensing with the tentative ifs and buts of academic discourse – depicts her as black.

Who were the Romans in Britain? And what have they to do with us, in the twenty-first century? I found myself remembering an article that the novelist Robin Yassin-Kassab had written after he and his family had visited Hadrian's Wall from their home in southern Scotland. They had been surprised to find traces of ancient Syrians there. 'Castle Douglas, our damp little town, seems very monocultural, and my family, being multicultural – my wife is Syrian, from Damascus and perhaps originally Palmyra, and I am an Anglo-Syrian mix – seem correspondingly out of place,' he wrote. 'Yet all those centuries ago there had been Syrians here, and north Africans, and Europeans of all descriptions.' Seeing their traces, he wrote, made him and his family feel that they were 'not alone'.

One of the artefacts that Yassin-Kassab saw was at Arbeia, a fort at the mouth of the Tyne in South Shields. It was a tombstone: a carved relief of a woman sitting in a high-backed wicker chair, beneath a little classical folly of Corinthian columns topped by a pediment. It is nicely preserved, except that she has no face. In her lap she holds a distaff and spindle, and by her left foot sits a basket containing balls of yarn. With her right hand she opens a chest with a lock – perhaps a jewellery casket. She wears a long, flowing, deeply draped dress, and on each wrist is a bracelet. Beneath her, in clear-cut letters, is the inscription:

> *DM REGINA LIBERTA ET CONIUGE BARATES*
> *PALMYRENUS NATIONE CATUALLAUNA AN XXX*

Or:

> To the shades of the dead: Barates the Palmyrene
> [set this up] to Regina, his freedwoman and wife,
> of the nation of the Catuvellauni, aged 30.

She had a Latin name – Regina, which means queen – but she came from the important British tribe of the Catuvellauni, whose homeland was roughly where Hertfordshire is now. She had become a slave – we can only speculate as to how. At some point Barates, a man from Syria, had bought her, then freed and married her. It is a reminder that the membrane between slavery and non-slavery could, for some people in the Roman world, be fine. Scribes, doctors, teachers – many of the jobs that we in the modern world would regard as high-status – were often undertaken by slaves. Some former slaves, such as those who had belonged to, and been favoured by, emperors, could earn vast wealth, such as Claudius's Pallas, who was given the honours equivalent to the high political rank of praetor and voted a fortune by the Senate. Ordinary people – such as Regina – could spend part of their lives as slaves, and end up manumitted. At any rate, Regina had died, a free woman, aged thirty, far from her homeland in south-east England. And her husband, a Syrian from precisely the opposite end of the Roman empire, had chosen to depict her on her tomb as the quintessential Roman matron – spinning her own wool, as the emperor Augustus's wife Livia was said to have done as a self-conscious act of traditional womanly virtue.

Underneath the Latin inscription is another line of text, which to the untrained eye is simply a series of squiggles. It is in Palmyrene, the version of Aramaic spoken in the Syrian city of Palmyra. The fluency and accuracy with which it is incised suggests that either Barates himself, or another native speaker, carved it. Translated, it reads: 'Regina, the freedwoman of Barates, alas.' There is in existence a tombstone to a Barates – perhaps this same man – that was found thirty miles away, in Corbridge. It records his death aged sixty-eight, and obscurely describes him as a *vexillarius*, which usually means a standard-bearer, but since no army unit is recorded, it is thought that he may rather have been some kind of trader or merchant. Here, then, were two lives intertwined. Here were grief, and love, and pride.

In Roman Britain, you do not have to look far to find traces of people sprung from every corner of the empire. Because of the Romans' insatiable desire to memorialise their lives and deaths, they left their mark. Some fell in love, had children, stayed. Many, no doubt, were brief visitors, posted to Britannia and then off to the next job, in Tunisia, perhaps, or Hungary, or Spain. In the Yorkshire Museum is an inscription made by a man called Nicomedes, an imperial freedman and probably Greek, to go by his name. He placed an altar to the tutelary spirit of the province – *'Britanniae sanctae'*, sacred Britannia. Also in York, a man called Demetrius erected two inscriptions in his native Greek – one to Oceanus and Tethys, the old Titan spirits of the sea; the other to the gods that presided over the governor's headquarters. The Roman empire was multicultural in the sense that it absorbed people of multiple ethnicities, geographical origins and religions. But Roman-ness – becoming Roman, living as a Roman – also involved particular and distinctive habits, architecture, food, ways of thinking, language, things that Romans held in common whether they were living in York or Gaza. At the same time, Roman-ness, and the Roman empire, survived so long because of its very impurity; because of its willingness to incorporate all but the most threatening foreign influences and cults. (The problem with Christianity, for example, was that it valued an exclusive relationship with God above allegiance to the Roman state gods and emperor.) And although the Romans, as we have seen, were not short of prejudices about the nature of the uncivilised peoples beyond the imperial borders, they do not appear to have differentiated between people based on the colour of their skin. Emperors were Italian, Spanish; later African, German, Arabian, Gaulish (if not British).

Every age has had its own answers to the question of what the Romans in Britain have to do with 'us'. For Camden, setting out on his tour of the counties of Britain in the 1580s, his humanist project was to gather information from the landscape, buildings, inscriptions and artefacts that he encountered, using them, and his knowledge of ancient texts, as a way of discovering the truth about a past lost through the 'negligence of writers and credulitie of the common sort'. It was, he wrote, a process of 'recovery' – Britain's history was to be wrenched back from the grip of the mythographers and subjected to proper scholarship. His attitude to the Roman invaders was ambivalent. The occupying military, he wrote, 'alwaies with terror were ready to command the Inhabitants', and the tax-collectors, 'that is to say, greedy cormorants and horsleeches . . . confiscated their goods and exacted tributes in the name of the dead'. But in the end, Camden wrote, the Romans 'governed [the Britons] with their lawes, and framed them to good maners and behaviour, so as in their diet and apparell they were not inferior to any other provinces'. Importantly for Camden, the Romans introduced 'that healthsome light of Jesus Christ' that 'shone withal upon the Britans'. Ultimately, the 'brightnesse of that most glorious Empire . . . chased away all savage barbarisme from the Britans minds'.

That the Romans had civilised the untutored, primitive natives was to become a strong thread in later discussions of their influence on Britain. And for those inhabiting the borderlands of Roman influence – the Scottish Lowlands – these discussions seem to have been especially heavily freighted. Sir John Clerk of Penicuik was sure of a line of inheritance from his beloved Romans to the (Lowland) Scottish present. With his friends and correspondents, Clerk was a member of a short-lived club-within-a-club of the Society of Antiquaries, known as the Equites Romani, or Roman Knights. Each member took a classically inflected, usually rather revealing nickname. Clerk called himself Agricola, the governor who had briefly conquered all Britain – appropriately for a commissioner for the Act of Union. William Stukeley was Chyndonax, after a supposed Druid whose tomb had been discovered in France in the sixteenth century. Alexander Gordon, a protégé of Clerk's, gave himself the name Galcagus – or Calgacus – after the heroic but doomed Caledonian chieftain of Tacitus's account of Mons Graupius.

In his work on the antiquities of Scotland, *Itinerarium Septentrionale*, Gordon took patriotic delight in the Romans' failure to keep lasting control of his homeland. The very existence of Hadrian's Wall and the Antonine Wall, he decided, were 'Proof of the Scots never having been conquered'. He argued passionately against the view that it had simply not been worth the Romans' while to hang on to Scotland. If it had been 'so despicable a Country in the Eyes of the Romans', he wrote, 'can it be reasonable to suppose that Julius Agricola would have spent seven whole Years in that Country, and that his Army should be so eager to penetrate to the utmost Bounds thereof, which in all that Time they never could?'

Indeed, Gordon argued, Scotland's terrain was a blessing – and here he was paraphrasing Calgacus's Tacitean speech at Mons Graupius – since 'these very Mountains seem by Nature to have been placed as so many Bulwarks, for the better defending their Independancy and Freedom, and preserving them from the griping Tallons of the grand Plunderers of the World'. Clerk clearly found this Scottish patriotism an embarrassment. In a letter to Roger Gale (in the Roman Knights

Venutius, named for Cartimandua of the Brigantes' divorced husband) he wrote: 'Mr Gordon's high respect for his countrey hath carryed him too far, & made him commit a sort of laudable fault . . . I am, I confesse, of the opinion of some learned men that it is a reproach to a nation to have resisted the humanity which the Romans laboured to introduce.' Rome's history of intervention in Scotland could, it seemed, be co-opted both as evidence for the country's fierce and long-lasting independence, and for the graciousness of its enlightened eighteenth-century capital. Clerk regarded himself as an inheritor of the 'humanity' that he believed the Romans had implanted in the Lowlands. ('Humanity' is also the Scots word for Latin; such that the professor of Latin at the University of Glasgow, for example, is traditionally known as the professor of humanity.)

Gordon's entertainingly written work was soon superseded, in 1732, by the magisterial *Britannia Romana*, by John Horsley. The meticulousness and accuracy of his recording of Britain's Roman remains caused the work to be regarded as authoritative well into the nineteenth century. For him, the Romans had provided not so much a literal inheritance as a set of moral lessons: 'no doubt a great many things may be learned from those antique monuments, which are both instructive and useful. At least there is nothing, that can give us a more affecting sense of the vanity of this world, and of all that is in it. Such vast works, suitable to so powerful and extensive an empire, all laid in desolation! *Ipsae periere ruinae!* [The very ruins perish!] What surprising revolutions and catastrophes may we read not only in history, but in these very monuments! How many men rais'd on a sudden, and then more suddenly cast down again, disgrac'd and murder'd!' It is as if within the stones are the traces of human stories of tragedy and reversal; they are a repository of narratives of Shakespearean grandeur. The Latin words '*ipsae periere ruinae*' come from Lucan's *Pharsalia*, an epic poem written in the reign of Nero. The scene is Troy and Julius Caesar is visiting the stage of the events of the Homeric age – a little like Aeneas's visit to the site of the future Rome in the *Aeneid*. Troy's glories are forgotten and gone; the scene is savagely comic. Caesar tramples over the tomb of Hector, not knowing what it is.

Britannia Romana: the very phrase 'Roman Britain' is uncomfortable, a hybrid open to all kinds of awkward questions. Historians and archaeologists still intensely debate whether these islands became in any meaningful sense 'Romanized', to use the term elaborated by the historian Francis Haverfield. In his famous paper, *The Romanization of Roman Britain* (first published in 1905, and expanded in 1912), Haverfield argued that in the western Roman empire, the conquered peoples essentially became Roman. The relationship between imperial power and imperial subjects, he argued, was quite different from that which prevailed in contemporary empires, such as in the case of what he described as 'the rule of civilized white men over uncivilized Africans, who seem sundered for ever from their conquerors by a broad physical distinction'. By contrast, 'it was possible, it was easy, to Romanize these western peoples'.

The historical pendulum has swung, and the history of the Romans in Britain looks rather different from a post-colonial purview. The study of Roman Britain has, if anything, become more political, rather than less so, over the past fifty years. Some historians argue that the Roman-ness of Britain was at best a thin veneer imposed by the occupiers, the presence of whom made very little difference at all to these islands in the long term. The Romans have loomed disproportionately large in the vision of earlier historians and archaeologists, goes the argument, largely because previous generations were steeped in the classics and thus, naturally, found classical things when they went searching for the deep past. In the nineteenth and early twentieth centuries, the argument continues, historians tended to overempathise with the Romans, because Britain's empire found a model in Rome's. This sympathy for the Romans – who, of course, won the propaganda war, with their great trail of histories and poems and stories and buildings and *things* – caused historians to underplay the true nature of the Roman encounter with Britain, which, in truth, was one of exploitation, violence and resistance. The literary equivalent of the historiographical argument is *The Romans in Britain*, Howard Brenton's 1980 play, in which the Roman encounter with Britain is, literally, a rape (the scene in which a Roman soldier violates a young British man earned the work instant notoriety when it premiered at the National Theatre).

But I wonder whether this view is too simplistic. It is a little late, and a little naive, to think of the Romans in Britain as a Good Thing, or a Bad Thing, in the style of *1066 and All That*. There is a fascinating tendency now – both among historians and in popular culture – to imagine Roman Britain as a kind of inversion of Britain's modern wars with faraway lands. One prominent historian has, slyly, called Britain 'Rome's Afghanistan'; and the identification has not been lost on storytellers. When film-maker Kevin Macdonald came to adapt Rosemary Sutcliff's *The Eagle of the Ninth* into his 2011 film *Eagle*, he consciously cast it as a story of a vulnerable military keeping only a tenuous hold on a treacherous, barely understood landscape: it vibrated with modern resonances. Neil Marshall's 2010 film *Centurion* also took the supposed massacre of the 9th Legion as its starting point; in genre terms it resembled a western, with Caledonians taking the place of Apaches. But it was also, Marshall told me, about 'a superpower invading a country and encountering guerrilla warfare'; again, it was hard not to think of recent conflict in Afghanistan.

So much for post-colonial treatments of Roman Britain: but the pro-Roman fervour of Victorian and Edwardian writers has, it seems to me, been overstated. Even when apparently vainglorious assertions are produced – that they, the nineteenth-century empire-makers, are the new Romans, that Britain is the new Rome – there is frequently a lurking anxiety. Roman Britain became a place through which to express imperial doubts rather than imperial confidence. If British colonial administrators were marinated in the classics through a public-school education, they would struggle to find in ancient texts on Britain – especially if they happened to read Tacitus – a clear endorsement of the imperial project from a Roman perspective. And the Roman empire, even at a cursory glance, surely presents a troubling model: in the end it failed, and after becoming Christian, too.

Britain's status in that empire, as a subjugated province of it – not very important and not very close to the centre – has also been far from straightforward. For example, the preface to Collingwood Bruce's 1851 *Guide to Hadrian's Wall* compares the British to the Roman empire, sagging somewhat beneath the weight of its purplish prose. 'In that island, where, in Roman days, the painted savage shared the forest with the beast of prey – a lady sits upon her throne of state, wielding a sceptre more potent than Julius or Hadrian ever grasped!' he wrote, continuing: 'The mighty people who reared these structures, and were masters of the world, have passed away. And why? Because they gave way to luxury, impurity, and sin of every kind.' It is a formulation that looks triumphal – we are not only the new Romans, but we have surpassed them – but is, in reality, a warning: if Rome fell, so too could Britain. 'Luxury, impurity and sin' – these are Collingwood Bruce's fears about his own imperial world; just, in fact, the kind of anxieties that imperial Romans tended to harbour about themselves.

Nowhere, I think, is this anxiety expressed more clearly, and harnessed more knowingly, than in the opening passages of Joseph Conrad's *Heart of Darkness*. The novel begins with the narrator and his companions aboard a boat on the Thames. The river is a grand and, in its way, comforting sight – over the centuries, it has done 'unceasing service' for those who ply it. But then dusk falls. The landscape changes. As the light fails, so does the familiarity of the terrain, which quite suddenly appears brooding and unknowable. Now comes Marlow's immortal line: 'And this also has been one of the dark places of the earth.' Marlow, recalls the nameless narrator, says he is thinking of the days of old, when the Romans came to Britain 'nineteen hundred years ago – the other day . . .' Imagine what it was like for a military commander posted here, he continues: 'No Falernian wine here, no going ashore. Here and there a military camp lost in a wilderness, like a needle in a bundle of hay – cold, fog, tempests, disease, exile, and death, – death skulking in the air, in the water, in the bush. They must have been dying like flies here.' Or imagine some young Roman citizen arriving to trade, he says. 'Land in a swamp, march through the woods, and in some inland post feel the savagery, the utter savagery, had closed round him, – all that mysterious life of the wilderness that stirs in the forest, in the jungles, in the hearts of wild men.'

Marlow goes on to enumerate differences between the Roman and British empires: what saves the British project is 'efficiency'; whereas the Roman, lacking a redeeming central idea, is simply 'aggravated murder on a grand scale', a phrase that Tacitus could almost have written. Conrad is using the Thames as an introductory foil to his main narrative to come, which concerns the savage, barbaric landscape of the contemporary river Congo – a landscape that will both cause, and form the backdrop to, Kurtz's mental disintegration. But despite the superficial insistence on the difference between the two rivers, there is, as the novelist and critic Chinua Achebe put it, 'a lurking hint of kinship' – for if the Thames too had once been one of the dark places of the earth, with its 'jungles' and 'wild men', could it not become so again? Could it not, as Achebe wrote, fall 'victim to an avenging recrudescence'?

What Conrad recognised was the fatal fragility of human affairs. And all this, he seems to be saying, will fall away. Like Horsley, he saw that the Romans' lesson to us is 'the vanity of this world, and of all that is in it'. For Conrad was wise, and he knew that 'nineteen hundred years ago' *was* 'the other day'.

Cumbria and the Lakes

Obscure provinces, like Roman Britain, always rather appeal to me.
Their obscurity is a challenge; you have to invent new methods for
studying them.

R. G. Collingwood, 1939

One hot June evening, Matthew and I brought the camper van north
from Ribchester, a beautiful little Lancashire town on the Ribble,
with an ancient churchyard dotted with solemn table-tombs. The
town also has Roman columns to support its pub doorway, the remains
of a Roman bathhouse near the banks of the river, and a lovely little
museum of antiquities, containing, among other things, an altar
dedicated to Apollo and his Celtic counterpart, Maponus, for the
safety of a cavalry unit from Sarmatia, in modern Hungary. We drove
from there up to the estuary of the river Esk in Cumbria, where we
found an empty campsite on a low-lying farm near a bend in the
river, with friendly dogs nosing around. Later, under a midsummer-
evening sky, we went for a stroll, along a lane tunnelling through
deep hedgerows. They were thick with dog roses and honeysuckle
that we could smell before we saw the elegant, curlicued blooms.
Foxgloves – the interior of each thimble-flower freckled and downy
– stood unbending amid the scrambling profusion of campion, vetch
and Queen Anne lace. In the east, as the sky darkened to mauve, a
swollen moon rose and paused heavy over the skyline. The night was
so clear, and the moon so bright, that I could still write in my notebook at half past ten. Behind us rose the hills of the Lakes: Ulpha
Fell, Whitfell, Stainton Fell. There was no sound but for a mournful
curlew's cry, till the creeping night stilled all.

The next morning we drove a few miles north to the estuary at the little village of Ravenglass, once an important Roman harbour, long ago silted up, though a few bright-painted fishing boats bobbed around. A short walk through a copse of birch brought us to a Roman bathhouse, so well preserved that the walls stood nearly four metres tall, some still with their Roman rendering. We wandered through the grass-carpeted rooms, our only company a couple of cyclists who asked us to take their photograph by the high red walls. These are the best-preserved Roman remains in the north of England: there was even a wall-niche intact, perhaps where a statue had once stood. From there we took the van and set forth along the line of the Esk. We stopped at a petrol station where, miraculously, they sold fresh Muncaster crab and local strawberries, which we bought for our lunch. We climbed and climbed along the route of the Roman road that runs from Ravenglass to Ambleside. Eventually the camper van began to complain at the steepness of the incline, and to stagger unnervingly at each change down of the gears, so we continued the climb on foot until we reached the Roman fort of Hardknott Castle.

It was one of the most beautiful places I had ever encountered in England. To the west, the road ribboned back down to the sea, over hills whose harsh contours were muffled by bracken that collapsed down the slopes like green snowdrifts. To the east, the road unfurled higher and higher again, curling through a mountain pass into the peaks of the Lake District, which were lightly laced with clouds against a flawless sky. The camper van was a comforting blue rectangle a considerable distance below us. Around us stood the low remains of the fort walls, presiding over the pass. Lambs sheltered in their scanty shade; the sharp, hard stone of them looked as if it had been dressed yesterday. Near the ruins was a patch of artificially levelled-off turf, a parade ground 140 metres by 80 metres, built for the execution of military exercises. Around most Roman forts have been discovered the traces of a 'vicus', or civilian settlement. No such evidence exists in this isolated spot. A fragmentary inscription, now in Tullie House Museum in Carlisle, tells us that the fort was built during the reign of Hadrian by a cohort of Dalmatians from what is now Croatia, and abandoned perhaps twenty years afterwards, its building presumably relating to the consolidation of the northern frontier at Hadrian's Wall. Camden described Hardknott as 'an high steepe mountaine, in the top whereof were discovered of late huge stones and foundations of a castle, not without great wonder, considering it is so steepe and upright that one can hardly ascend up to it'. It was here that R. G. Collingwood had his first experience of archaeology. It was the spring of 1889; he was three weeks old and his father was excavating the north-west gate of the fort. 'They took me in a carpenter's bag,' he wrote in An Autobiography.

Collingwood is a significant, but in many ways curious figure in the history of British scholarship. He was a major contributor to the study of Roman Britain: with J. N. L. Myres, the Anglo-Saxon expert and sometime youthful admirer of Tessa Verney Wheeler, he wrote the first volume of the Oxford History of England; and he collated much of the material for the exhaustive collection of epigraphic material called The Roman Inscriptions of Britain (published posthumously, it remains an essential resource for historians of the period). But he was also the Waynflete professor of philosophy at Oxford; a metaphysician; a writer on philosophical method; a philosopher of art and, most significantly, of history. Such was the breadth of his learning that many people now working in one of his disciplines barely know of his work in the other; or even, sometimes, realise that Collingwood the philosopher was the same person as Collingwood the Roman Britain expert.

In 1938, not yet aged fifty, he suffered a stroke. In some ways this appalling experience was the defining moment of his academic career. It was the first of several; the same complaint had carried off his father. From this point onwards, until his death five years later, Collingwood wrote as if he were living on borrowed time. Granted leave from Oxford, he poured out writings, and it is the work from this period that is now his most influential, including the posthumously published *The Idea of History*, which, although its ideas have been superseded in many respects, still stands as a classic. The year after that first stroke he also produced his rather startling autobiography – not a conventional story of a life at all, but an account, barely concealing the enormous passions stirring beneath its rigorous, donnish prose, of the development of a mind. Distilling his most important ideas, it announced his intention to redeploy his intellectual powers in a single direction: the defeat of Nazism. By turns noble and arrogant, it also accused his fellow philosophers of being stooges of fascism, and condemned the wider establishment and media of an unforgivable indifference to the cause of Spanish republicanism.

Collingwood was a child of the Lakes. Born at Cartmel, he soon moved with his family to Coniston, to a comfortable house called Lanehead, a mile away from Brantwood, where John Ruskin lived. Both houses overlooked the grand heights of the Old Man of Coniston. His father, W. G. Collingwood, a painter, writer, local historian and archaeologist, had been Ruskin's pupil, biographer and devoted last secretary. His mother, Dorrie, was a painter of miniatures and a wonderful pianist. The young Robin and his sisters would wake up every morning to the sound of her playing Beethoven or Chopin before breakfast. A painting by Burne-Jones – *Two Angels* – hung in the drawing room. Robin was taught at home by his father until the age of thirteen. He read his way through his father's library. Aged eight, he picked up a copy of Kant's *Theory of Ethics*, and was 'attacked by a strange succession of emotions. I felt that things of the highest importance were being said about matters of the utmost urgency . . . then, with a wave of indignation, came the discovery that I could not understand them . . . Then, third and last, came the strangest emotion of all. I felt that the contents of this book, although I could not understand it, were somehow my business . . . I felt as if a veil had been lifted and my destiny revealed.' By the age of thirteen, he had excellent Greek and Latin and 'spoke and read French and German almost as easily as English'. He was a prolific writer of stories and poems, and edited a family magazine for private circulation. He was, too, 'a neat-fingered boy, skilful at making all sorts of things; active in walking, bicycling, or rowing, and thoroughly practised in sailing a boat'. His father wrote a children's story, *Thorstein of the Mere*, set among the Vikings who settled at Coniston. It was dedicated to his son, with a verse inscription including the lines: 'Thanks, Robin: for the wide world o'er/ A writer asks no finer flattery,/ No kinder fate of all in store,/ Than Five-years-old's assault and battery/ Demanding more and more.' When R. G. advocated home-schooling in his Hobbesian work of political philosophy *The New Leviathan*, published in 1942, one can see why. He was utterly miserable at Rugby, and seemed to regard his undergraduate days at Oxford as an opportunity for long bursts of private reading, relatively undisturbed by actual teaching. Everything that he regarded as important about his education had begun at home.

If his Lakeland upbringing sounds almost too idyllic to be true, at least one outsider was also caught up in its spell. One day, W. G. Collingwood, walking home from a painting trip up on the Old Man, saw what he thought was a body washed up on a wide flat stone in Copper Mines Beck. He called out and was relieved when the apparent corpse lifted its head. The young man in question later recalled: 'He asked me what I was doing and I told him I had been trying to write poetry. Instead of laughing, he seemed to think it a reasonable occupation, and we walked down to the village together.' This was the young Arthur Ransome, who had caught the train north 'with Hazlitt in one pocket, Keats in the other' to take his first holiday from his job at a London publisher's. Ransome fell in love with the whole family. His favourite children's book had been *Thorstein of the Mere*, and he immediately felt that his own literary efforts would be taken seriously by this family of writers, musicians and painters; in his own father, now dead, he had prompted nothing (he felt) but exasperation and disappointment.

The elder Collingwoods became the 'touchstones by whom to judge all other people that I met'. This was the life creative and the life of the mind; a kind of paradise for Ransome. Recalling W. G.'s study, he wrote: 'I can see it now, the books from floor to ceiling, the enormous long table piled with books and manuscripts, the unfinished canvas on an easel, the small table at which he was writing and, over the fireplace, his lovely portrait of his wife, in a small boat with two of the children.' Here art was made for its own sake. 'He wrote and they both painted with complete disregard of possible sales.' Soon Ransome was out on Coniston Water, sailing with the Collingwood girls, Dora and Barbara. 'In the afternoon we went down to their boathouse and out in the *Swallow*, a one-time fishing-boat, monstrously heavy to row but not bad under sail, the first of a long dynasty of *Swallows* in my sailing life.' The two boys, Robin and Arthur, would race *Swallow*, and a friend's 'half-decked, sloop-rigged' boat, the *Jamrach*, across Coniston Water. When Ransome was issued with a writ for libel by Lord Alfred Douglas, after the publication of his *Oscar Wilde: A Critical Study*, R. G., by then a young don, offered up all his savings to his friend. Fortunately his (presumably meagre) resources were not needed, since the jury at the 1913 trial found in Ransome's favour. Ransome was not the only young man to receive the warm hospitality of the Collingwoods. Wilfred Owen, a devotee of Ruskin, 'blew in upon them one stormy night' from Keswick, where he was staying in the summer of 1912, 'and as soon as I had warmed myself in their geniality, blew out again and over the moors'. He had been 'a little drunk on Ruskin', he recalled. Perhaps Owen and the Collingwoods also spoke of their shared love of archaeology.

R. G. Collingwood did his First World War service in London, in naval intelligence. In common with Mortimer Wheeler, he felt a sense of profound responsibility after the conflict. He was the only one of Francis Haverfield's students to survive, and the great historian himself died in 1919. Haverfield's work, wrote Collingwood, had to be continued 'in piety to him'.

Collingwood's efforts as a practical archaeologist on his home turf of Cumbria are often overlooked, or regarded as a mere vacation pastime compared with his 'real' work as a philosopher in Oxford. But his bibliography records publication after publication on archaeo-logical matters, many for the Cumberland and Westmorland Antiquarian Society, for which his father served as president. By Coniston Water and in Eskdale his mind was forged. It was his 'great good place', to borrow Auden's phrase. It was here that he returned to write his autobiography when invalided out of academic duties; it was here that he died; it was here that one feels he was happiest and most truly himself. 'Of all the valleys of England there is none lovelier than Eskdale, from its wild beginnings among the precipices of Scafell to its quiet ending in the land-locked harbour of Ravenglass,' he wrote in his little guidebook, *Roman Eskdale*, published in the late 1920s. Of Hardknott, he wrote: 'The fort commands a splendid view. To the visitor who cares for magnificence of scenery, the sudden revelation of the Scafell range, as he reaches the edge of the spur and looks over the precipices and the valley below him at the mountains beyond, is an unforgettable experience.' In the scholarly R. G. there still clung the traces of the schoolboy Robin, romping by the lake and demanding more of his father's stories. Recalling Camden's remark that there were some who thought the old bathhouse at Ravenglass to be the court of the legendary King Eveling, Collingwood expanded in his guidebook: '. . . people thought it was the Lyons Garde of the Arthurian romances, the Castle Perilous beside the Island of Avillon, where dwelt the Lady of the Fountain; or they said it was the castle of King Eveling or Avaloc, the husband of the sea-fairy Morgan le Fay, who was king over the island in which lived the blessed dead'.

Collingwood was one of the first to argue that archaeology should be precise and directed. One should dig in order to discover the answer to specific questions, not simply as a speculative exercise or as a search for beautiful things. Intellectually, it was also the place where his academic interests met. His Cumbrian digs became the crucible for his philosophy of history, the place where theory could be put to practical test. At his most likeable – at least in so far as he emerges from his own writings – he was a person who thought matters through in the doing of things: as a violinist, a sailor, a walker, and most importantly as a digger. In his autobiography he described himself as the sort of person who, 'when I read . . . the beautifully illustrated handbook that tells me how to look after a certain kind of motor, my brain seems to stop working. But . . . leave me alone with the motor and a box of tools, and things go better.' Archaeology was the box of tools that helped him formulate his philosophy of history.

The strongest example, in his view, of the way this worked was through his views on the history of art – here was the 'rapprochement' between the two sides of his scholarship, between history and philosophy. His writings on art, he wrote, he would 'gladly leave as the sole memorial of my Romano-British studies, and the best example I can give to posterity of how to solve a much-debated problem in history, not by discovering fresh evidence, but by reconsidering questions of principle'. His particular theory related to what he believed was the suppression of Celtic art during the Roman period and then, as the evidence suggested at the time, its revival after many centuries. The history of man, he argued, was the history of thought, of purposive thought. The job of the historian was to recapture, or re-enact, these past thoughts. The past never truly went away; it lay 'incapsulated' in the present. As he saw it, the artistic habit of the Celts had not died out under the Romans, but had been passed down by 'the transmission by example and precept of certain ways of thinking and acting from generation to generation'. The Celts' skills and their desire to make art had lain dormant – 'incapsulated'.

If his ideas seem outmoded, it is still striking to witness the passion with which he wrote, and the absolute urgency of his thinking in the late 1930s. In Collingwood's philosophy of history, the past was not a distant, dead thing, but stood in the closest possible relation to contemporary life. Science had brought us extraordinary technology, but the primary use to which we had put it was the invention of deadly weapons and the pursuit of war, he argued. History was the true science of human affairs, and must be marshalled to make sense of the present; it was only history that could help put a stop to the disasters that he rightly saw amassing in the immediate future. In the end, it was the ideas forged as R. G. Collingwood dug about in the Roman forts of Cumbria that caused him to break up 'my pose as a detached professional thinker' and throw himself, however impotently, however imperfectly, into an open political struggle. In the end, it was his encounter with Roman Britain that made a passionate anti-fascist of him.

Collingwood's writings also impel us to ask whether it is more appropriate to treat the Roman things brought forth from the British soil as objects of aesthetic veneration, or as the purposive jigsaw fragments of history. He himself developed fierce views on the quality of artistic production in Roman Britain. In his part of the *Oxford History of England* he asserted that 'the history of Romano-British art can be told in a couple of sentences. Before the Roman conquest the Britons were a race of gifted and brilliant artists: the conquest, forcing them into the mould of Roman life with its vulgar efficiency and lack of taste, destroyed that gift and reduced their arts to the level of mere manufacture.' There was more: 'On any Romano-British site the impression that constantly haunts the archaeologist, like a bad smell or a stickiness on the fingers, is that of an ugliness which pervades the place like a London fog: not merely the common vulgar ugliness of the Roman empire, but a blundering, stupid ugliness that cannot even rise to the level of that vulgarity.'

It is a remarkably extreme sentiment for someone who spent so much of his life among those 'blundering, stupid' remains. In truth, the aesthetic qualities of Romano-British art and craftsmanship had often caused anxiety, and still do: are the stubby little walls of Roman ruins in Britain worth admiring, when we have the magnificent, sombre depletions of medieval abbeys? It is these buildings that were officially sanctioned as picturesque by the eighteenth-century lovers of the Gothic, and lovingly depicted by artists such as Turner. Horace Walpole, who realised his Gothic appetite magnificently at Strawberry Hill, his villa near Twickenham, was derisively unequivocal about the taste for Romano-British things. 'Roman antiquities . . . such as are found in this island, are very indifferent, and inspire me with little curiosity,' he wrote in a letter of 1780. 'I do not say the Gothic antiquities I like are of more importance; but at least they exist. The site of a Roman camp, of which nothing remains but a bank, gives me not the smallest pleasure.' Not everyone was a Sir John Clerk of Penicuik or a William Stukeley, extolling the beauties of Romano-British things.

In 2010, such questions of aesthetics came into sharp focus when, on the east side of the Lake District, in a field near the hamlet of Crosby Garrett, a metal detectorist pulled out from the mud a piece of crushed metal that he assumed was a Victorian ornament. It was, in fact, a Roman cavalry sports helmet – an ornate and precious thing, which would have been used on the parade ground on ceremonial occasions, too decorative and impractical for wearing on the field of combat. It was a find of immense rarity, and a thing of great visual power: the helmet had a visor cast into the form of a youthful, beautiful face. When news of its discovery was announced, the *Daily*

Telegraph put a photograph of it on its front page. Only two other helmets of this type are known in Britain: the Newstead helmet found in the Scottish borders, now in the National Museum of Scotland; and the Ribchester helmet, which is in the British Museum. The Crosby Garrett helmet was curious in another way. Despite its undoubted rarity, it fell through the cracks of laws designed to protect archaeological finds. Had the helmet come within the legal definition of 'treasure', the finder and landowner would have been awarded compensation at a price agreed by a panel of experts, and the helmet would in all likelihood have been privately bought by the Tullie House Museum in Carlisle, the most important Cumbrian museum for Roman antiquities. However, only gold or silver objects, or groups of bronze objects, fall within that definition. The bronze helmet, found on its own, was not 'treasure'. Which is how it came to be sold on the open market, the star object of Christie's antiquities sale in London, in autumn 2010.

On the day I went to Christie's to see the Crosby Garrett helmet, the auction house was about to host a fire-sale of remnants from the offices of Lehman Brothers, the bank that had collapsed in 2008, triggering an international financial crisis. Potential bidders, catalogues in hand, wove around the salvage from the bank's offices: pieces of furniture, works of art of varying quality, and even a plaque marking the building's opening by the then chancellor, Gordon Brown. (This would a few days later sell for just over £28,000.) In the middle of all this, somebody set up a plinth. Then, from the back of the room, and not without a sense of theatre, strode a young woman in an elegant shocking-pink dress. In her gloved hands she held the Crosby Garrett helmet, which she gently placed on the plinth. It was the life-size face of a beardless boy of impossible beauty, wearing a tall Phrygian cap, the headgear that gave its name and shape to the *bonnet phrygien* of the French Revolution. His slightly parted lips were sensuous and delicate, the chin round and a little chubby. His hair was set in perfect whorls, as if piped by an expert patissier. His eyebrows were long and thin, the fine hairs picked out in a herringbone pattern. The back of the helmet was engraved with a starburst, and on the high proud peak of the cap sat a griffin, balancing a little amphora under its right paw. The griffin's tail was neatly tucked but its beak was wide open in a kind of screaming ferocity quite unlike the blank serenity of the human face beneath. The whole thing had an uncanny, vacant perfection to it.

I asked the woman who had carried in the helmet – Georgiana Aitken, Christie's head of antiquities – what sort of person or organisation might buy it. It was estimated to sell for £200–300,000. She said that there had been interest from private buyers as well as museums, and observed that antiquities can look very fine amid a collection of modern art. I considered the helmet as an elegant sculptural piece, setting off a Richter, say, or a Twombly, and saw that it would do very well. I asked the Christie's people how much work had been done on the helmet to present it thus. Not much, they said breezily.

This, it seemed, depended on how you might define 'not much'. According to Dr Ralph Jackson, curator of Romano-British collections at the British Museum, it had been 'hugely changed'. The flawlessness of the helmet was an illusion. When it was found by the detectorist in May 2010, the visor was face down in the mud, 25cm below the surface. The chin was gashed and the curling hair was missing chunks.

The helmet itself (which would have been attached to the visor mask with hinges) was in sixty-eight pieces, its greater part folded up lengthwise, like a closed book. Jackson told me this folding must almost certainly have been deliberate, that the helmet had, he believed, most likely been bent and buried as part of some kind of ritual.

Christie's commissioned a restorer, Darren Bradbury, to work on it. It was a 'complex and delicate task', he told *British Archaeology* magazine, that took 'some 240 hours'. He reshaped the helmet, carefully opening out the fold. He closed cracks. He made moulds of existing curls of hair and cast them in resin to replace the missing ones; the same process was used to re-create the missing section of chin. He gilded the resin with silver leaf and distressed it, so that the whole object had a smooth, seamless patina with no visible joins. He reattached the griffin.

The artefact now occupied a kind of limbo between the state in which it was found and its original appearance. Its surface was an agreeably antique-looking greenish-silverish, more or less as it had been when the Cumbrian sod had been fully cleaned away. When it was first made, the helmet would have been golden and the visor tinned, so that it would have shone like silver. When I asked Jackson what the British Museum would have done, had the helmet fallen into their hands, he told me they would have worked much more slowly on its conservation, analysing it and studying it as they went. They would probably not, he said, have reshaped it, but would most likely have had a replica made to suggest its original appearance. 'We would not have interfered with the state of its ultimate demise,' he said. Half a century ago, the museum might have thought differently. Fashions in the acceptable levels of re-creation change, and the territory between conservation and restoration is disputed. In cases such as that of the Crosby Garrett helmet, there is no such thing as a definitive, 'authentic' object.

Tullie House Museum set about raising funds to buy the helmet, which had been the cause of great excitement locally. The campaign did well, and at the sale, on 7 October 2010, the museum was able to bid up to £1.7m. But the helmet went to an anonymous buyer for the hammer price of £2m. The buyer has not, up to the time of writing, responded to the museum's requests for a loan, or accurate measurements so that a replica can be commissioned. All that is known is that the buyer is in Britain: if he or she were overseas, the artefact would have been subject to an export stop and the museum would have had another chance to try to buy it. The helmet has made only one public appearance, at the Royal Academy of Art's Bronze exhibition in autumn 2012; otherwise it has disappeared as completely as if it had been swallowed up once more by the Cumbrian sod. When Tullie House Museum reopened its Roman galleries in 2011 after a refurbishment, the space they had hoped it would occupy was taken by another Roman cavalry helmet, on loan from a museum in the Netherlands.

As it is, the most fascinating object in Tullie House Museum's Roman gallery is also one of its least visually arresting. Found in 1891, in the bed of the river Peterill, just south of Carlisle, the artefact is a rough piece of stone, just under two metres tall, rather narrower at one end than the other. In the centre of the slab was once an inscription. There is nothing there now except a faint trace of a single letter. At the slightly fatter end, roughly incised, are the words:

> IMP CM
> AUR MAUS
> CARAUSIO PF
> INVICTO AUG

Or, 'for the Emperor Gaius Marcus Aurelius Maesaeus Carausius Pius Felix Invictus Augustus'. At the other, slightly thinner end, and with the letters facing in the opposite direction, the inscription reads:

> FLVAL
> CONS
> TANT
> NONOB
> CAES

Which translates as: 'for Flavius Valerius Constantinus, most noble Caesar'. Both extant inscriptions are made in rather wobbly, drunken letters; the stone looks more like a country gatepost than a slab of Roman officialdom. In fact, the ramshackle look of the whole artefact belies the extraordinary story that it tells. For this Roman milestone brings us a fragment of the curious history of Carausius – Britain's breakaway Roman emperor.

The written historical record on Carausius is sparse. In the late third century, there was no historian of the stature of Tacitus to tell his story. What we know of him is gleaned from two brief passages in the work of the historians Aurelius Victor and Eutropius, both composed at different points during the fourth century and both, it is thought, relying on a lost single source from earlier in the century. Also surviving are panegyrics – speeches delivered in lavish praise of emperors – in this case to Maximian, Constantius Chlorus and Constantine. None of these literary sources was produced by a voice favourable to Carausius, but by those deeply invested in his downfall.

The facts, such as we have them, are that Carausius was a humbly born Menapian, from the area around the mouth of the Rhine in the modern Netherlands. Having distinguished himself in campaigns against the Bagaudae, rebels in northern Gaul, he was given command of a fleet in charge of ridding the Channel and North Sea of Saxon pirates and raiders. He was accused, though, of corruption: of allowing raiders to carry off booty before attacking them, and then keeping the loot for himself rather than restoring it to either its owners or the emperor. When Maximian – joint emperor in the west, ruling alongside Diocletian – learned of this alleged abuse, he ordered Carausius's execution. Carausius's response, in AD 286 or 287, was to seize Britain with, crucially, its three garrisons, who must have had their own reasons for giving him that loyalty (whether it was bought, or whether it related to a real respect for his military abilities, we will probably never know). He also had the fleet at his disposal, and substantial forces in northern France.

An initial attempt by Maximian to haul Britain back seems to have ended in failure, judging by the silence of the panegyrists, who had previously boasted of the lavish preparations being made for the province's reconquest. The precise chronology is uncertain, but it is probable that Constantius Chlorus recovered Boulogne in AD 293, after which Carausius was assassinated by a figure called Allectus, who in turn assumed control of Britain. Of Allectus we know little: Aurelius Victor calls him Carausius's minister of finance; Eutropius refers to him simply as an ally. Some three years later, an invasion force under Constantius Chlorus crossed the Channel in a thick fog that enabled them to pass Allectus's fleet, lying in wait off the Isle of Wight, without detection. They defeated Allectus's ill-prepared land army, and a further force, initially separated from the main seaborne force by the fog, later reached London in time to finish off the remnants of Allectus's Frankish troops, who were in the process of sacking the city. After an intriguing decade of self-rule, Britain was finally brought back into the imperial fold.

But what of the story from Carausius's side? The Tullie House inscription is one of the few hints towards what he felt he was trying to achieve, and in what manner he was attempting to project himself as a ruler. It is an extraordinary survival: by the third century, the Romans in Britain were losing the 'epigraphic habit', the urge to inscribe stones with markers of deaths, great events, building projects. In fact, this artefact is the only surviving inscription that mentions Carausius at all. On it, we see him bedecked with all the pompous titles of an emperor. The imperial-sounding Pius Felix Invictus Augustus – 'dutiful, happy, unconquered Augustus' – will certainly have been adopted to give his rule the sheen of legitimacy. 'Marcus Aurelius' may just have been his names at birth; it is more likely, though, that he adopted them to recall the philosopher-emperor whose reign, over a century before, looked like a golden period of stability given the decades of barbarian unrest, imperial succession problems and civil wars that had dogged the empire in mainland Europe and Asia during the middle decades of the third century. What becomes clear is that Carausius was attempting to make his stolen reign feel reassuringly traditional.

A further reason this inscription is so rare is that normal Roman practice after the downfall of a figure such as Carausius was to erase his name from all inscriptions: the kind of *damnatio memoriae* to which Caracalla's brother Geta had been subject earlier in the century. The blanked-out central section of the stone slab, indeed, may relate to some previous *damnatio memoriae* – perhaps even of Maximian, erased by Carausius's people. But Carausius's inscription remains, and the clue to its survival is the fact that the words on the other half of the block, relating to Constantius, are upside down. What happened, we may infer, is that after Carausius fell, instead of the inscription being scraped off in the usual way, the stone was simply upended, the old lettering buried in the earth, and the new inscription carved. The Constantius here may be Constantius Chlorus, who oversaw the invasion force that brought the erring Britain back into the empire proper in AD 296. Or it may refer to his son, Constantine the Great, who was acclaimed emperor in York a decade later.

There exists another source for Carausius's side of the story. During his period in power, he minted money from London and, probably, Colchester. Coins were a powerful means of trait projection for any ruler. Even if not everyone handled or had money, or could read the legends inscribed upon it, there were plenty for whom coins were an important part of life – not least the army, through whom the bulk of money in Roman Britain flowed as pay before entering the wider economy. At their most basic, coins were a way of circulating the name and face of the emperor. In the case of the usurping Carausius, the very fact that he appeared on the coinage lent him an air of imperial legitimacy. One rather daring issue had his head in profile alongside those of the co-emperors Maximian and Diocletian, with the legend '*Carausius et fratres sui*', 'Carausius and his brothers'. He was claiming to stand alongside these legitimate rulers as an equal.

Yet more intriguing, perhaps, was what happened on a coin's reverse. Here was the place for a further message, a burst of propaganda, a world view. Carausius's coinage was highly suggestive and utterly distinctive. One of his issues called him '*restitutor Brit(anniae)*' – the restorer of Britain. Another showed him hand in hand with the personified Britannia, as if in mystical marriage. He was, it seems clear, projecting himself as a restorer of traditional values, of Britannia as it had once been, before the current turbulent age. On one coin are inscribed the words '*expectate veni*', 'come, oh awaited one'. It is, as William Stukeley recognised, an adaptation of a line of Virgil, from the second book of the *Aeneid*, in which Aeneas dreams that he encounters the dead hero Hector – the 'awaited one'. It is not, perhaps, a wildly appropriate allusion, since the Hector that he conjures in his dream is battle-worn and bloody and rather terrifying, a god-sent vision to persuade him to abandon the defeated Troy. But the message of the coinage becomes clearer: Carausius seems to have been presenting himself as an almost messianic saviour of Britain. The coins were literally embodiments of the values of a better time: in an era of debased coinage and soldiers' pay inflation, he brought back the silver content of his precious-metal issues to levels not seen since the reign of Nero 200 years earlier.

Another of the coins is inscribed with the words '*renovat(or) Roman(orum)*' – 'the restorer of the Romans'. The image is of a she-wolf, suckling two infants – Romulus and Remus. The appeal is, again, to the old brew of history and mythology that created the very idea of Rome. Beneath are the initials R.S.R. The letters appear on many of the precious-metal issues of Carausius, and have been interpreted as standing for the name of a mint, though they do not suggest any known town or city; or for the words '*rationalis summae rei*', meaning 'financial minister', though they do not match the standard abbreviation for the phrase. Neither of these speculations has ever seemed completely satisfactory as a way of explaining R.S.R.

These letters are not the only enigmatic initials, unknown in the coinage of other reigns, to crop up on Carausius's issues. In 1931, a young boy brought to the British Museum a medallion, given to him by his grandfather but otherwise of unknown origin. One day in the spring of 2012, I visited the British Museum coin department, where curator Richard Abdy brought it out for me to look at. He let me pick it up; it felt heavy and clumpy in my palm. On the obverse was an image of Carausius in a consular toga. That was a piece of fiction: Carausius awarded himself the title. On the reverse was Victory in a chariot, with the legend '*victoria Carausi Aug(usti)*' – 'victory of Carausius Augustus'. Below the image were the letters I.N.P.C.D.A. Generations of scholars were baffled by this bizarre string of initials: no one could work out what they might mean, or stand for. Until one day a historian and author called Guy de la Bédoyère saw the solution staring him in the face.

When I wrote to de la Bédoyère to ask him how he had solved the mystery of the letters R.S.R. and I.N.P.C.D.A., he gave me a rather surprising answer. In the early 1990s, he said, he had become bored by his study of Roman Britain, and had put it to one side in order to concentrate on something entirely unrelated: the seventeenth-century diary and correspondence of John Evelyn. In doing so, he wrote, he 'became used to ploughing through endless Latin texts to trace [the] unattributed quotes and asides' that the diarist, with the learned ease of his age, had used quite freely and naturally. 'But one day in, I think, 1997 I picked up a Roman coin book and looked at the coins of Carausius and those mysterious exergue legends. I remember quite distinctly thinking, "Well, everyone knows that Carausius alluded to

Virgilian imagery on his coins so I expect those initials represent some Virgilian text."

'Then I had to run the bath for the kids. While the water was running I decided to skim through Virgil as I had done for all of Evelyn's quotes. But first of all I thought the easy thing to do would be to skim through the *Oxford Dictionary of Quotations*. I had an old 1950s copy (which I still possess) and scanned through what they had. On page 557 column (a) I found I.N.P.C.D.A.

'I can still recall the skin crawling on the back of my neck when I saw it. I returned to the bath and stopped the taps. Then I remembered R.S.R. and I hardly dared look at the book. My eyes slowly drifted up and there was R.S.R . . . So I never even had to look up Virgil properly . . . In short I had done nothing clever. I know a bit about coins, a bit about Carausius and a bit about the classics and I hadn't been tied by an academic post only to work on Roman Britain . . . John Evelyn took me to Virgil and Carausius by a roundabout route. The whole thing took about twelve minutes.'

He had simply seen that R.S.R. are the initial letters of the words 'redeunt saturnia regna', 'the Golden Age returns'; and I.N.P.C.D.A. of 'iam nova progenies caelo demittitur alto', or 'now a new progeny is sent from Heaven'. The two phrases constitute the most famous line and a half of Virgil's fourth *Eclogue*, an ecstatic poem foretelling an era in which a miraculous child will be born and the earth will bring forth its bounty unbidden. If de la Bédoyère's leap was right – and it seems too great a coincidence not to be – it provides another hint towards how Carausius was trying to project himself: he was using Virgil's poetic language to suggest that he would preside over nothing less than the rebirth of the Augustan values of the Roman empire, now tarnished and tired. But nothing more of Carausius is known. Whether he really did wish to restore old virtues, or whether he was using these Virgilian references as mere empty propaganda, is obscure. It seems unlikely that his reign was imagined, in its time, as the beginnings of a proudly independent Britain: Carausius will more likely have had his eye on the greater prize of being accepted as some kind of legitimate joint ruler of the empire, as the coin showing him with Maximian and Diocletian suggests. But our fragmentary knowledge of the Carausius episode remains intriguing. Could old Rome really have been reborn? In Britannia? This is fertile ground for the historical novelist: Rosemary Sutcliff's sequel to *The Eagle of the Ninth*, *The Silver Branch*, is set during Carausius's British reign.

It was John Evelyn, as it happened, who had first proposed that the phrase *'decus et tutamen'* – 'an ornament and a safeguard' – should be engraved on the edge of Charles II's silver coins. The phrase, somehow inevitably, also comes from Virgil, from the *Aeneid*, book five; it is a description of the beautiful cuirass that Aeneas bestows on one of his men as a prize in the funeral games that he holds in honour of his father. Evelyn had been inspired to suggest the phrase after seeing it, of all places, on the binding of one of Cardinal Richelieu's books in 1644. It was surely this coincidental Virgilian connection that had steered de la Bédoyère unconsciously towards solving the riddle of R.S.R. and I.N.P.C.D.A. The words *'decus et tutamen'* are still inscribed around the rim of our one-pound coin, though the practice of clipping coins, which the inscription was meant to discourage in the seventeenth century, has long ceased. Collingwood, I think, would not have approved of the route by which de la Bédoyère reached the fourth *Eclogue*: it would have been insufficiently scientific and systematic for his taste, I imagine. But the intuitive threads that connect Carausius, the seventeenth century and our own ordinary pound coin – I hope that he would have enjoyed that, as the child Robin, if not as the don R. G. 'Suppose,' he wrote in his autobiography, 'the past lives on in the present; suppose, though incapsulated in it, and at first sight hidden beneath the present's contradictory and more prominent features, it is still alive and active?'

11

The Cotswolds and the South-West

That it was a famous place, the Romane coins, the cherkerworke pavements, and the engraven marble stones that now and then are here digged up (which have beene broken, and to no small prejudice of Antiquitie) do evidently testifie.

William Camden, 1607

In the second half of the fourth century, Roman Britain was decades away from collapse. Things were changing. Populations in many of the now 200-year-old towns were dipping. The wealthiest inhabitants' urge to endow municipal buildings and set up inscriptions was fading. Towns were ceasing to be thriving centres of civic life: in Silchester, the grand basilica, once the scene of regional administration, seems to have ended up being used for industrial metalworking. On the other hand, some people, in some parts of Britain, were enjoying more prosperity than at any other time under Roman rule, and a lifestyle that would not be equalled in wealth or sophistication for another 800 years. In the Cotswolds and the south-west came a great flowering of grand country estates – rural villas, some of enormous size, luxuriously appointed, probably controlling great swathes of agricultural land. When Matthew and I puttered along the dead-straight Fosse Way to visit the villa remains at Chedworth, and those at nearby Great Witcombe (among whose low walls wild orchids were pushing up their purplish spears), I could not help but be reminded of eighteenth-century country gentlemen, and of the twenty-first-century super-rich, in the Gloucestershire fastnesses of later centuries.

Often, Roman remains have survived precisely because of the care taken by the gentry of a later age – and their access to cheap labour. 'The discovery of Roman villas in these woods originated with an under gamekeeper, engaged in ferreting rabbits,' wrote James Farrer, the antiquary who excavated the Chedworth villa in the 1860s. The gamekeeper showed a handful of tesserae to the heir to the local estate, Lord Eldon. Recognising them as Roman, Lord Eldon brought in Farrer, his uncle, to supervise an excavation. Fifty labourers and foresters were employed to clear the surrounding trees and to unearth the remains. What they found was a palatial fifty-room villa with two bathhouses, and numerous hypocaust-heated rooms with elaborate, still-bright mosaics. The family built a museum and opened the site to the public; it is now owned by the National Trust.

When we visited the Cotswolds, we stayed in a borrowed shack in a woodland clearing. A wren was nesting in the room where we slept; from the bed I could hear its tiny wings thrumming above me and see its tremendous, tremulous bursts of flight. The cottage was hard by the walls of one of the great Gloucestershire estates, Barnsley Park. In the grounds had once been excavated a Roman villa, among whose remains was found a gemstone engraved with an image of Orpheus. With certain feelings of feudal anxiety, I knocked on the door of the early-eighteenth-century Palladian house, and we were let into the entrance hall, the walls of which bristled with icy Italianate stucco plasterwork. We were politely sent away without being allowed to look at the site of the villa.

Cirencester – the epitome of a snug Cotswolds market town, built in golden, sun-washed stone – was once the capital of Britannia Prima, the south-western province of Britain after its division into four administrative sections in the late third or early fourth century. We left the camper van in the bathetically named Forum car park. Just south of here once stood a magnificent basilica, 102 metres long, the second largest in Britain, after London's. I found it almost impossible mentally to project a Roman grid and buildings on to the winding streets of this genteel town, with its gentlemen's outfitters and antique shops. In the centre, Quern Lane and Lewis Lane tentatively pick up the line of the Roman Fosse Way, and point towards the high, grassed-over remains of one of the largest Roman amphitheatres in Britain, on the south-western edge of the town. (Beyond, the Fosse Way marches south-west to Bath, and north-east to Leicester and Lincoln.) Apart from these traces, the most intriguing signs of Cirencester's Roman past are to be found in the Corinium Museum.

Here is the 'Septimius stone', whose inscription gives weight to the idea that Corinium, Roman Cirencester, was a provincial capital; it is a dedication to Jupiter by *'primae provinciae rector'*, the 'governor of the first province'. An immense Corinthian column capital, wreathed in carved acanthus leaves, gives a notion of the scale of the town's public architecture. Nearby is displayed an ingenious word square, scratched into a bit of wall plaster, which reads:

```
R  O  T  A  S
O  P  E  R  A
T  E  N  E  T
A  R  E  P  O
S  A  T  O  R
```

It means 'Arepo the sower holds the wheels by his labour', and the words are palindromic, such that they can be read from left to right, right to left, top to bottom or bottom to top. There may have been magic in this arrangement of letters. Such word squares have been found in Pompeii and in Syria. There is a sculpted trio of stone Matres, the Celtic mother-goddesses, their laps swelling with cakes, fruit and bread. A cavalry tombstone tells us that Sextus Valerius Genialis was Frisian and served for twenty years in a Thracian cohort. As I read the inscription, I realised the sculptor had slipped, and misspelled THRAEC as TRHAEC.

The most wonderful things here, however, are the mosaics, brought to the Corinium Museum from beneath the streets of the town or from the great country villas. Found under Dyer Street in 1849 was a remarkable pavement, its layout a three-by-three series of octagons in a guilloche frame. Within the octagons are depicted intricate scenes – four of them badly damaged, but the remaining five clear and bright. In the corners are the four seasons. Winter is obliterated, but the others are there. Spring is especially lovely: she has flowers in her hair, and on her shoulder perches a swallow with a red flash at its throat and streamers for a tail. The finest of the medallions shows the hunter Actaeon, who, in Ovid's poem on mythical transformations, the *Metamorphoses*, chances upon the chaste goddess Diana as she bathes. His punishment for this unwitting violation is to be turned into a deer. As Ovid wrote: *'dat . . . vivacis cornua cervi'* – 'she gave him the antlers of a mature stag'. In the mosaic they are beginning to sprout from his still-human body, just as they do in the poem. He is already being ripped apart by his own hunting dogs, who tear into his thighs, their little fangs dripping tesserae of blood.

Better still is the Barton Farm mosaic, found in 1824 when workmen removed a tree from a spot just outside the old town walls of Cirencester. In its central, circular panel is Orpheus, who sits upon a rock strumming a lyre, his cloak stretched out behind him. He wears a Phrygian cap; and a fox leaps away from him. Around him, arranged in two concentric circles, are the animals that he has charmed with his unspeakably seductive music. Nearest him are the birds: a peacock with its tail furled; a peahen or pheasant; a swan or a goose. In the next band are great animals: tiger, leopard, lion and – the only mytho-logical beast – griffin. The felines have the powerful necks, low-held heads and stealthy tread of real cats. Between the animals are trees, for in the *Metamorphoses* they too are charmed by Orpheus's song: according to Ovid, the oak, the poplar, the hazel; the plane, the willow, the arbutus; the beech, the willow, the pine. Even in its damaged state, with whole passages of it destroyed, it is wonderful.

Further west into Gloucestershire, near Stroud, is another version of this Orpheus mosaic. It lies under the graveyard of the village of Woodchester – perhaps a church was built here because of the gran-deur of the spot, for the mosaic, which would have covered the floor of the most spectacular room of the villa here, is nearly fifteen metres square. Local antiquaries knew of its existence from the late seven-teenth century and from time to time portions were revealed – and appallingly damaged – when graves were dug. Finally, over the course of four summers from 1793, it was studied in detail by Samuel Lysons, one of the most significant figures in the development of Romano-British archaeology.

The son of a clerical family from Gloucestershire, Lysons studied law in London, and also painting, under Joshua Reynolds. His own portrait, made by Thomas Lawrence, shows a plainly dressed, wirily handsome man with a penetratingly intelligent gaze. His skill as a draughtsman and his love of the antique united gloriously in his masterpiece: *Reliquiae Britannico-Romanae*, a three-volume work published between 1813 and 1817 in lavish elephant folio. It contains exquisite engravings of the remains he excavated, including a representation of the Woodchester mosaic over two spreads, the pages folding out to reveal the design on a luxurious scale. Orpheus sits this time not in the very middle of the composition (as in the Barton Farm mosaic, which is so stylistically similar it must have been produced by the same workshop, and possibly for the same client) but just off centre, among the birds. He is encircled again by great prowling felines and a griffin, as well as by a stag and a shaggy-coated bear. That outer circle is banded by a guilloche and a generous acanthus border. In the spandrels – the corners of the enclosing square – are nymphs, pale-skinned on a dark ground, barely draped in fleeting lengths of fabric.

Lysons devoted a complete work to his study of Woodchester: it is another splendid volume, beginning with an engraving of himself sketching, in breeches and frock coat, among the villa ruins, the church in the background. Dispassionately, he explained how he was able to access the Orpheus mosaic: 'On the digging of a vault for the inter-ment of the late John Wade esquire, of Pudhill, at the depth of four feet below the surface of the ground, so considerable a portion of the same pavement was laid open, as, together with other openings, which were made in the course of that and the following year, enabled me to ascertain its form and dimensions.' He concluded that the pave-ment was, 'for size and richness of ornament . . . equalled by few of those discovered in other provinces of the Roman Empire, and is undoubtedly superior to any thing of the same kind found in this country'. He called it the Great Pavement.

Lysons's account and careful recording of what he found is of immeasurable importance – not least because the mosaic rests to this day under the earth, among the dead of Woodchester. It has from time to time been uncovered: the last occasion was in 1973, when 141,000 people visited and the village groaned under the footfall. There are no plans for it to be revealed again. Among those who did see it then was a local builder called Bob Woodward. He then owned a construction firm with his brother, John; when we met, in the summer of 2010, he was the very image of the prosperous retired businessman, in neatly pressed trousers and sports jacket, speaking with a Bristolian's angular vowels. In 1973, the brothers were then working at Wotton-under-Edge, a market town on the southern edge of the Cotswolds. When a friend of theirs came to visit from Brighton, Bob decided to take him to Woodchester to see the mosaic. 'In fact it didn't mean much to me,' he told me, 'because I had never seen a Roman mosaic before.'

When he got there, 'I was absolutely mesmerised by it,' Woodward said. 'Being in the building trade and looking at a building that had been there for sixteen or seventeen hundred years, I was amazed at the craftsmanship of the men who had made the mosaic. At the same time I was so angry that so much of the original was broken up, mostly by gravediggers. You could see coffin-shaped areas where tesserae were missing. When I was driving back to Wotton-under-Edge I said to my friend: "I've got to do something about that; what a great challenge it would be to remake it." My friend answered, "You'd have to be crazy to do that." And I thought to myself, perhaps I've got the qualifications.'

So began a project magnificent in its ambition. Woodward persuaded his brother that they were to transform themselves from builders into accomplished mosaicists. They managed it: it took a decade and 1.6 million tesserae to re-create, at full size, the fourth-century Great Pavement. While Woodward and I were talking, we were standing on his mosaic, as big as a ballroom, its surface both cool and inviting and somehow as thickly luxurious as a carpet. At the time, it was on display at Prinknash Abbey, outside Gloucester, just before being put up for auction by its then owner (Woodward had long ago sold it). It was bought by an anonymous buyer for £75,000. The villagers at Woodchester had tried to acquire it, but were outbid, and it has now disappeared from public view.

Remaking the mosaic presented innumerable technical challenges. While the original was still exposed, the brothers were granted permission by its legal owner, the rector of the parish, to have it carefully photographed. After endless experimentation and many false starts, they invented a process whereby a projector sunk some feet below ground would reproduce the image of a section of the mosaic on to tracing paper placed atop a sheet of armour-plated glass. 'We wanted to make something that was really authentic,' he said. 'We didn't want people to say, "It probably looks from a distance like the one at Woodchester, it gives the overall impression of it." No, we wanted to do an in-depth study into the mosaic and to be able to explain our idea to people who know far more about mosaics than we were ever likely to know and to get their backing.' Rather than sourcing coloured stone for the tesserae, they commissioned a potter in south Wales, who provided clay in the various shades they required. 'We got five tons fired up and ended up using twelve tons.' They made the mosaic in sections, so it could be jigsawed together. At first the tesserae buckled and curled on their backings; this, like many other problems, the brothers solved by patient trial and error.

Forty per cent of the original mosaic had been destroyed over the centuries; so Woodward set about researching the lost sections – from drawings made by Lysons and his predecessors, and when that failed, from other similar mosaics made nearby, such as that from Barton Farm. 'I left school at fourteen, so I had no idea about how you go into the Bodleian Library and how you get the right book. My old headmaster used to say to me, "Keep your head up, Woodward, there's nothing in it."' But Woodward found himself metamorphosing into a scholar, working in the libraries at the Ashmolean Museum and the Society of Antiquaries in London. He pursued the theory, first put forward in the 1960s, that the reason Orpheus was not dead centre of the composition was that there had once been a fountain set there – which is now generally accepted by archaeologists. After the mosaic was re-created, 'I was invited to speak at the Getty Museum in Malibu in 1985 – and I think, though I say it myself, I stole the show,' he said.

Remaking the mosaic taught the brothers to look – really look – at it. 'If you are going to make it, you have to understand it,' he said. As they went on – embodying, re-enacting the work of the original craftsmen – they discovered the mosaicists' tricks. For example: the elaborate square panels that border the composition must have been made from the outside working in, for in their centre comes what Woodward called a 'release panel' – a rectangular section that could work at any width, thus accommodating variations or inaccuracies in the neighbouring panels. Woodward paced around, showing me his favourite parts: 'the gorgeous pheasant with a ring around his neck'; 'the colours in the tigress and the lion's flowing mane'. He told me how he had reconstructed what in the original was a headless, limbless Orpheus, using the Barton Farm mosaic as his guide. As we spoke, I remembered the full story of Orpheus's death in Ovid's *Metamorphoses*: he was ripped apart, his limbs scattered, by furious maenads. Only in the afterlife was he reassembled, a ghostly metamorphosis.

What is striking to me about the mosaics of Roman Britain is how completely *Roman* they are. The Orpheus pavements of the Cotswolds are not greatly different from those of Sicily, in Palermo and Piazza Armerina – certainly in terms of their iconography if not in complexity or skill of execution. There are some Romano-British mosaics, though, that strike a rather different note. In the Hull and East Riding Museum there is an exceptional collection, including a vivid depiction of a chariot race, found when gardeners were digging a kitchen garden at Horkstow Hall in Lincolnshire in 1797, a print of which was published by Lysons in 1801. But the mosaic known as the Rudston Venus is something quite distinct. Here Venus is not an elegant classical creature, but a rather curious pear-shaped figure, with a large belly and bottom, tiny feet and breasts, and a crudely depicted pubic triangle.

In her right hand, apparently balanced on the very tip of her finger, is a round object that might be the golden apple from the Garden of the Hesperides that she claimed when Paris judged her to be the most beautiful of goddesses. From her other hand drops a large tennis-racquet-shaped item, which may be a mirror. Next to her – perhaps what has caused her to let fall her mirror in surprise – is a triton,

fish-tailed and human from the waist up. Around this central section
are scenes from the amphitheatre. A lion, somewhat resembling a
dachshund with its long body and short legs, has a spear protruding
from its body. There is a bull, with the words 'TAURUS OMICIDA'
picked out in tesserae, meaning the 'murderous bull', or 'the bull
called Man-eater' – except that the M and the Us have been given
cross-strokes (like the letter A), suggesting, perhaps, that the craftsman
was unlettered. A rectangular panel at one end of the composition
shows the head and shoulders of a figure with Mercury's snake-
wreathed staff, the caduceus. But from his helmet, oak leaves rather
than wings sprout, as if the craftsman has mistaken a detail he has
seen in a pattern book. The work looks very much as if it has been
made by local, British craftsmen. Even so, despite the apparent crude-
ness of the depiction, there is nothing un-Roman about the iconography of the Rudston Venus. The scenes shown here would be readable
to anyone in the Roman empire.

The heirs to the work of Samuel Lysons are two archaeologists,
David Neal and Stephen Cosh, who have recorded, illustrated,
described and discussed every single known Roman mosaic in Britain,
gathering evidence, too, about those long ago destroyed. Over the
course of fifteen years (and two lifetimes of expertise) they have
together produced *Roman Mosaics of Britain*, a four-volume work
published by the Society of Antiquaries. By the time they reached the
final volume, they were obliged to add an appendix containing discoveries that had been made since they began. The work is a remarkable
act of devotion to the objects that give us the clearest idea of the
nature of artistic work in Roman Britain.

Turning the pages of Neal and Cosh's volumes, it seems extraordinary
that so many tessellated pavements have survived, from the three entries
from Scotland (one recording two lonely glass tesserae found in
Castlecary on the Antonine Wall) to the bafflingly peculiar mosaic of
Brading, on the Isle of Wight, which shows a cockerel-headed man
beside a pair of griffins, interpreted variously as an Egyptian religious
scene, a North African-style gladiatorial contest, or the Gnostic deity
Abraxas. But there have also been tremendous losses. Obliteration is as
much a feature of Romano-British mosaics as survival.

In 1805, Edward Donovan, an Irish scholar best known for his
twenty-volume work on the zoology of Britain, published an account

of a journey he had taken through Wales, including a visit to Caerwent, the Roman town of Venta Silurum, which lies a little east of Chepstow in Monmouthshire. Unlike Silchester, Wroxeter and Caistor St Edmund, a village sprang up on the site of the town – but a modest one, so that the encircling Roman walls run at times through open fields. Wandering round the village and the local farms, Donovan noted the 'mutilated remains of a noble capital, and shaft of a pillar' that served 'to support a wheat-stack'. The pillar's ignoble recycling was, he thought, 'evidently derogatory to the first intention of the sculptor' but at least rendered the crops 'above the reach of the host of little plunderers, which the cautious farmer has to guard against'. He then made his way to the orchard of one Mr Lewis, where two 'highly celebrated' mosaics were said to be viewable. But Donovan was to be disappointed. 'Passing through the orchard, we soon perceived that the first of these pavements, having lain exposed in the open ground, was nearly all demolished; part of the broad external border, and some portion of the inner quadrangle, alone remaining.' The other was reduced to a few tesserae 'scattered promiscuously through the grass, and nettles'. Donovan recorded the reason for the disaster: the landowner's initial enthusiasm for the mosaic had 'suffered a very sensible diminution'. He had dismantled the structure built to protect the mosaic from the ravages of the weather, and used the materials to make a new brewhouse.

When I visited Cosh in his well-ordered modern house in Surrey, the walls hung with some of his beautifully drafted drawings, he told me of a myriad possible deaths for a mosaic. Exposure to the elements was the most serious: Lysons, for example, had recorded the fate of a section of the Great Pavement, 'containing the figures of an elephant and several birds', that had been unearthed and left unprotected a decade before he visited in the 1790s. 'The wet and frost have long since entirely destroyed it,' he wrote. Then there is the danger of looting by souvenir-hunters, damage by livestock, soil erosion, or destruction to make way for building projects. Deep modern ploughing is another threat: in the final volume of *Roman Mosaics of Britain* is a poignant drawing of a mosaic found in 2002 in Pillerton Priors, Warwickshire, gouged by recent plough lines like giant clawmarks. Or there is simple human neglect. 'In York there's a pub called the Jolly Bacchus,' Cosh told me. 'They found a mosaic, and thought, that's a nice attraction for people coming to the pub – let's charge people a penny. This was in the 1800s. That didn't make them any money. So they used it as stables instead, and it was trampled to smithereens.' He told me, too, about the building of the Great Western Railway, which 'had a habit of going right through Roman villas'. A mosaic was discovered at Newton St Loe in Somerset during the building of the Bath to Bristol line in 1837. Fortunately, one of the young engineers, Thomas Marsh, was an enthusiast for Roman things. He made plans and drawings of the site, and traced the finest mosaic – another Orpheus panel, probably dating from the late fourth century. 'Marsh had the mosaic lifted and set into Keynsham railway station,' Cosh said. 'Eventually, for whatever reason, the mosaic had to go. It was set in concrete – they hacked it up with a pickaxe, and gave the pieces to what became Bristol City Museum. There it was damaged in a fire in the museum stores, so it was not only broken up, but blackened, too.' In 2000, it was pieced back together and put on display – but is now back in store. Aside from the technical difficulties of lifting mosaics, they are often too large and unwieldy to be displayed well in museums. Of one of the most famous mosaics ever to be excavated in Britain – the Hinton St Mary mosaic, from Dorset – only the central part is on show, at the British Museum. Most experts believe that the figure at its heart, a head-and-shoulders backed by a chi-rho, is meant to depict Christ. But there is no room to display the rest of the pavement, with its vigorous, lively scenes of deer-hunting, its corner panels of four men who might be the four Evangelists, and its panel showing Bellerophon slaying the Chimaera – a heterogenous composition that, seen as a whole, might complicate a straightfor-wardly Christian interpretation of its iconography.

The luckiest mosaics, perhaps, are those that have been carefully looked after *in situ*. In 1811, a farmer called George Tupper stumbled on the remains of a villa when ploughing on his farm at Bignor on the South Downs, a short step away from Stane Street, the Roman road from Chichester to London. Nearby, at Bignor Park, lived John Hawkins, whose family had grown rich from mines in his native Cornwall. Hawkins, a well-travelled man of botanical and antiquarian leanings, took charge of the excavations – since, in his words, Tupper was 'a man of very low education and manners'. (The villa is still owned by

Thomas Tupper, the great-great-great-great grandson of the original George.) The remains were quickly secured from 'nightly depredations' by a 'Hovel in which one of [Tupper's] sons can sleep'. Later, sturdy thatched-roof buildings were put up, which still stand – and indeed are regarded as rare surviving examples of early-nineteenth-century agricultural buildings, valuable in their own right.

In a pattern now familiar, Lysons was brought in to study and record the excavations. Visitors began to flock to see the mosaics: between March and November 1815, there were 904 signatures in the visitors' book. Hawkins and Lysons became firm friends, corresponding copiously: on one occasion Lysons gave an all-too-vivid hint of the discomforts of even gentlemanly archaeology, noting (in March 1813) that 'I have been so much troubled with my old complaint of the Rheumatism in my hip, that I was afraid of venturing to stand about in the open air, unless there had been a greater probability of the absence of the East or North wind.' In 1819, Lysons died suddenly – a shock and an 'irreparable' loss to Hawkins. The following year a guidebook by Lysons was posthumously published 'for the accommodation of [the proprietor's] visitors; many of whom were desirous of obtaining more information on the subject, than it was in his power to afford'. The book described the mosaics as 'in a good taste, and the figures are better executed than any which have been before discovered in similar remains in this island'. The villa – now surrounded by vineyards, giving it an oddly Mediterranean atmosphere – has been attracting visitors ever since.

The high point of the mosaics at Bignor is a depiction of the rape of Ganymede by Jupiter, disguised as an eagle. The boy was taken to Olympus, to become cup-bearer to the gods. One of the eagle's wings is blotted out, but the other is a bright sweep of ruby and rust and cream. The eagle grasps Ganymede carefully – a claw around the boy's sexily naked hip, the beak nuzzling his scarlet Phrygian cap. The boy wears a crimson cloak, its folds and shadows carefully picked out. He holds out his right hand, as if in surprise, and he still carries his shepherd's crook in the other, for the unsuspecting Trojan prince had been herding a flock of sheep on Mount Ida. In Ovid's *Metamorphoses*, the story of Ganymede's abduction is the first of the tales that Orpheus tells in his poem-within-a-poem, as he sits in the grove of listening trees, surrounded by animals and birds.

> And off he swept the Trojan lad; who now
> Mixing the nectar, waits in heaven above
> (Though Juno frowns) and hands the cup to Jove.

Ovid's stories seem to run through so many mosaics: but were these really readers' mosaics, meant to be associated with poems – or just images to be plucked from a pattern book, entirely divorced from their literary associations? Often it is hard to tell. But one famous mosaic discovered in England cannot be understood without a poem. Indeed, it demands to be read like a poem.

One day in 1938, Herbert Cook was digging a hole to bury a dead sheep on his farm near Low Ham, in Somerset, when he came across an unfamiliar-looking terracotta tile. He took it to the local museum, where it was identified as part of a pilae stack for a hypocaust system. The site was excavated in 1946 and a villa, probably dating from the late fourth century, was revealed – including a mosaic that is now one of the great objects of the collection of the Museum of Somerset at Taunton. Alongside the mosaic, the museum shows a Pathé newsreel shot during the excavation. Against a soaring, Elgar-like score, the voiceover intones: 'Even in this atomic age, the richness and grace of the mosaics are of great significance in the recording of Britain's long history . . . When the excavation is completed, experts hope to perpetuate this relic of an age that had no such things as prefabs and housing problems.'

The mosaic is divided into five panels, two running the length of the mosaic at each side, and three occupying the central strip. They tell a story sequentially, like a graphic novel. It begins with one of the long flanking panels, which shows three ships ploughing the sea, the boats with beaky figureheads, and the faces of little men emerging rather comically above the decks. One of them, in the centre boat, wears a Phrygian cap: which shows that these people, like Ganymede, are Trojans. From the first boat, the leading figure hands an object – perhaps a necklace or diadem – to a man who, rather awkwardly, stands on the shore at right angles to the rest of the composition.

The next panel makes the subject of the mosaic perfectly clear. It is a family group of sorts. On the left stands Aeneas, bearded, leaning on a spear. Beside him is a young boy, also with a spear, and also wearing the distinctive Phrygian cap. It is his son, Ascanius. Next is a tall, elegant creature, white-skinned and naked but for her jewels: armlets, a necklace, a diadem, and a body chain, which fits over her neck and under her arms, connected between the breasts – there is one just like it in the British Museum's Roman Britain gallery. This is Venus, goddess of love, who is also Aeneas's mother. And at the right, a female figure, draped in scanty fabric, her hair bound in a topknot: Dido. This, then, is the story of Dido and Aeneas, the doomed love between the queen of Carthage and the prince of Troy, which is told in the early books of Virgil's *Aeneid*.

Venus, flanked by two Cupids (one holding his flaming torch pointing down, the other raising his aloft), also sits in the panel at the centre of the mosaic – for it is she who is orchestrating this story, the spider at the heart of the web. In the *Aeneid*, when the exhausted, storm-tossed Trojans turn up on the north African shore, Venus fears a hostile reception for her beloved Trojans, and so she disguises her son Cupid as Ascanius, and he inflames Dido with what turns out to be a disastrous love for Aeneas.

The next scene shows three galloping horses. Mounted are Ascanius, Aeneas and Dido. They are out hunting, all three of them at full pelt, their cloaks streaming behind them. Ascanius gallops out in front, his mount's hooves pounding. Aeneas comes next, his head turned back towards Dido, who follows on a white horse. The final panel shows the culmination of Venus's plans. As the hunt continues, a storm breaks. Dido and Aeneas take shelter together in a cave, and there they make love. The mosaic shows them embracing, kissing: he has lifted her bodily from the ground.

'*Ille dies primus leti primusque malorum/ causa fuit*' – 'that was the first day of her death, the first day of her sorrows, the cause of everything', says the poem. Dido is completely engulfed by her love for Aeneas. And the Trojan is in love, too, up to a point: until Jupiter sends Mercury, the messenger of the gods, to remind him of his destiny, which is not here building Dido's new city (for she too is an exile, a traveller from Phoenicia in the east who must establish a new home for her people). Aeneas must leave her and go on, back to sea, and to Italy, where destiny decrees he will establish the dynasty that will one day found Rome.

What happens next is not on the mosaic. Aeneas orders his men to prepare the ships in secret: he will find a moment to tell the queen

of his departure. But Dido senses what is afoot. She rages through the city, like a furious maenad, and then confronts him. 'Did you think you would keep this a secret? Did you think you'd steal away from my shores?' she asks. Aeneas replies that their love was no marriage; that Italy must be his darling desire now. Nothing moves him. He is resolved; the Trojans leave. Dido builds herself a funeral pyre, takes Aeneas's sword, which he has left behind him, and stabs herself: '*ensemque cruore spumantem sparsasque manus*' – 'the sword is spattered with blood, her hands are soaked in it'. It is a cruelly symbolic suicide, penetrated by her lover's weapon. The pyre burns; the Trojans, as they put out to deep water, see it flaming in the distance. Later, Dido and Aeneas meet again when he makes the perilous journey to the Underworld, the realm of the dead. She turns her back on him. It is then that Aeneas tries, at last, to express his real love for her: too late.

There is nothing quite like this mosaic elsewhere in Britain. It is, you could argue, the first object in Britain that tells a complete story:

a set of images that reveals, and is to be read alongside, a literary text. It has been argued that the owner of the villa at Low Ham might have commissioned the mosaic based on images he himself knew: there is a manuscript of the *Aeneid* in the Vatican, for example, whose illuminations are similar to the scenes in the Low Ham mosaic. That can be no more than speculation: but what seems clear to me is that someone in what we now call Somerset loved a poem so much that they wished it to be picked out in fragments of stone: a set-piece of learned, literary, utterly Roman taste on the fringe of the empire. And just a few decades later, everything that the mosaic and the poem stood for fell apart.

Norfolk, again, and Sussex

But we are moving in a dim land of doubts and shadows. He who wanders here, wanders at his peril, for certainties are few, and that which at one moment seems a fact, is only too likely, as the quest advances, to prove a phantom. It is, too, a borderland . . .

Francis Haverfield, 1905

It was a gloomy June day in Great Yarmouth, beneath the infinite Norfolk sky that sank into the flat and treeless fens. Matthew and I had come to the edge of England, and to the end of a month-long journey in search of the remains of Roman Britain. We drove through the outskirts of the town, past endless rows of static caravans poised for occupation by those with a taste for the bleak. At length we arrived

at Burgh Castle, the name of both a village and the Roman ruin that
lies at its edge. When we saw it, we were quieted by its sheer force.
Even from a distance the fort walls – standing as tall as they were
built, and outridden by fat, tubular towers – were daunting.

New clouds had flooded the sky; it was cooling, and threatening
to rain. As we approached the fort on foot, through fields of calf-
length grass, we began to get a sense of the landscape beyond. With
the sweep of the river Waveney in the foreground, and a windmill in
the distance, it resembled a scene, more sky and water than land, by
one of the more austere seventeenth-century Dutch landscape painters:
Jacob van Ruisdael, perhaps. When Burgh Castle was built, probably
in the third quarter of the third century, there was none of this land
to be seen: it guarded the southern tip of a great estuary, where Great
Yarmouth stands now. The northern edge was presided over by another
fort, at Caister-on-Sea.

We walked to the south wall of the fort, which rose an imposing
four and a half metres tall. Five neat courses of terracotta tiles, in the
usual Roman style, ran at regular intervals through the flint-and-mortar
walls. Some of the smartly squared-off flints used to face the wall
were still in place, though many had been plundered over the years,
revealing its rubbly innards. I ran my hand over the unforgiving sharp
grittiness of it – the familiar texture of East Anglian buildings of
almost any age. A large chunk of wall, in all its massy two-metre
width, leaned out at a disconcerting angle from the main run, like a
slice of cake ready to be levered on to a plate. We were the only
people here, except for a dog-walker and two joggers who ploughed
determinedly round and round the walls.

Burgh Castle is one of the Roman forts, dating from the third
century, that dot the east coast of England from the Wash to the
Solent. The *Notitia Dignitatum*, a Roman document outlining all the
military commands held in the empire in the late fourth century, notes
the existence of a post called the Count of the Saxon Shore. It is
because of the existence of this post that the great coastal remains
of the east have come to be known as the 'Saxon shore forts'. In fact,
the forts – including those at Brancaster, Reculver, Lympne, Dover
and Pevensey – cannot be ascribed confidently to a single, coherent
building plan. They seem to have been built at different dates and
fallen out of use at different times. But they point clearly to a threat

from the sea: pirates from the east; Saxon raiders. Burgh Castle is not a romantic or picturesque remain: it is the remnant of a vast and glowering military installation.

It was here, in 1962, that some of the latest objects that can be associated with Roman Britain were discovered: a set of exquisite glass vessels – drinking cups, beakers, jugs and bowls – in milkily aqueous shades of green. They had been set inside a bronze dish and buried. Some of them had survived intact; others were restored from fragments. They can now be seen in the Roman Britain gallery of the British Museum. On stylistic grounds, they have been dated to the early fifth century, the very end of the age of Roman Britain; they are the newest things on display in the gallery. But they are, otherwise, deeply mysterious objects. Were the glass vessels set here for safe keeping against a better time? If so, by whom? And why were they placed here, in Norfolk, in a pit beneath a rampart in a century-old fort?

No one can give secure answers to such questions. There are many theories, speculations and fantasies about the end of Roman Britain, but few certainties, and no consensus. It is not clear precisely why Roman rule ceased in about AD 408 and was never resumed. Or to what extent, and in what parts of Britain, and for how long, vestiges of Roman-ness persisted: some have argued that in the west of Britain, a Roman way of life continued even into the seventh century, while others have claimed that most Roman towns were already derelict by AD 408. Nor is it clear precisely when, and in what numbers, the Saxons, Angles and Jutes came to Britain, and whether as peaceful settlers or violent aggressors. Nor is it known to what extent myths of British resistance to the Saxons – such as the legend of King Arthur – are tinged with truth. The written evidence, bar a handful of problematic texts, quickly dries up. Britain fades out of the historical record, slipping into a literary darkness almost as complete as that which obtained before the Romans began to write about it – a darkness only to be lifted with the composition, in AD 731, of Bede's *Ecclesiastical History of the English People*.

The archaeology draws a similar blank. Inscriptions virtually ceased to be produced; the few new coins that circulated were poor, reduced specimens, some manufactured from the clippings of old ones. Pottery factories were stilled. The sturdy stone buildings of Roman Britain were no longer built. Londinium itself was virtually deserted, the walled city not to be fully reoccupied until the reign of Alfred the Great nearly half a millennium later. This silence and absence is itself eloquent: it points towards the collapse of civic life, of the money economy, of the secure and busy world of Roman *things*. It is hard not to stare into the deep white blankness of Roman Britain's end and to see a calamity that was swift and complete; a limb destroyed as it was sundered from the blood supply of the imperial body.

The reign of Constantine the Great, from his acclamation in York in AD 306 to his death in 337, saw a generation of stability in Britain, and perhaps its high-water mark of prosperity. After his death, a familiar pattern of warring sons vying for power asserted itself. By 343, one of them was dead and the empire was divided between the remaining two: Constans in the west and Constantius II in the east. But Constans – who made an unusual winter Channel crossing to Britain that year, perhaps to deal with some stirring trouble – was ousted, and the pagan Magnentius raised in his stead. By 353, Magnentius's forces had in turn been defeated by Constantius II in Illyricum in the Balkans, and in Gaul. Now, as sole emperor, Constantius II sent his representative, Paul 'the Chain' Catena, to Britain to quash Magnentius's remaining sympathisers – apparently so brutally that Martinus, the vicar of Britain (the civil administrator who oversaw the four provinces of the island), attempted to attack him with a sword, before committing suicide. In 355, Constantius appointed his obscure young cousin, the brilliant pagan Julian, to rule the western empire. He appears to have used the rich agricultural land of Britain, perhaps the chief cause of its prosperity, to supply the Roman troops who were slugging it out against the Germanic insurgents on the Rhine. In 367 came the so-called Barbarian Conspiracy, an unusual instance of various interest groups co-operating for an all-out assault on Roman territory. Picts from Caledonia and Scots and Attacotti from Hibernia raged in Britain, while Saxons and Franks assaulted Gaul. The leader of the Roman troops in Britain, Fullofaudes, was put out of action; the *comes maritimi tractus* – the 'count of the maritime region' – was killed. The revolt seems to have been completely put down by Theodosius, the father of the emperor Theodosius the Great, who is also said to have restored the otherwise undocumented province of Valentia, perhaps in northern England.

But any respite from instability was temporary. On two subsequent occasions over the next few decades, troops in Britain elevated pretenders to the purple – Magnus Maximus and Constantine III, the latter apparently chosen by the soldiers at least partly on the basis of his name, perfumed as it was with the glory of the old emperor (to whom he was not related). According to the sixth-century cleric Gildas – whose sermonising work *On the Destruction of Britain* is the only near-contemporary source describing the end of Roman rule – Maximus depleted the island of troops, who were never to return.

The empire in the north-west was now embroiled in wars with foreign insurgents, riven by civil war, and locked, by reason of military and diplomatic necessity, into endlessly complex and often mutually duplicitous relationships with 'barbarian' allies such as the Goth Alaric, who, when relations turned sour, was to sack Rome itself in 410. At length, while Constantine III was campaigning in Spain in around 408, a serious barbarian invasion racked Britain. According to the Byzantine historian Zosimus, writing at the turn of the sixth century, 'the barbarians beyond the Rhine made such unbounded incursions over every province, as to reduce not only the Britons, but some of the Celtic nations also to the necessity of revolting from the empire, and living no longer under the Roman laws but as they themselves pleased. The Britons therefore took up arms, and incurred many dangerous enterprises for their own protection, until they had freed their cities from the barbarians who besieged them. In a similar manner, the whole of Armorica, with other provinces of Gaul, delivered themselves by the same means; expelling the Roman magistrates or officers, and erecting a government, such as they pleased, of their own.'

It is not at all clear that the Britons regarded this move as a final break from Rome. There are hints that on subsequent occasions they appealed to the empire for help: in his narrative, Zosimus noted that the emperor Honorius 'sent letters to the cities of Britain urging them to take measures to defend themselves'. This, known as the 'rescript of Honorius', usually dated to 408, has traditionally been regarded as the moment at which Britain was permanently cast adrift from the empire. In fact, as with so much about the last days of Roman Britain, its status is unstable: the manuscript is now thought by most scholars to be corrupt, referring to Brittium, in modern Calabria, rather than Britannia.

It is impossible to know what the aftermath of all this felt like from the inside, except by way of the merest chinks illuminating the darkness. The *Confession* of St Patrick, believed to date from the mid fifth century, begins with Patricius, the son of a deacon (elsewhere he describes his father as a *decurion*, a Roman magistrate), being taken captive from his small villa near the settlement of Bannavem Taberniae, the location of which is unknown. '*Hyberione in captivitate adductus sum, cum tot milia hominum, secundum merita nostra, quia a Deo recessimus*' – 'I was abducted in captivity to Ireland, like so many thousands of men, as we deserved, because we had turned away from God,' he wrote. He served as a slave, he added, for six years.

Gildas – whose tone is fire and brimstone rather than one of scholarly detachment – painted a grim picture. As the Romans left, he wrote, the Scots and the Picts arrived in their coracles like '*fusci vermiculorum cunei*', 'dark swarms of worms'. The people were torn apart '*sicut agni a lanionibus*', 'like lambs by butchers'. Later, after a period in which the Britons gave way to decadence and luxury, the Saxons came, he wrote, in three warships. They were paid off, but in time their demands for land and provisions became heavier and heavier.

In the later, even more insecure source traditionally ascribed to the monk Nennius, perhaps writing in the ninth century, the story is that the British king Vortigern granted the island of Thanet to the Saxon mercenaries Hengist and Horsa, who eventually grabbed more and more territory in the south-east. At any rate, according to Gildas, violence erupted. Fire blazed from sea to sea; settlements were destroyed, bishops, priests and people lay dead in the streets. Some fled to the mountains, some gave themselves up to slavery. The Britons finally rallied under Ambrosius Aurelianus – 'a modest man, who alone of the Romans had by chance survived the shock of such a storm, a storm in which his parents had evidently perished', according to Gildas. They took on the Saxons at Mount Badon – the whereabouts of which is unknown – and won a great victory.

In Nennius, it is Arthur who leads the troops at Badon; his text is the wellspring for the great medieval elaborations of the Arthurian legends. R. G. Collingwood, for one, was a believer: not in Geoffrey of Monmouth's tales of magic and knights and chivalry, to be sure, but in Arturius as a likely historical reality, a figure who, against the backdrop of 'a country sinking into barbarism', was likely to have been the last remnant of 'Roman ideas'. However that may be, Collingwood was surely right when he wrote that it was in the figure of Arthur in which 'the British people has embalmed its memory of Roman Britain'. It was the historiographical void left by the end of Roman rule that created the conditions for the weaving of Britain's most powerful and wonderful myths: the knights of the Round Table, Camelot, Lancelot and Guinevere. As if this terrifying lacuna, this great Dark Age of nothingness, needed to be filled with stories in which good fought against evil, in which magic vibrated through the forests of the island, in which heroes valiantly strove. Perhaps the Arthurian legends also reflect the wonderment of the English at the grand, decaying Roman towns and buildings, which must have been built by supernatural means. The melancholic Anglo-Saxon poem 'The Ruin' begins:

> Snapped rooftrees, towers fallen,
> the work of the Giants, the stonesmiths,
> mouldereth.

One early spring day I visited the British Museum to look at an object that, like the Burgh Castle glass, stands at the very end of the Romano-British period. Curator Richard Hobbs had offered to show me the Great Dish of the Mildenhall Treasure, an elaborately decorated late Roman platter made from eight kilograms of silver. Unusually, the Great Dish had been removed from its display case in the Roman Britain gallery so that Hobbs could study it in detail. It is the most impressive item in a spectacular trove of thirty-four silver objects – platters, dishes, ladles, spoons – that was found buried on the outskirts of West Row, a fenland village near the town of Mildenhall in Suffolk.

The Mildenhall Treasure is one of a number of buried hoards that date from the last years of Roman Britain. Among them is the Hoxne Treasure, also found in Suffolk: it was discovered in 1992 by a man searching for his lost hammer using a metal detector. He found the hammer, too: it is now part of the British Museum's collection, along with the cache of coins, jewellery and precious tableware, including a silver pepperpot in the shape of a grand Roman lady, her eyes and lips picked out in gold. The richness and beauty of these hoards is startling. 'It turns out that the place to go for fourth-century precious metal is Britain,' said Hobbs. Such finds vastly outnumber those from neighbouring Gaul: attesting, it seems, to the wealth of the province in the dying decades of Roman rule – and perhaps also to unusual levels of trouble. For no one knows for sure why such hoards were buried. They may have been the hastily concealed wealth of families on the run from Saxon raiders, or the breakdown in civil society. They may have been ritually buried, offerings to the gods (though some of the hoards seem to have been buried by Christians).

We were in a book-lined study room in the British Museum, behind one of those mysterious locked doors in the galleries through which curators are occasionally glimpsed emerging or disappearing as they go about their business. Hobbs took the Great Dish out of a drawer, unwrapping it from layers of tissue paper, and placed it on a table. It caught the light from the window behind us, and seemed to illuminate the whole room. It appeared larger, a more hefty physical presence, than when I had seen it in its glass case. Hobbs explained how its intricate decoration had been made by a craftsman pushing the metal into shape with chasing tools. Wearing cotton gloves, we traced the scenes with our fingers.

At the centre was the face of a sea god, with dolphins sprouting from his hair and beard. Around him circled a playful, erotic scene of sea creatures cavorting with naked nymphs, all edged with a row of scallop shells. Here were fishtailed tritons; a hippocamp, a creature that was half fish, half stag; a merman with a snapping lobster claw protruding from his groin instead of a penis. The decoration was exquisitely detailed: the scales on the fishtails were individually rendered, even the hair on the aureoles of the men's nipples carefully suggested. The largest scene ran around the edge of the dish. Here Bacchus, with his emblematic panther, leaned on his thyrsus, while deep-browed Silenus, the satyr, held out his bowl to the god. Hercules – his lionskin and club lying next to his feet – staggered drunkenly. A naked youth played the double pipes while a maenad threw her head back as she danced, the fine fabric of her dress swirling behind her and catching against the flesh of her thigh. All was movement and clamour and the wild, abandoned worship of the god.

The discovery of the Mildenhall Treasure is one of the most notorious sagas in twentieth-century British archaeological history, trailing unsolved puzzles and igniting conspiracy theories. Hobbs has

researched its history, sifting through documents and correspondence
and interviewing the protagonists' surviving relatives. It was Dr Hugh
Fawcett, an amateur antiquary from Buckinghamshire, who first
alerted the British Museum to the existence of a number of ancient
objects that he had seen at Easter 1946 in the home of a fellow enthusiast, Sydney Ford, who ran a small but successful contract ploughing
firm in Suffolk. Fawcett, aware of the law of treasure trove, which
obliged finders to declare precious-metal finds to the authorities, had
urged Ford to report his discovery. This, with enormous reluctance,
Ford eventually did – not before claiming that 'I don't feel I have
committed a crime by picking up something of value off my land.'
This apparently simple statement was not the least of a number of
obfuscations perpetuated by Ford. In actual fact, he had not himself
discovered the hoard: that had been done by one Gordon Butcher,
who had struck the silver with his plough one January afternoon in
1942 and had immediately summoned Ford. Nor was it 'my land': the
field in question, at least according to the location that Ford finally
pinpointed, belonged to one Sophia Aves, whose tenant was one Fred
Rolfe, who contracted Ford to do the ploughing, who had employed,
on this occasion, Butcher to drive the tractor.

In July, an inquest was held at Mildenhall police station. A photograph from the *Bury Free Press & Post* shows two local coppers unloading the silverware from the boot of their police van with considerably less ceremony than was apparent in Hobbs's cotton-gloved handling of the Great Dish. Giving his evidence, Ford told how he and Butcher had dug up the objects and put them in a sack before he, Ford, had taken them home. He said he thought they were pewter. (Had they been, treasure trove legislation would not have applied.) Butcher's involvement in this process was unelaborated. The objects were 'all black and very dirty with a thick crust', Ford told the coroner. Over the years after the discovery, he gradually cleaned them up – the platters, the dishes, the spoons with their chi-rho engravings. It took him nearly two years to complete his work on the Great Dish, and British Museum scientists think that he may have used a blowtorch to help clean off the encrusted grime. The fact that precise records were not taken of how the objects lay in the ground, as well as Ford's crudely amateur cleaning, means that countless details about the hoard that could have been gathered from a slow, careful excavation have been lost for ever. In the end, Butcher and Gordon were each awarded £1,000 compensation for the hoard – a sum substantially less than the silver's market value, to reflect its illicit four-year concealment.

After the inquest – at which the hoard was duly declared treasure trove and thus, under normal practice at the time, the property of the British Museum – a report of the discovery appeared in the *Times*. The young writer Roald Dahl saw the article and, as he recalled thirty years later, 'leapt up from my chair without finishing my breakfast and shouted goodbye to my mother and rushed out to my car'. He drove his nine-year-old Wolseley the 120 miles to Mildenhall along 'small twisty roads and country lanes'. There he found Butcher's cottage, and knocked on the door. Butcher told him he was fed up of reporters; but Dahl explained that he was a short-story writer. 'I went on to say that if he would tell me exactly how he found the treasure, I would write a truthful story about it,' recalled Dahl. Butcher agreed to be interviewed, but later that day, when Dahl went to see Ford, the door was closed in his face. 'But by then I had my story and I set out for home . . . I wrote the story as truthfully as I possibly could.'

Dahl published his story in a magazine, and thirty years later included it in his collection *The Wonderful Story of Henry Sugar*. As may be expected from the nature of his encounters, the narrative strongly favoured Butcher as the hero of the piece – a man whose simple honesty had caused him unthinkingly to hand over the treasure to the crafty Ford, who by contrast had a 'clever foxy look about his face' and a 'mouth that never smiled'. None the less, Hobbs believes there is no particular reason to doubt the details Dahl gives about the discovery itself: the plough set to make especially deep furrows for the planting of sugar beet rather than wheat; the share hitting something in the ground that turned out to be a piece of metal; Butcher's summoning Ford and then the two men working, as twilight fell, to uncover all thirty-four pieces while a blizzard whirled around them and six inches of snow fell. But Dahl gave particular texture to the two men's final encounter that night, with Ford grasping the sack of booty like a child 'closing his fingers over the biggest chocolate éclair on the plate', and saying, 'Well, Gordon . . . I don't suppose you'll be wanting any of this old stuff.' At this distance, it is impossible to tell how much Dahl embroidered this event to suit his own narrative needs. There is clearly a paradox in his insistence that he was 'not a reporter' but a writer of fiction who would tell the tale 'as truthfully as possible'. He uses this phrase twice, in his memoir about writing the story, perhaps protesting too much.

Dahl's implication was that Ford was a villain. And yet it seems unlikely that this was, in any straightforward sense, true. Ford treasured the Roman silverware – aside from the years he spent cleaning it, there are photographs in existence that show the Great Dish and some of the smaller vessels in pride of place on his dresser. According to his grandson, the Great Dish was used as a fruit bowl at Christmas, piled high with apples, oranges, pears and nuts; and Ford used one of the spoons every day for his breakfast and dinner. He clearly loved the objects: it is just that he wanted very badly to keep them for himself. On the other hand, his concealment of the hoard, his failure to declare it until virtually forced to do so, and his inconsistent, dishonest accounts of its discovery have greatly added to the mystery that surrounds the objects. Some people have doubted, for example, whether he handed over every single piece of the hoard – there was some later talk of coins, which never materialised. As for the precise spot where the treasure was found, it has never been satisfactorily established. When the respected local archaeologists Gordon Fowler and Thomas Lethbridge attempted to excavate according to Ford's sketched map and instructions, they found nothing, except for three pieces of late Georgian base metal – the handle of a tureen, the lid of a water jug and part of a teapot – all of which had the air of having been planted there with intention to deceive, or mock. They never found any trace of the hole that Ford and Butcher said they had dug.

Had there been foul play? Conspiracy theories abounded. One – to which Lethbridge and Fowler became strongly attached – concerned another local mystery. In the 1920s, a Suffolk solicitor had received a letter from Canada claiming that at some time in the 1860s a hoard of treasure had been buried in a field near Mildenhall by a shadowy figure called 'Black Jack' Seaber. The solicitor instigated a search, but found nothing. Fowler and Lethbridge eventually came to the conclusion that Ford had himself secretly worked out the burial place, and waited several decades before digging it up for himself: the Mildenhall Treasure and 'Black Jack' Seaber's hoard were one and the same. Others speculated that the hoard was in fact war loot, flown from Africa or Italy to the air-force base at Mildenhall, and then buried in Rolfe's field. This was, it seems, a not infrequently expressed suspicion in archaeological circles immediately after the war, partly because the objects seemed to bear no traces of damage from a plough (in fact there is a dent in the footring of the Great Dish, and other damage to the objects, that very likely is the result of having been so struck). This theory was also fuelled by a notion that late Roman Britain was too backward and poor to have contained anything so spectacular as this elaborate silverware. Hobbs rejects these conspiracy theories; but the mysteries that cling to the Mildenhall Treasure – as to so much about the dying days of Roman Britain – may never be quite resolved.

There is a painting by John Everett Millais called *The Romans Leaving Britain*, which was exhibited at the Royal Academy in 1865. In it, a fierce, pale-faced, bare-footed young woman sits in a landscape that is recognisably the chalk cliffs of the Sussex or Kent coast. She is in profile; she stares fixedly into the middle distance, and her hair is a cloud of auburn. Kneeling at her feet, his face in her lap, and his arms clasped around her waist, is a dark-skinned man dressed in Roman armour. In the distance, other soldiers can be seen heading down to the beach; boats embark from the shore. Millais's painting is a heartbreak story – lovers wrenched apart. It is also a narrative of two people who are utterly unalike: the Celtic girl, with that ivory skin and rosy blush, kissing goodbye to her foreign lover, the soldier with his southern colouring. The myth that the 'Romans' were, after 400 years, a distinct layer of people, probably Italians, who left en masse in AD 408, has been remarkably persistent. In reality, in the fifth century all free men of Britain were citizens of Rome; and though it is conceivable that some officials may have left the province, any idea of some mass exodus should be put aside. In addition, the numbers of actual Italians in British civil or military administration at this point in history will have been tiny. As we have seen, 'Romans' were drawn from all parts of the empire, anywhere from Gaul and Germany to Greece and Gaza.

But then the end of Roman Britain is a shadowy, half-understood borderland, the explorers of which are apt to see phantoms and conjure ghosts. If classics-mad authors of the eighteenth century, such as William Stukeley and Sir John Clerk, saw an unbroken line of inheritance between the 'civility' of the Romans in Britain and the civic virtues of their own day, then others have regarded the collapse of Roman rule – and the subsequent silence of the sources – as a *tabula rasa*, preparing the ground for the real start of British history, or more precisely, English history. The 'departure' of the Romans, and the loosening of the chains that bound slavish Britannia to the empire, has, in some minds, created the blank page on to which the doughtily Germanic Anglo-Saxons might now burst unencumbered – ready to take up their position as the originators of the English nation, the creators of its earliest institutions, the harbingers of its monarchy, the ancestors of a firmly northern race, and the founders, via Augustine's mission in 597, of its Church.

In 1841, in his inaugural lecture as professor of modern history at the University of Oxford, Thomas Arnold, the headmaster of Rugby School, argued that 'our history clearly begins with the coming over of the Saxons; the Britons and Romans had lived in our country, but they are not our fathers; we are connected with them as men indeed, but, nationally speaking, the history of Caesar's invasion has no more to do with us, than the natural history of the animals which then inhabited our forests.' He added: 'We, this great English nation, whose race and language are now overrunning the earth from one end of it to the other, – we were born when the white horse of the Saxons had established his dominion from the Tweed to the Tamar. So far we can trace our blood, our language, the name and actual divisions of our country, the beginnings of some of our institutions.' Modern history, he argued, was a biography of the living, and the Saxons, through a direct blood inheritance, were indeed living still. 'Beyond, it is but the biography of the dead,' he said. According to this formulation, Roman Britain has nothing to say about our island story. It is a specifically Anglo-Saxon, English polity that has mattered: it has subsumed the identities of the other nations of Britain, and forged their joint destiny: the creation of empire. In the wake of the break-up of that empire, it is no wonder that, lacking this sense of common purpose, Great Britain seems to be fracturing into its constituent nations. But no one talks about where the idea of Britain was first recorded – an island sighted across a grumbling grey ocean by traders and invaders long before the Scots and the English sailed to it across the western and eastern seas.

Seven years before Arnold delivered his lecture, the medieval Palace of Westminster, which had been remodelled in the neoclassical style by Sir John Soane, burned down. The young Gothic architect and designer Augustus Pugin was among the crowd that watched, a little in dread and mostly in wonder. (Turner was among the spectators too, later producing a vivid sequence of watercolours depicting the disaster.) For Pugin, there was 'nothing much to regret & a great deal to rejoice in' at the destruction. 'A vast quantity of Soanes mixtures & Wyatts heresies have been effectually consigned to oblivion, oh it was a glorious sight . . .. the old walls stood triumphantly amidst this scene of ruin while brick walls & framed sashes slate roofs etc fell faster than a pack of cards.' In the years of reconstruction, a Fine Arts Commission was set up by Prince Albert to encourage the kind of national history painting that might be commissioned for the new building – which, under Charles Barry and Pugin, was to be rebuilt in the Gothic rather than neoclassical style, emphasising the notion that the origins of English civil institutions were in the nation's medieval and Anglo-Saxon past and effacing any notion of a classical inheritance. A series of competitions was held: for the first, in 1843, nineteen designs relating to Roman Britain were entered, including George Frederick Watts's painting of Caratacus led in chains through Rome.

Eleven scenes of St Augustine and Ethelbert were received; and thirteen depicting incidents in the reigns of the first three Edwards. The prizewinners included Watts, as well as Edward Armitage for his *Caesar's First Invasion of Britain* and H. C. Selous for his *Boadicea Haranguing the Iceni*.

In the end, however, despite the early enthusiasm among artists for Romano-British subjects, not a single fresco depicting Britain's Roman period was executed. A scene of Boudica and her troops was commissioned from Daniel Maclise for the Royal Gallery, a great chamber that was to be lined with battle scenes. But Maclise's contract was cancelled after the completion of the first two works, on the battles of Trafalgar and Waterloo. Another series of scenes that touched on Romano-British history – though almost determinedly *not* from a Roman point of view – also remained unexecuted. This sequence, intended for the Central Corridor of the palace, was meant to draw attention to a contrast between ancient Britain, 'sunk in ignorance, heathen superstition and slavery', and enlightened, Christian Britain, 'instructing the savage, abolishing barbarous rites, and liberating the slave'. It was to begin with the 'Phoenicians in Cornwall' and continue, via 'A Druidical Sacrifice' and 'Anglo-Saxon Captives Exposed for Sale in the Market-place of Rome', to 'Cook in Otaheite', 'English Authorities Stopping the Sacrifice of a Sutee' and 'The Emancipation of Negro Slaves'.

One could put it down to chance that no scenes from Caesar or Tacitus decorate the Houses of Parliament. If Maclise had chosen to paint his martial series in chronological order, then perhaps the monarch would process past a scene of Iceni valour, rather than of Nelson's death, as she opened Parliament. As it is, there is neither brave Briton nor glorious Roman. Instead, Saxon kings are converted to Christianity, Shakespearean heroes play out their stories and Good Queen Bess reigns again. Boudica must drive her chariot towards the Houses of Parliament from Westminster Bridge; she will never storm it. In a building whose fabric was conceived as an expression of national virtues and history, Britain's four centuries in the orbit of Rome were felt to have nothing to say.

Perhaps the problem is, and has been since antiquity, that Roman Britain is too jagged and unsettling and ambiguous to be pulled into line. It will never settle into telling us one thing: it will just as soon tell us the opposite. Like Edward Nicholson's lead tablet, plucked from the goddess's sacred spring at Aquae Sulis, Roman Britain can be read well enough if you stare at the traces. Turn it around, though, and it will offer another story.

One cloudy early summer day I went back to Sussex, this time to Pevensey Castle, one of the Saxon shore forts, built in the late third century. Like Burgh Castle, its vast expanse is circled by thick flint walls still standing to their original Roman height. Not far from here, Puck of Pook's Hill appeared to the children of Kipling's story, and brought them tales of a land formed by Romans, Saxons, Danes and Normans: a land drenched in old magic, whose 'windy levels' and 'stilly woods' held the scars of ancient battle, and were marked by the tread of gods.

Inside the Roman walls are the ruins of a medieval keep, gap-toothed and jagged and louring. William the Conqueror's army landed here in 1066. Later, his half-brother Robert held it along with the Rape of Pevensey, a wedge of its hinterland. In the 1190s, Richard I paid for building work. Later, a stone-built bailey was constructed, and it held out for over a year when besieged by Simon de Montfort's forces in 1264. In the fourteenth century it belonged to John of Gaunt; in the fifteenth, Henry V imprisoned his stepmother, Joan of Navarre, here. Under Elizabeth I, a gun emplacement was erected to ward off Spanish invasion. During the Second World War, the castle was refortified. A blockhouse for anti-tank weapons was built in the Roman west gate. Pillboxes were slotted in among the ruins. They were carefully constructed from the same flint as the rest of the castle, and so are inconspicuous. Look hard enough, though, and you will see the slits of machine-gun posts, moments of modernist rectilinearity among the collapsed angles of ancient masonry.

I think of Roman Britain and its curious bequest to us: how it has become a place where we may play out our uncertainties and anxieties about the perils of empire; a place where we might, if we choose, consider a meaning for Britain that complicates, and long pre-dates, the national boundaries and identities that are now so strongly reasserting themselves. I think of Roman Britain above all as the place where these islands were begotten in writing. In a landscape that vibrates with stories, where every crag and moor, city and suburb, wasteland and industrial tract has been written into being, the Romans were the first to mould the land in prose. If it is to medieval literature that we owe the idea of Britain as a busy and productive and domesticated land, a 'fair field full of folk', then it was the Romans who first made it wild, a land of sudden mists and treacherous marshes, a territory of mountains and impassable rivers. A land as ferocious as its people.

As I wandered about the ruins of Pevensey, the village was preparing for a celebration, putting up a stage in the castle precincts and warming up a barbecue. A trunk road throbbed, out of sight. I walked across the levels, where a solitary cuckoo marked time, to the Martello towers by the grey and corrugated sea.

Notes

(*RIB* = *The Roman Inscriptions of Britain*. See Bibliography, p.252.)

Chapter One: Kent and Essex

• **Page 5** epigraphs: Solinus, 22.1; Shakespeare, *Richard II*, II, i; Brenton. This is the first line of *The Romans in Britain*, which was first produced in 1980. • **Page 6** 'Terrified by the situation': Caesar, 4.24. • **Page 6** 'many ages since absorpt by the ocean': Stukeley, 1776, p.127. • **Page 7** 'sluggish and heavy': Tacitus, *Agricola*, 10. • **Page 7** Britons had close links with their neighbours across the Channel: Caesar, 4.20. • **Page 7** '*ultimosque Britannos*': Catullus, 11, 11–12. • **Page 8** '*toto divisos orbe*': Virgil, *Eclogues*, 1.66. • **Page 8** the Cassiterides: Herodotus, *Histories*, 3.115. • **Page 9** Diodorus Siculus on Britain: the *Library*, 5.21 ff. • **Page 11** Roman road turns out to be Iron Age: Pitts. • **Page 12** Cassius Dio: only books 36 to 60 (inclusive) remain. The rest exists as fragments, or otherwise 'epitomes', or abridgements made in the medieval period. For Roman Britain, the most important figure here is Xiphilinus, a Byzantine monk, who in the 1070s made an epitome of books 46 to 80, and who is the main authority for books 61 to 80 (including the events after the invasion of Britain by Claudius). • **Page 12** '*imperium sine fine*': Virgil, *Aeneid*, 1.279. • **Page 14** Richborough in the First and Second World Wars: see Butler; Grenville. • **Page 14** '*exo tes oikoumenes*': Cassius Dio, 60.19 • **Page 19** 'By laying all the circumstances together': Morant, p.12. • **Page 21** Colchester's chariot track: on the archaeology, see especially pp.1344 ff. in the report by Pooley et al.

Chapter Two: Norfolk

• **Page 25** epigraph: *The Tragedie of Bonduca*, 1.1. • **Pages 25–26** Tacitus on Caratacus: *Annals*, 12.33–8. • **Pages 27–28** Tacitus's account of Boudica: ibid., 14.29-37. • **Pages 32–33** Horace's Ode 1.37, 'Nunc est bibendum', on the defeat of Cleopatra. • **Page 33** Cassius Dio's account of Boudica, *History of Rome*, 62.1–6. • **Pages 33–34** Holinshed, 4.12 • **Page 36** Elgar and *Caractacus*: I am grateful to the participants in the University of Bristol's interdisciplinary Caractacus Day, held on 18 March 2012, for their penetrating thoughts on Elgar's *Caractacus*; in particular to speakers Tim Berringer, Richard Hingley and Ellen O'Gorman. • **Pages 36–37** On the composition of *Caractacus*: Moore, p.230. • **Page 37** 'I made old Caractacus stop as if broken down': letter of 21 August 1898, quoted in ibid., p.238.

Chapter Three: London

I am grateful for help with this chapter to Jenny Hall, formerly of the Museum of London, who generously walked me around the Roman city; and to Roy Stephenson, head of archaeological collections at the Museum of London.

• **Page 43** epigraphs: Camden, 'Midle-sex'. Here, and throughout, page numbers for Camden are not given. Readers are advised to consult the searchable online text at www.philological.bham.ac.uk/cambrit/. Macaulay, p.453 • **Page 44** *'copia negotiatorum et commeatuum maxime celebre'*: Tacitus, *Agricola*, 14.33. • **Pages 44–45** on the heads in the Walbrook Stream: Geoffrey of Monmouth, *A History of the Kings of Britain*, 5.5. • **Page 46** 'great Plain of Ashes and Ruins': Wren, p.267. • **Page 46** 'the most remarkable Roman Urns': ibid., p.266. • **Page 46** 'Having rummaged all the Ground thereabouts': ibid., p.296. • **Pages 47–48** Penelope Lively's description of the bombed-out city comes at the very end of her memoir. • **Page 48** on 'the new ruins': Macaulay, pp.453–4. • **Pages 53–54** Roach Smith's unpublished diaries are held in the British Museum.

Chapter Four: Silchester

I am grateful to the editors of the *Guardian* for allowing me to adapt material from the article 'Re-reading Rosemary Sutcliff's *The Eagle of the Ninth*' (2 April 2011) in the latter part of this chapter.

• **Page 60** epigraph: Propertius, 4.10.25–8. • **Page 62** Boudica on the foodstuffs of the Britons: Cassius Dio, 62.5. • **Page 62** Isle of Wight, as well as twenty hill forts: Suetonius, *Vespasian*, 4. • **Pages 62–63** 'Agricola gave private encouragement': Tacitus, *Agricola*, 21. • **Page 64** Stukeley on Silchester: Stukeley, 1776, p.178. • **Page 64** 'sometimes surprizd the whole College': quoted in Haycock, p.40. • **Page 65** 'a mighty conceited man': Lukis, vol. 73, p.170.

• **Pages 70 and 72** Novels readable by anyone from nine to ninety; 'I think that I am happiest of all in Roman Britain': Sutcliff interviewed by Raymond H. Thompson, 1986, http://www.lib.rochester.edu/camelot/intrvws/sutcliff. htm. • **Pages 70 and 71** 'I don't write for adults, I don't write for children'; 'Fortunately, I have got a very good memory': Rosemary Sutcliff interviewed for the *Independent* by Giselle Green, 18 April 1992.

Chapter Five: Wales and the West

• **Page 75** epigraph: From Hardy's *A Tryst at an Ancient Earthwork*. • **Page 75** 'It lieth low near merry England's heart': Wilfred Owen, 'Uriconium: An Ode'. • **Page 75** 'Hurry, Harold, hurry': quoted in Jon Stallworthy's biography of Wilfred Owen. • **Page 76** Charles Dickens wrote up his visit to Wroxeter in an article called 'Rome and Turnips', for *All the Year Round* magazine. • **Pages 78 and 80** Quotations from Owen's letters: Owen's correspondence can be found in full in Owen and Bell. • **Page 80** Wheeler's memories of Housman are recorded in Wheeler, 1955, p.29. • **Page 80** Wheeler's memorial address by Sir Max Mallowan: quoted in Hawkes, p.9. • **Pages 80–81** Wheeler's taste in women: ibid., p.10. • **Page 81** I am indebted to Dr Lydia Carr for her generosity in allowing me to read her unpublished DPhil thesis on Tessa Verney Wheeler, which was an invaluable resource in the writing of this chapter. It has since been published by Oxford as *Tessa Verney Wheeler: Women and Archaeology Before World War Two*. • **Page 82** J. N. L. Myres's memories of the dig at Y Gaer: quoted by Hawkes, pp.90–1. • **Page 82** Sir Flinders Petrie's letter to Mortimer Wheeler: quoted by Carr, p.76. • **Page 84** *South Wales News* reports the Wheelers departure: quoted in ibid., p.80. • **Page 85** 'Caerleon is of unquestioned antiquity': Gerald of Wales, p.114. • **Page 86** Verney Wheeler's to-do list: ibid., p.93. • **Page 88** Mortimer Wheeler discovers the '*minimi*': Wheeler, 1955, p.86. • **Page 90** the *Daily Mail* on Verney Wheeler at Verulamium: Carr, p.188. • **Page 90** 'a satiety of Roman things': Wheeler, 1955, p.91. • **Page 90** William Wedlake's recollections of Maiden Castle: quoted in Hawkes, p.168. • **Page 90** Wheeler's account of learning of Tessa's death: Wheeler, 1955, pp.50–1. • **Page 91** 'the magic of the great hill': Carr, p.288. • **Page 91** Wheeler's description of the 'massacre' at Maiden Castle: Wheeler, 1943, pp.62–3. • **Page 91** The graves are no longer thought of as a 'war cemetary': see Sharples, pp.124–5: '[Wheeler's] vivid description of the sack and slighting of the hillfort, followed by the hasty burial of the dead is not altogether consistent with the evidence on the ground.'

Chapter Six: Bath

• **Page 93** epigraph: from Carter. • **Page 95** 'There once many a man': Alexander. • **Pages 95–96** On the benefits of the waters: Guidott, p.131; Stukeley, 1776, p.146. • **Page 96** Soft-porn Bath: the reader is referred to Anon, 1700. • **Pages 96–97** Jan Morris – from her essay on Bath in *Among the Cities*. • **Page 97** 'a grand place of Assembly', Wood, 1749, p.232. • **Pages 97–98** Leland in Mearne, 1768, p.62. • **Page 98** Sylvia's suicide: Wood, ibid., p.446. • **Page 98** 'a silly pack of stuff': Lukis, vol. 73, p.337. • **Pages 98–99** Geoffrey of Monmouth and Bladud, *The History of the Kings of Britain*, p.81. • **Page 99** 'skipping from one remote Part of the Island to another': Wood, 1749, p.14. • **Page 99** Bladud/Abaris riding on a sacred arrow: ibid., p.33. Abaris is in Herodotus's *Histories*, 4.36; Herodotus claims he will 'make no mention' of this fantastic story. • **Page 99** Bladud and Zoroaster: Wood, 1749, p.36. • **Pages 99–100** Bladud and the Druids, ibid., p.137. • **Page 100** Strabo on Druids: *Geographia* 4.4, 4–5 • **Page 100** Suetonius on Druids: *Claudius*, 25.5. • **Page 100** Sibbald on flint arrowheads: see Piggott, 1989, p.9. • **Page 100** Stukeley's Druidic temple in his garden: Lukis, vol. 73, p.208. The description comes in a letter to Samuel Gale, of 14 October 1728. Stukeley goes on to remark that the temple is near his treasured Roman altar, where once he buried his wife's miscarried foetus, 'about as big as a filberd' (hazelnut), 'with ceremonys proper to the occasion'. • **Pages 100–101** 'struck dead upon the spot'; Stanton Drew as a model of the planets: Wood, 1749, p.148. • **Page 101** 'furnish'd the various Sorts of Building': Wood, 1741, p.74. • **Page 101** the Romans communicate architecture to the Britons: Anderson, p.27. I am grateful to Jacqueline Riding for the steer to Anderson, and to Mowl and Earnshaw's biography of Wood. • **Page 101** 'If we were to scrutinize': Wood, 1741, p.221. • **Page 102** the idea of a link between Stanton Drew and the Circus was put forward by Mowl and Earnshaw, in their fascinating biography of John Wood the elder. See especially p.179 ff. • **Page 103** 'whether pagan or Christian': see Tomlin, 'The Curse Tablets', in Cunliffe, 1988, p.232. • **Page 103** theft of a cloak: ibid., p.198. • **Pages 103–104** eating, drinking, defecating or urinating: ibid., p.160. • **Page 104** the goddess can debilitate as well as cure: ibid., p.102. • **Pages 104–106** the whole story of Edward Nicholson here is indebted to Tomlin, 1994. I feel sure that his article, a splendid conjunction of razor-sharp scholarship and vivid pen-portrait, is the best (or nearest to) fun that can be had with the otherwise dead-serious journal *Zeitschrift für Papyrologie und Epigraphik.*

Chapter Seven: Hadrian's Wall

• **Page 111** epigraphs: W. Hutton, p.312; Collingwood Bruce, p.40; Long, p.16.
• **Page 114** farmers complain about disruption caused by tourists: H. Davies, p.160. • **Page 118** Warburton's manuscripts 'unluckily burnd': quoted in the *Dictionary of National Biography*, 1885–90, vol. 59. • **Page 118** Warburton, p. iii. • **Page 118** travel 'with me, though by your own fire-side': W. Hutton, p.vii. • **Page 118** 'feeds upon withered husks': ibid., p. vi. • **Pages 119–120** destruction of the wall at St Oswald's: ibid., p.202. • **Page 120** beef at the Twice Brewed: ibid., p.230. • **Page 120** Stanwix, a beauty and fleas: ibid., p.285. • **Page 121** the first 'pilgrimage': Collingwood Bruce. • **Page 122** Revd John Auden (1860–1946): he appears as the 'Rev Prebendary Auden, Church Stretton' in the subscribers' list in Bushe-Fox. He was the author of *The Little Guide to Shropshire*, a copy of which W. H. Auden owned. John Auden first published the book in 1912 and revised it (1918) while he was a serving soldier.
• **Page 122** 'fearfully badly'; 'an uncomfortable pause': see Mitchell, p.522, who notes that 'the haunting quality of the blues melody was such that Peter Pears in later life was still able to sing the first few bars'. • **Page 123** Britten's music . . . was thought lost: see the Britten-Pears Foundation website, http://brittenpears 2.org/?page=news/index.html&id=57. *Guardian* news story: http://www. guardian.co.uk/uk/2006/feb/27/topstories3.arts. The newly rediscovered song was performed, with simple piano accompaniment, for a profile of Auden made for *The South Bank Show*, broadcast on 18 February 2007, directed by John Mapplebeck. My thanks to Matthew Cain and Siobhan Panayiotou for tracking down a DVD. • **Page 124** 'Roman Wall Blues'. Colin Matthews also very kindly arranged for a recording to be made of the Britten song with his new piano accompianment, sung by Mary Carewe, with Huw Watkins. It is available to download on the NMC website: http://www.nmcrec.co.uk/roman-wall-blues
• **Page 127** Had Auden been writing his radio drama today: Bowman (p.79) makes the connection between 'Roman Wall Blues' and the tablets; as does Beard, 2006. • **Pages 127–128** on finding the first Vindolanda tablet: R. Birley, p.32. • **Page 129** the Vindolanda tablets have been digitised – with images, translations and commentary – at http://vindolanda.csad.ox.ac.uk/. Most of the individual tablets I have mentioned are browsable in the 'highlights' section.
• **Page 130** *Appendix Vergiliana/Georgics*: Bowman, Thomas and Tomlin.

Chapter Eight: Scotland

• **Page 137** epigraph: Skene, p.82. • **Page 137** over 200 sites north of Hadrian's Wall: according to Fraser Hunter, principal curator archaeology, Iron Age,

Roman and early history at the National Museum of Scotland. I am indebted to Dr Hunter's paper given at the Roman Society Septimius Severus day at the British Museum, 26 November 2011. • **Page 139** Agricola advances north: Tacitus, *Agricola*, 23ff. • **Page 139** The shift from Graupius to Grampius: Keppie, 'Legacy of Rome', p.8. The edition in question was published by Franciscus Puteolanus in 1476. • **Page 140** *'Perdomita Britannia et statim omissa'*: Tacitus, *Histories*, 1.2. • **Page 140** a stage on which his subject could be the Roman he needed to be: this passage is indebted to the analysis of the *Agricola* at the end of Woolf, 2007. • **Page 141** Wade's bridge: Breeze, Roman Scotland p.108, compares the Roman and Hanoverian experiences of Highland Scotland. • **Pages 141–142** 'Marvel at this military road'. The Latin inscription, replaced in 1932, runs:

> MIRARE
> VIAM HANC MILITAREM
> ULTRA ROMANAE TERMINOS
> M PASUU CCL. HAC ILLAC EXTENSAM
> TESQIS & PALUDIB' INSULTANTEM;
> PER RUPES MONTESQ: PATEFACTUM
> ET INDIGNANTI TAVO
> UT CERNIS INSTRATAM
> OPUS HOC ARDUUM SUA SOLERTIA
> ET DECENNALI MILITUM OPERA
> AN AER X 1733 PERFECIT G WADE
> COPIARUM IN SCOTIA PRAEFECTUS
> ECCE QUANTUM VALEANT
> REGIA GEORGII 2 AUSPICIA!

• **Page 142** William Roy – a factor's son from Lanarkshire: Hewitt, p.14. Her introduction and first chapter provide a vivid account of the production of the *Military Survey of Scotland* in the wake of the 1745 uprising. • **Page 142** William Roy's *Military Survey of Scotland* (1747–55) can be viewed online at http://maps.nls.uk/roy/index.html. • **Page 143** 'Military men . . . in reasoning': Roy, 1793, p.iv. • **Page 146** the hero Gryme: Skene, p.82. • **Pages 146–147** Alexander Gordon on Croy Hill and Bar Hill: Gordon, pp.136–7. • **Pages 148–149** Fordun on Arthur's O'on: Skene, p.46. • **Page 148** *'rotundam casulam'*: I am indebted to Darrell Rohl of the University of Durham, whose unpublished MA dissertation, which he kindly allowed me to read, brings together accounts of Arthur's O'on from the twelfth century onwards (p.53 ff.). • **Page 149** 'dedicated to Romulus the parent': Stukeley, 1720, p.27. • **Page 149** 'some may think we have done the Caledonian Temple too much

Honour': ibid., p.19. • **Page 149** 'a Place for holding the Roman Insignia': Gordon, p.31. • **Page 150** Stenhousemuir football club: an observation made by Lawrence Keppie (personal communication). • **Page 150** 'No other motive induced this Gothic knight': from the minute book of the Society of Antiquaries, 21 July 1743. • **Page 150** 'I like well your project': letter from Gale to Clerk, 20 August 1743; 'barbarous demolition': copy, in Clerk's hand, of a letter to William Stukeley, 16 July 1748. Both in the National Archives of Scotland, GD18/5018 and GD18/5027. • **Page 151** 'occasioned by eating too much cabage broth': Clerk, p.146. • **Page 151** 'my publication of Arthurs Oon': letter from Stukeley to Clerk, 21 March 1724/5, National Archives of Scotland, GD18/5027. • **Page 152** 'full of compliments, as usual with foreigners'; 'I press'd Mr Bertram to get the manuscript': Stukeley, 1757, pp.12-13. • **Page 153** 'He gives us more than a hundred names of cities': ibid., p.15. • **Page 154** 'which I shewed to my late friend Mr Casley': ibid., p.13. • **Page 154** 'scrupulously exact', Hatcher, p.vii. • **Page 154** 'be useful to distinguish this ridge of mountains': Conybeare and Phillips, p.365. • **Page 155** 'more or less good idiomatic English': see Woodward, vol. 220, pp.620 and 445. • **Page 156** 'his silk-dyer father': J. A. Farrer, p. 26, has a biographical sketch of Bertram. • **Page 156** 'The World oftener rewards the Appearances of Merit: see Bertram, 1751, pp.9, 13, 15. • **Page 156** Bertram's contribution to linguistics: Linn, p.190.

Chapter Nine: York

• **Page 161** epigraph: from Camden's *Britannia*, on York. • **Page 161** 'No city or town': Hargrove, p.17. • **Page 162** When archaeologists were brought in to dig': Ottaway, p.18. • **Page 164** Let no one escape sheer destruction: epitome of Cassius Dio, *History of Rome*, 76.15. • **Page 164** Julia Domna: ibid., 76.16. • **Page 164** a gang of centurions: ibid., 77.2. • **Page 165** 'If anyone so much as wrote the name Geta': ibid., 77.12. • **Page 167** Corellia Optata inscription: *RIB* 684. • **Page 167** She was a little over five feet tall: Leach et al., 2010, p.135. • **Page 168** 'In cosmopolitan Eboracum': ibid., p.141. • **Page 170** 'Castle Douglas, our damp little town', Yassin-Kassab. • **Page 170** 'DM REGINA LIBERTA': *RIB* 1065. • **Pages 171–172** 'Britanniae sanctae': *RIB* 643. • **Page 172** Demetrius: *RIB* 662 and 663. • **Page 173** 'placed as so many bulwarks': Gordon, p.138 • **Page 174** 'a great many things may be learned', Horsley, p.iv. • **Page 176** 'Rome's Afghanistan': Mary Beard, writing in the *Sunday Times*, February 2012. • **Pages 177–178** Conrad: Woolf, 2007, pp.18–19, brilliantly discusses Conrad's *Heart of Darkness* in relation to Roman ideas about Britain – a passage on which these paragraphs are dependent.

Chapter Ten: Cumbria and the Lakes

• **Page 179** epigraph: Collingwood, 1939, p.86. • **Page 182** Collingwood and Kant: ibid., pp.3–4. • **Page 183** 'spoke and read French and German': ibid., p.6. • **Pages 183–184** Ransome and the Collingwoods: Ransome, p.80 ff. • **Page 184** Ransome and Collingwood racing boats: ibid., p.130. • **Page 184** Collingwood offers up his savings: ibid., p.147. • **Page 184** Wilfred Owen and the Collingwoods: Hibberd, 1982, pp.286–7. The short description of the visit comes in a fragmentary draft of a letter, recipient unknown, written when Owen was recovering from shell-shock in Scotland. • **Pages 185–186** 'rapprochement' between history and philosophy: Collingwood, 1939, pp.144–5. • **Page 186** 'the transmission by example and precept': ibid., p.142. • **Pages 186–187** 'the history of Romano-British art': Collingwood and Myres, Chapter 15. pp.247–8. • **Page 187** 'Roman antiquities . . . are very indifferent': Walpole, p.246. The letter is quoted in Hingley, 2008. • **Pages 187–191** the Crosby Garrett helmet: *Guardian* articles about its discovery and sale, Kennedy, 2010a, b, c. • **Pages 189–190** Ralph Jackson's remarks: personal communication. The account of its restoration is drawn from Worrell et al. • **Page 191** Carausius milestone: *RIB* 2290–2. • **Pages 192–197** The sources on Carausius, including the relevant passages from the panegyrics, Aurelius Victor's *Liber de Caesaribus*, and Eutropius's *Breviarum*, are collected in a translation by R. S. O. Tomlin in Casey, pp.191–8. • **Page 194** '*restitutor Brit(anniae)*': ibid., p.65. • **Page 194** levels not seen since the reign of Nero: de la Bédoyère. This article lays out de la Bédoyère's theory about the letters R.S.R. and I.N.P.C.D.A., and also contains the note about John Evelyn and '*decus et tutamen*'. I am grateful for the author's generous response to my enquiry about how he made the Virgil connection. Some doubt has been cast on the authenticity of the three known I.N.P.C.D.A. medallions (Williams), none of which have long provenances. Williams's argument depends on demoting the '*expectate veni*' to a coincidental, rather than knowing, echo of Virgil, and to the inherent unlikeliness of legionaries' and German mercenaries' being familiar with Virgil. In de la Bédoyère's defence, it may be noted that the literary origin of the phrase '*decus et tutamen*' on our pound coins may not be recognised by the bulk of the modern British population. • **Page 197** 'the past lives on in the present': Collingwood, 1939, p.100.

Chapter Eleven: The Cotswolds and the South-West

• **Page 198** epigraph: from Camden's *Britannia*, on Cirencester. • **Pages 198–199** 'The discovery of Roman villas in these woods': J. Farrer. • **Page 199** icy

Italianate stucco plasterwork: the decorations are well-known, and attributed to Artari and Bagutti, according to Mander, p.124. • **Page 202** 'On the digging of a vault for the interment of the late John Wade esquire': Lysons, 1797, p.2. • **Page 205** found when gardeners were digging a kitchen garden at Horkstow Hall in Lincolnshire in 1797: D. J. Smith, p.34. • **Page 205** the mosaic known as the Rudston Venus: for a discussion of the mosaic see Neal and Cosh, vol. 1, pp.353–6. • **Page 206** the Brading mosaic is discussed by Neal and Cosh, vol. 3, pt. 1, pp.265–8. • **Page 207** 'mutilated remains of a noble capital, and shaft of a pillar': Donovan, p.78.• **Page 207** 'containing the figures of an elephant and several birds': Lysons, 1797, p.2. • **Page 207** Pillerton Priors, Warwickshire: see ibid., vol. 4, p.396. • **Page 208** John Hawkins: his obituary is in the *Gentleman's Magazine*, September 1841, pp.322–3. • **Page 208** 'a man of very low education and manners': letter from Hawkins to Lysons, 11 February 1812, in Steer, p. 1. • **Page 209** there were 904 signatures: ibid., p. vi. • **Page 209** 'I have been so much troubled': ibid., p.9. • **Page 209** 'irreparable' loss: ibid., p.47. • **Page 209** 'for the accommodation of [the proprietor's] visitors': Lysons, 1815, advertisement. • **Page 209** 'in a good taste, and the figures are better executed': ibid., pp.8–9. • **Page 210** 'And off he swept the Trojan lad': Ovid, *Metamorphoses* 10.155–61. (trans. A. D. Melville, Oxford Classics). • **Page 210** The mosaic is divided into five panels: for a detailed description, see Neal and Cosh, vol. 2, pp.253–7. • **Page 211** *'Ille dies primus'*: Virgil, *Aeneid*, IV.169–70. • **Pages 212–213** manuscript of the *Aeneid* in the Vatican: discussed by Neal and Cosh, vol. 2, p.257.

Chapter Twelve: Norfolk, again, and Sussex

• **Page 214** epigraph: from Haverfield. • **Page 218** 'the barbarians beyond the Rhine': Zosimus, 6.5 2–3. • **Page 219** the Scots and the Picts arrived in their coracles – Gildas, 19 ff. • **Page 219** 'a modest man, who alone of the Romans had by chance survived': ibid., 25. • **Pages 219–220** country sinking into barbarism'; the last remnant of 'Roman ideas': Collingwood and Myres, p.324. • **Page 220** the lines from 'The Ruin' are taken from Michael Alexander's translation. • **Page 221** The discovery of the Mildenhall Treasure: Hobbs, 2008, pp.376–420. This passage draws deeply on Hobbs's patient detective work, described in a fascinating article in *The Antiquaries Journal*. • **Page 223** 'leapt up from my chair': Dahl, p.5. • **Page 224** piled high with apples, oranges, pears and nuts: Hobbs, 2008, p.410. • **Page 225** a not infrequently expressed suspicion in archaeological circles: Ashbee. • **Page 225** John Everett Millais, *The Romans Leaving Britain*: http://www.christies.com/LotFinder/lot_details.aspx?intObjectID=4026906 (a reduced version of the original, which is in a private collection); http://www.victorianweb.org/painting/millais/ drawings/33.html (a sketch towards the painting). • **Page 227** 'nothing much to regret & a great deal to rejoice in': Hill, 2007, p.129. • **Page 227** nineteen designs relating to Roman Britain: Robertson, p.62. • **Page 228** 'sunk in ignorance, heathen superstition and slavery': ibid, p.334. • **Page 230** 'fair field full of folk': the quote is from William Langland's poem *Piers Plowman*.

Places to Visit

The essential resource for visiting the places mentioned in the book is R. J. A Wilson's *A Guide to the Roman Remains in Britain*, which at the time of writing was out of print, but available from second-hand sellers, including Amazon and Abe. For Scotland, Lawrence Keppie's *The Legacy of Rome: Scotland's Roman Remains* is similarly indispensable.

Many Roman remains are in the care of the national heritage organisations. Details of entry to sites can be found on the relevant websites: for English Heritage www.english-heritage.org.uk; for Cadw (Wales) cadw.wales.gov.uk; for Historic Scotland www.historic-scotland.gov.uk. Membership brings free entry to sites in their care, and is strongly recommended if several visits are planned. There are reciprocal arrangements between the national organisations, meaning you should have to join only one – check online for details.

Depending on how many museums you visit in a year, membership of the Art Fund may be worthwhile – it gives free entry to over 200 museums and galleries in Britain: www.artfund.org.

If you are within reach of London, a first port of call must be the British Museum (free) – www.britishmuseum.org – whose Roman Britain gallery contains some of the most significant artefacts from the period.

Please check opening dates and times for all sites and museums before setting out. They are liable to change, and some visiting regimes are eccentric; for example, not all local-authority-run museums open on a Sunday.

Chapter One: Kent and Essex

As described, there are no Roman remains to see at Deal, though it is a pleasant place (with a lovely Henrican clover-leaf castle, in the care of English Heritage). Nearby Richborough, however, is spectacular (entry charge, free for English Heritage members).

Fishbourne Roman Palace (entry charge) on the outskirts of Chichester, in Sussex, is one of the most important Roman sites in Britain: sussexpast.co.uk. If you are in the area, it's good to combine with a visit to Bignor Roman Villa (see Chapter Eleven).

In Colchester, not to be missed are the walls and, particularly, the Balkerne Gate, near the Mercury Theatre. Colchester Castle Museum (entry charge) has a superb collection of Roman finds from the town, and is itself constructed on the base of the Claudian temple. Additional guided tours of the Roman 'vaults' are also available: www.cimuseums. org.uk. The following site, www.visitcolchester.com/Roman-Colchester.aspx, has plenty of information and links.

Colchester town hall, with its statue of Boudica, is on the high street, while the preserved remains of the theatre can be seen any time on Maidenburgh Street, visible through the window of a building on the left if approaching from the high street. At the corner of Maidenburgh Street and St Helen's Lane is St Helen's Chapel, built on the line of the theatre. It is sometimes unlocked: orthodoxcolchester.org.uk.

Work is in progress to develop the remains of the amphitheatre as a site for visitors. Latest developments on this and Colchester's archaeology in general can be found at www.thecolchesterarchaeologist. co.uk.

Chapter Two: Norfolk

The Roman town at Caistor St Edmund (free) is in the care of Norfolk Archaeological Trust: www.norfarchtrust.org.uk/Caistor.html. More information about Roman Caistor, and news about the latest archaeology, can be found at caistorromanproject.com.

Norwich Castle Museum (entry charge) has an excellent Iron Age and Roman collection, including part of the extraordinary Snettisham hoard of gold torques: www.museums.norfolk.gov.uk. The remainder is in the Roman Britain gallery of the British Museum (free). While you are in Norwich, do not fail to visit the cathedral with its spellbinding cloister: www.cathedral.org.uk. You can give the Iceni Village a miss.

Chapter Three: London

The first port of call for an investigation of Roman London is the Museum of London (free), at the Barbican. The galleries, with their excellent collection, set the scene; the map of Roman London, available to buy in the shop, is ideal for anyone wishing to set forth into the streets. The museum arranges tours of sites otherwise closed to the public, such as the fort gateway near London Wall car park, and the Lower Thames Street baths. It has also produced a Londinium app to guide users around Roman London: www.museumoflondon. org.uk. There are downloadable maps and leaflets at www.museumoflondon.org.uk/Collections-Research/Research/Your-Research/Londinium/Today/.

The British Museum's Roman Britain gallery holds important material relating to Roman London, including Fabius Alpinus Classicianus's tombstone.

Only fragments of the Roman city wall (often medieval above the foundations) remain. A tract of it can be seen in London Wall car park, bay 52, near to the Museum of London. Alphage Gardens, near the Barbican, is cared for by the Corporation of London. It is a pleasant place to stop, sit, and admire the wall. A decent length is visible on Noble Street, and there is a chunk right next to Tower Bridge tube. A walk can be made of the entire circuit, guided by the Museum of London map. Imagination is necessary.

The remains of the Roman amphitheatre may be seen in the Guildhall Museum and Art Gallery (free): www.guildhallartgallery.cityoflondon.gov.uk. Don't forget to look at the tiles in the courtyard that mark out the line of its perimeter.

The Bank of England Museum (free) has a Roman mosaic by the ticket desk, and the other mosaic in the basement can be visited by arrangement: www.bankofengland.co.uk.

A fragment of the basilica of the Roman bastion can be seen in the basement of Nicholson & Griffin hairdresser's at 90 Leadenhall, during opening hours on request: www.nicholsonandgriffin.com.

The Mithraeum and the London Stone were, at the time of writing, awaiting their new London home, and not on public view.

Chapter Four: Silchester

Silchester is an atmospheric place to visit (free), and a stroll around the town walls is especially pleasant. Don't miss the amphitheatre. In addition, each year the excavators from the University of Reading hold an open day. For information, news and a blog on the site and current archaeology, go to www.silchester.rdg.ac.uk.

Most of the finds from Silchester, including the bronze figure of Harpocrates and the eagle that inspired Rosemary Sutcliff, are in Reading Museum (free).

Chapter Five: Wales and the West

Wroxeter Roman City is in the care of English Heritage (entry charge; free for members), and has a small on-site museum. Do walk down to the village church, whose gate is supported on Roman pillars and whose font is a Roman column. It has a lovely Tudor tomb. There is also Roman masonry built into the walls.

More finds are at the Shrewsbury Museum and Art Gallery (free), housed in two seventeenth-century buildings: www.shrewsburymuseums.com.

Y Gaer: detailed directions and description of the site (free) can be found in Wilson's *Guide to the Roman Remains in Britain*.

The Brecknock Museum in Brecon, which houses the Maiden's Stone and other Roman inscriptions and finds, was sadly closed to the public as this book went to press.

Caerleon: there is much to see (and for free) here: the remains of the Roman barracks, perhaps the most spectacular amphitheatre in Britain, and the baths complex. They are jointly managed by the National Museum of Wales and Cadw: www.museumwales.ac.uk/en/roman/ruins.

The National Roman Legion Museum based here (free) has an excellent collection: www.museumwales.ac.uk/en/roman.

While in the area, also think of visiting Caerwent, twelve miles away (mentioned in Chapter Eleven, page 207). The village is encircled by the Roman walls of the town of Isca Silurum (the capital of the Silures tribe). You can wander freely through the remains of its basilica and temple, and see an important Roman inscription in the church porch. Carved Roman stone blocks are visible in the church walls.

Lydney Park Gardens, including the temple of Nodens, open to the public each spring (entry charge) to coincide with the flowering of the azaleas and rhododendrons. They also open on further selected days under the National Gardens Scheme. Highly recommended: it is an enchanting spot, and the family museum, with Roman finds from the temple site, is charming. Good cake, too. For details and future opening dates, go to www.lydneyparkestate.co.uk.

Maiden Castle: a walk up its windy heights is highly recommended. Hod Hill, some thirty miles north-east, near Child Okeford is another Iron Age hill fort with Roman interventions and a beautiful view. Both can be visited at any reasonable time. (If you like an Iron Age hill fort, Hambledon Hill, opposite Hod Hill, is also lovely, with impressive earthworks, though nothing Roman.) Finds from Maiden Castle are housed in the Dorset County Museum (entry charge), Dorchester: www.dorsetcountymuseum.org.

Chapter Six: Bath

A wander round the streets of Bath is always a pleasure: seek out Wood's masterpieces, the Royal Crescent and Circus. As one of Britain's most significant Roman sites, the Roman Baths are a must (entry charge). They have been recently refurbished: www.roman-baths.co.uk. After all that, tea in the elegant Pump Room above the Roman remains is recommended, and it would be churlish not to try a glass of the Bath water. It tastes so awful it must be doing you good.

For the full spa experience (entry charge), do visit the Thermae Baths Spa: www.thermaebathspa.com. Sessions of a minimum of two hours can be bought (no pre-booking, except for treatments and special packages).

Chapter Seven: Hadrian's Wall

Individual sites can be enjoyably visited along Hadrian's Wall, but by far the most rewarding thing to do is to walk it end to end (about six days' walking), or at least the bulk of it that lies between the train stations at Newcastle and Carlisle. Traditionally, walkers go east to west, following the direction of the first pilgrimage in 1849. We did it the other way around. At the Newcastle end, the trail veers away from the route of the wall and takes you along the banks of the Tyne, meaning, if you do it our way, a dramatic descent into the city beneath the beautiful bridges.

The best information to help you plan a walk along all or part of the wall is found at www.nationaltrail.co.uk/hadrianswall. One of its features is an interactive map of accommodation, which we used to book B&Bs in advance. B&Bs we enjoyed included Greencarts Farm (the campsite is also good) and Matfen High House. The website also has details of bag-handling services, in case you don't want to carry your own all the way. The B&B owners usually recommended pubs where we could get some supper. Sometimes they even gave us a lift to them. The website also provides details of various circular walks if you have only a day.

The Great North Museum (free) at Newcastle has the most important collection of inscriptions and sculptures from the wall: www.twmuseums.org.uk/great-north-museum.html. Also in Newcastle is Segedunum Roman Fort, with its reconstruction of a bathhouse (entry charge): www.twmuseums.org.uk/segedunum. At the other end, Tullie House Museum (free) at Carlisle has recently refurbished its Roman gallery: www.tulliehouse.co.uk. Near the centre of the wall are the privately run archaeological site of Vindolanda, where the writing tablets were excavated, and the Roman Army Museum (entry charges): www.vindolanda.com.

Chesters Roman Fort and Museum is a lovely site (entry charge; free to English Heritage members). Look out for the phallus sculpted into one of the paving stones. The bathhouse near the river is well worth seeing, and the museum, built by local antiquary John Clayton in the nineteenth century, is charming.

Further west, Housesteads, near the centre of the wall, and in a dramatic spot, is perhaps the best-preserved fort hereabouts, and has those Roman toilets that so interested me when I was twelve (entry charge; free to English Heritage and National Trust members). It has a new museum on site. Further west again, Birdoswald Roman Fort (entry charge; free to English Heritage members) is worth seeing. There is much more, including the temple at Brocolitia, the fort of Great Chesters (not to be confused with Chesters), various milecastles, etc., which can be seen as you go.

For the footsore, a bus service, the AD122 (get it?), runs along the military road south of the wall during the summer, between Newcastle and Carlisle stations. The timetable is on the national trail website above.

The most useful book to have in your pocket is probably the English Heritage guidebook *Hadrian's Wall*, by David Breeze.

Chapter Eight: Scotland

Walking the entire length of the Antonine Wall is not for the faint-hearted, but there are plenty of individual sites along the route that are worth seeing. The most spectacular part is around Bar Hill. A circular walk can be made, from Croy railway station or by parking near the canal, that takes in Croy Hill, Bar Hill (and its fort) and a length of the Forth–Clyde canal towpath. Rough Castle is perhaps the site where there is most to see, including the *lilia* pits, and is convenient for taking a look at the Falkirk Wheel, a feat of modern engineering on the canal. The bathhouse at Bearsden is also worth a visit (all of these can be seen freely at any reasonable time). David Breeze's book *The Antonine Wall* is an excellent guide, as is Lawrence Keppie's *The Legacy of Rome: Scotland's Roman Remains*. The Royal Commission on the Ancient and Historical Monuments of Scotland has published a map of the Antonine Wall, though it is also clearly marked on the relevant two sheets of Ordnance Survey Pathfinder maps.

The excellent galleries at the National Museum of Scotland (www. nms.ac.uk) in Edinburgh (free) and the Hunterian Museum (www.gla. ac.uk/hunterian) at the University of Glasgow (free) are the places to find out more about Roman Scotland. The distance slabs of the Antonine Wall have been recently given an impressive redisplay at the Hunterian. Both are wonderful museums aside from their Roman Britain collections.

There is a very small but nicely done display at the Auld Kirk Museum at Kirkintilloch (free): www.museumsgalleriesscotland.org.uk/member/auld-kirk-museum. The museum (free) in the seventeenth-century stable block of Kinneil House, through whose grounds the wall runs, tells the story of the Kinneil estate from the Roman period onwards: www.falkirkcommunitytrust.org/venues/kinneil-museum/.

The website www.antoninewall.org has plenty of resources, including an interactive map of the wall.

Aside from the Antonine Wall, Ardoch, in the village of Braco in Perthshire, is worth seeing, and can be visited at any reasonable time.

Walks can be taken in the pleasant grounds of the ruined Penicuik House south of Edinburgh (www.penicuikhouse.co.uk/ex_policies. aspx) and the version of Arthur's O'on, remade as the Clerks' dovecote, can be seen from a distance, though bear in mind that the stable block is a private house.

Chapter Nine: York

The place to start is the excellent Yorkshire Museum (entry charge) which has an exceptional collection, recently redisplayed: www.york-shiremuseum.org.uk. The multiangular tower, possibly built during Septimius Severus's stint in the city, is in the museum grounds. It's a short walk to York Minster (entry charge), where the undercroft (entry charge) can be visited, with its Roman sculptures and fragments of painted plaster: www.yorkminster.org.

A walk around the walls of York is pleasant, with beautiful views. The best book to have with you is Patrick Ottaway's *Roman York*. The following link also provides a leaflet about Roman York: www.histo-ryofyork.org.uk/tpl/uploads/1Roman.pdf.

The tombstone of Regina is at Arbeia Roman Fort and Museum at South Shields (free): www.twmuseums.org.uk/arbeia.html. There is also a good cast of it in the British Museum's Roman Britain gallery (free).

Chapter Ten: Cumbria and the Lakes

Ribchester is a delightful Lancashire town. The Roman baths on the edge of the Ribble and the Roman remains next to the church can be seen (free) and the little museum (entry charge) next to the church is excellent, containing, among other things, a good reproduction of the Ribchester parade helmet, the original of which is in the British Museum.

The bathhouse at the little village of Ravenglass is in the care of English Heritage and can be visited (free) at any reasonable time. The earthworks of the Roman fort are visible in the neighbouring field. Hardknott Castle, a few miles away, and in a spellbinding setting, can also be visited (free) at any reasonable time.

Not mentioned in the text, but certainly worth a visit, is the Senhouse Museum (entry charge) in Maryport, north of Ravenglass on the southern part of the Solway Firth. It has a spectacular collection of exceptionally well-preserved Roman altars. The enigmatic 'serpent stone' is a sculpture in the shape of a phallus (its authenticity has been questioned in some quarters). There is a charming sculpture of a running boar, emblem of the 20th Legion: www.senhousemuseum.co.uk.

The Coniston home of John Ruskin, Brantwood (www.brantwood.org.uk), can be visited (entry charge). Lanehead, the Collingwoods' house, is now an Outward Bound centre.

Tullie House Museum (free) in Carlisle contains the Carausius milestone and other Roman artefacts: www.tulliehouse.co.uk.

Chapter Eleven: The Cotswolds and the South-West

Great Witcombe villa (free) is in a lovely spot and can be visited at any reasonable time. So can the amphitheatre on the edge of Cirencester. Both in the care of English Heritage.

The collection at the Corinium Museum (entry charge) is excellent, and Cirencester is a very pleasant town to wander about in (the abbey is particularly lovely): coriniummuseum.cotswold.gov.uk.

Chedworth Roman Villa is a major site in a picturesque spot, in the care of the National Trust (entry charge, but free to members). Bob Woodward's reconstruction of the Woodchester Pavement is, unfortunately, no longer on view to the public; the real Woodchester Pavement lies protected under the earth of the village churchyard. The Dido and Aeneas mosaic is one of the highlights of the recently refurbished Museum of Somerset (free): www.somerset.gov.uk/museums.

Also mentioned in this chapter, though very much not in the Cotswolds, are the mosaics in the Hull and East Riding Museum (free entry) in Yorkshire, and the lovely Bignor Roman Villa (entry charge) on the Sussex downs south of Petworth: www.bignorromanvilla.co.uk.

Chapter Twelve: Norfolk, again, and Sussex

Burgh Castle, just south-west of Great Yarmouth, is one of Britain's most impressive Roman remains. It can be visited at any reasonable time (free), and is in the care of the Norfolk Archaeological Trust: www.norfarchtrust.org.uk/burghcastle.html. The Mildenhall Treasure and the late Roman glass from Burgh Castle can be seen in the Roman Britain gallery of the British Museum.

Pevensey Castle, in the care of English Heritage, is also extraordinary (entry charge but free to members).

Bibliography

ANCIENT TEXTS

Where possible, online resources are indicated. Translations of most of the sources on Roman Britain are also usefully collected in Ireland, *Roman Britain* (see p.257)

Julius Caesar, *Commentaries on the Gallic War*
Latin text: http://www.thelatinlibrary.com/caesar/gall5.shtml
Translation: http://classics.mit.edu/Caesar/gallic.5.5.html

Diodorus Siculus, the *Library*
Greek text: Loeb Classical Library (7 vols.), 1939
Translation: http://penelope.uchicago.edu/Thayer/E/Roman/Texts/Diodorus_Siculus/home.html

Vindolanda Tablets online
http://vindolanda.csad.ox.ac.uk/

Tacitus, *Agricola*
Latin text: http://www.thelatinlibrary.com/tacitus/tac.agri.shtml
Translation: *Tacitus: the Agricola and the Germania.* Translated with an Introduction by H. Mattingley. Translation Revised by S. A. Handford, rev. ed., London, 1970.

Tacitus, *Annals*
Latin text: http://www.thelatinlibrary.com/tac.html
Translation: http://penelope.uchicago.edu/Thayer/E/Roman/Texts/Tacitus/Annals/14B*.html

Cassius Dio, *History of Rome*

Greek text: http://remacle.org/bloodwolf/historiens/Dion/
Translation: http://penelope.uchicago.edu/Thayer/E/Roman/Texts/
    Cassius_Dio/

Solinus, *Collection of Marvels*
Latin text: http://www.thelatinlibrary.com/solinus.html
I have found no English translation in print or online.

St Patrick, *Confession*
Latin text: http://www.ucc.ie/celt/published/L201060/index.html
Translation: http://www.ccel.org/ccel/patrick/confession.toc.html

Gildas, *On the Destruction of Britain*
Latin text and English translation: http://www.vortigernstudies.org.uk/
    arthist/vortigernquotesgil.htm

Collingwood, R. G. O., Wright, R. P., and Tomlin, R. S. O., *The Roman
    Inscriptions of Britain (RIB)*, 3 vols., Oxford, 1965–2009.

UNPUBLISHED SOURCES

Smith, C. R., *Journals* (5 vols.), London, 1835–60. Held by the Department of
    Prehistory and Europe, British Museum.
Papers of the Clerk Family of Penicuik, Midlothian. Held by the National
    Records of Scotland, GD18/5018–5075: Antiquarian, general papers and
    correspondence, 1698–1845.

SECONDARY SOURCES

Achebe, C., 'An Image of Africa: Racism in Conrad's Heart of Darkness',
    Massachusetts Review, vol. 18, 1977.
Acworth, H. A., *Ballads of the Marathas: Rendered into English Verse from the
    Marathi Originals*, London, 1894.
Alexander, M., *The Earliest English Poems*, translated and introduced by Michael
    Alexander, 3rd edn, London, 1991.
Allason-Jones, L., *Women in Roman Britain*, London, 1989.
Anderson, J., *The Constitutions of the Free-Masons*, London, 1723.
Anon, *The History and Antiquities of Silchester in Hampshire*, Basingstoke,
    1821.
Anon, *A Step to the Bath: With a Character of the Place*, London, 1700.
Arnold, T., *Introductory Lectures on Modern History Delivered in Lent Term,*

MDCCCXLII, with the Inaugural Lecture, Delivered in December, MDCCCXLI, 4th edn, London, 1849.

Ashbee, P., 'Mildenhall: Memories of Mystery and Misgivings', *Antiquity*, vol. 71., p. 74.

Ayres, P. J., *Classical Culture and the Idea of Rome in Eighteenth-Century England*, Cambridge, 1997.

Beard, M., 'Rebel in Spirit', *Times Literary Supplement*, 24 June 2005.

—and J. Henderson, 'Rule(d) Britannia: Displaying Roman Britain in the Museums', in N. Merriman (ed.), *Making Early History in Museums*, Leicester, 1999.

—'How People Lived in Roman Britain', *Times Literary Supplement*, 4 October 2006.

—*The Roman Triumph*, Cambridge, Mass., & London, 2007.

—'The Rape of Britannia', A Don's Life blog, 30 January 2008: http://timesonline.typepad.com/dons_life/2008/01/the-rape-of-bri.html.

—'No More Scissors and Paste', *London Review of Books*, vol. 32 no. 6, 25 March 2010.

Bede, *Ecclesiastical History of the English People with Bede's Letter to Egbert and Cuthbert's Letter on the Death of Bede*, Sherley-Price, L. (trans.), Latham, R. E. (rev.), Farmer, D. H. (trans.), rev. edn, London 1990.

de la Bédoyère, G., *Roman Britain: A New History*, London, 2010.

—'Carausius and the Marks R.S.R. and I.N.P.C.D.A.', *The Numismatic Chronicle* 158 (1998), 79–88.

Bentwich, N., *They Found Refuge: An Account of British Jewry's Work for Victims of Nazi Oppression*, London, 1956.

Bertram, C. J., *An Essay on the Excellency and Style of the English Tongue: Wherein the Several Calumnies Raised Against It Are Examined and Answered*, Copenhagen, 1749.

—*Rudimenta Grammaticae Anglicanae*, Copenhagen, 1750.

—*Ethics from Several Authors, The Words Accented to Render the English Pronuntiation Easy to Foreigners*, Copenhagen, 1751.

—(ed.), *Britannicarum Gentium Historiae Antiquae Scriptores Tres*, London, 1759.

—(ed.), *Vorstllung der samtlichen Konigl Danischen Armee*, Copenhagen, 1762.

Birley, A. R., *The People of Roman Britain*, London, 1979.

Birley, R., *Vindolanda: A Roman Frontier Post on Hadrian's Wall*, London, 1977.

Bowers, F. (gen. ed.), *The Dramatic Works in the Beaumont and Fletcher Canon*, vol. IV, Cambridge, 1979.

Bowman, A. K., *Life and Letters on the Roman Frontier*, London, 1994.

—, Thomas, J. D., and Tomlin, R. S. O., 'The Vindolanda Writing Tablets (Tabulae Vindolandenses IV, Part 1)', in *Britannia* 41 (2010), 187–224.

—, Tomlin, R. S. O., and Worp, K. A., 'Emptio Bovis Frisica: the "Frisian Ox Sale" Reconsidered', *The Journal of Roman Studies*, vol. XCIX (2009), 156–170.

Breeze, D. J., *The Antonine Wall*, Edinburgh, 2006.

—*Roman Scotland*, rev. edn., London, 2006.

Brenton, H., *The Romans in Britain*, London, 1980.

Britten, B., *Letters from a Life: The Selected Letters and Diaries of Benjamin Britten, 1913–1976*, Mitchell, D. (ed.-in-chief), vol. 1, 1923–39, London, 1991.

Buchanan, G., *Rerum Scoticarum Historia*, Edinburgh, 1582.

Bushe-Fox, J. P., *Second report on the excavations on the site of the Roman town at Wroxeter*, Shropshire, 1913, London, 1914.

Butler, R., *Richborough Port*, Ramsgate, 1999.

Camden, W., *Britannia*, trans. Howard, P., London, 1607. (www.philological. bham.ac.uk/cambrit.)

Carr, L., *Tessa Verney Wheeler: Women and Archaeology Before World War Two*, unpublished DPhil thesis, Oxford, 2008.

Carter, A., 'Bathed in Englishness', in *Shaking a Leg: Journalism and Writings*, London, 1997.

Casey, P. J., *Carausius and Allectus: The British Usurpers*, London, 1994.

Clarke, K., 'Re-reading Tacitus' Agricola', *Journal of Roman Studies*, vol. 91 (2001), pp. 94–112.

Clerk, J., *Memoirs of the Life of Sir John Clerk of Penicuik, Baronet, Baron of the Exchequer, Extracted by himself from his own journals 1675–1755*, Gray, J. M. (ed.), Scottish Historical Society, vol. 13, 1892.

Collingwood, R. G., *Roman Britain*, Oxford, 1923.

—, *Roman Eskdale*, Whitehaven [publication date unknown, probably 1928].

—, and Myres, J. N. L., *Roman Britain and the English Settlements, The Oxford History of England*, vol. 1, Clark, G. (ed.), 2nd edn, Oxford, 1937.

—, *An Autobiography*, Oxford, 1939.

Collingwood, W. G., *Lake District History*, 2nd edn, Kendal, 1928.

Collingwood Bruce, J., 'The Roman Wall "Pilgrimage" of 1849', *Proceedings of the Society of Antiquaries of Newcastle-Upon-Tyne*, series II, vol. II, no. 17, 1885, pp. 135–141.

Conrad, J., *Heart of Darkness*, London, 2007.

Conybeare, W. D., and Phillips, W., *Outlines of the Geology of England and Wales*, London, 1822.

Cunliffe, B., *Roman Bath Discovered*, rev. edn, London, 1984.

—*The Temple of Sulis Minerva at Bath. Volume Two: The Finds From the Sacred Spring*, Oxford, 1988.

—*English Heritage Book of Roman Bath*, 3rd edn., 1995.

—*The Extraordinary Voyage of Pytheas the Greek*, 2nd edn, London, 2002.

—*The Celts: A Very Short Introduction*, Oxford, 2003.
—*Iron Age Communities in Britain*, 4th edn, London, 2005.

Dahl, R., *The Wonderful Story of Henry Sugar*, London, 1977.
Davies, H., *A Walk Along the Wall*, 2nd edn, 1984.
Davies, J. A., *Venta Icenorum: Caistor St Edmund Roman Town*, Norwich, 2001.
Dickens, C., 'Rome and Turnips', *All the Year Round*, vol. 1, no. 3, 1859.
Donovan, E., *Descriptive Excursions Through South Wales and Monmouthshire*, London, 1805.

Edwards, C., 'The Art of Conquest', in Edwards, C., and Woolf, G. (eds.), *Rome the Cosmopolis*, Cambridge, 2003.
Elgar, Edward: Opus 35, *Caractacus, A Cantata*, London, 1985.

Farrer, J., 'Notice of Recent Excavations in Chedworth Wood, on the Estate of the Earl of Eldon, in the County of Gloucester', *Proceedings of the Society of Antiquaries of Scotland* 6, ii (1865–6), pp. 278–83.
Farrer, J. A., *Literary Forgeries*, London, 1907.
Freeman, P. W. M., *The Best Training-Ground for Archaeologists: Francis Haverfield and the Invention of Romano-British Archaeology*, Oxford, 2007.
Frere, Sheppard, *Britannia: A History of Roman Britain*, 3rd edn., rev., London, 1987.
Fulford, M., 'Imperium Galliarum, Imperium Britanniarum. Developing New Ideologies and Settling Old Scores: Abandonments, Demolitions and New Building in South-east Britain, c. AD 250–300', in Clark, J., Cotton, J., Hall, J., Sherris, R., and Swain, H., *Londinium and Beyond: Essays on Roman London and its Hinterland for Harvey Sheldon*, York, 2008.

Geoffrey of Monmouth, *The History of the Kings of Britain*, translated with an introduction by Lewis Thorpe, London 1966.
Gerald of Wales, *The Journey Through Wales and the Description of Wales*, translated with an introduction by Lewis Thorpe, London, 1978.
Giles, J. A. (ed.), *Six Old English Chronicles*, London, 1848.
Goodall, J., *Pevensey Castle*, rev. edn, London, 2011.
Gordon, Alexander, *Itinerarium Septentrionale: Or, A Journey Thro' Most of the Counties of Scotland, and Those in Northern England*, London, 1726.
Green, M., *The Gods of Roman Britain*, Princes Riseborough, 1983.
Grenville, A., 'Saved By A Transit Visa', *Association of Jewish Refugees Journal*, May 2009.
Guidott, T., *A Discourse of Bath, and the Hot Waters There*, 2nd edn., 1725.

Hardy, T., *A Tryst at an Ancient Earthwork*, Detroit, 1885.

Hargrove, W. M., *History and Description of the Ancient City of York*, 1818.

Harris, S., *Richborough and Reculver*, London, 2001.

Hassall, M., 'London: the Roman City', in Haynes, I., Sheldon, H., and Hannigan, L. (eds.), *London Under Ground: the Archaeology of a City*, Oxford, 2000.

Hatcher, H. (ed.), *Description of Britain, Translated from Richard of Cirencester, with The Original Treatise De Situ Britanniae and a Commentary on the Itinerary, Illustrated with Maps*, London, 1809.

Haverfield, F., *The Romanization of Roman Britain*, Oxford, 2nd edn., 1912.

Hawkes, J., *Mortimer Wheeler: Adventurer in Archaeology*, London, 1982.

Haycock, D. B., *William Stukeley: Science, Religion and Archaeology in Eighteenth-Century England*, Woodbridge, 2002.

Hearne, T., (ed.) *The Itinerary of John Leland*, 3rd edn., Oxford, 1768.

—et al., *Letters Written By Eminent Persons in the Seventeenth and Eighteenth Centuries*, vol. 1, 1813.

Henig, M., *Religion in Roman Britain*, 1984.

Herendeen, Wyman H., *William Camden: A Life in Context*, Woodbridge, 2007.

Hewitt, R., *Map of a Nation: A Biography of the Ordnance Survey*, London, 2010.

Hibberd, D., 'Wilfred Owen's letters: Some Additions, Amendments and Notes', *The Library*, vol. 4, no. 3, 1982, pp. 273–87.

—, *Wilfred Owen: A New Biography*, London, 2002.

Hill, R., *God's Architect*, London, 2007.

—'Gentlemen Did Not Dig', *London Review of Books*, 24 June 2010.

Hingley, R., *Roman Officers and English Gentlemen: the Imperial Origins of Roman Archaeology*, London, 2000.

—and Unwin, C., *Boudica: Iron Age Warrior Queen*, London, 2005.

—*The Recovery of Roman Britain 1586-1906: A Colony so Fertile*, Oxford, 2008.

—and Hartis, R., 'Contextualizing Hadrian's Wall: the Wall as "Debatable Lands"', in O. Hekster and T. Kaizer (eds.), *Frontiers in the Roman World: Impact of Empire*, vol. 13, pp. 79–96, Leiden, 2011.

Hobbs, R., 'The Mildenhall Treasure: Roald Dahl's Ultimate Tale of the Unexpected?', *Antiquity*, vol. 71, 63–73.

—'The Secret History of the Mildenhall Treasure', *The Antiquaries Journal*, vol. 88, 2008, pp. 376–420.

—and Jackson, R., *Roman Britain*, London, 2010.

Holinshed, R., *Chronicles*, London, 1587.

Hopkins, K., *Conquerors and Slaves*, Cambridge, 1978.

Horsley, J., *Britannia Romana*, London, 1733.

Hume, D., *The History of England in Three Volumes, vol. 1, part a, From the Britons of Early Times to King John*, London, 1860.

Hutton, R., *Blood and Mistletoe: the History of the Druids in Britain*, New Haven and London, 2009.

Hutton, W., *The History of the Roman Wall, Which Crosses the Island of Britain, From the German Ocean to the Irish Sea, Describing Its Antient State, and Its Appearance in the Year 1801*, London, 1802.

Inglis, F., *History Man: The Life of R. G. Collingwood*, Princeton, 2009.

Ireland, S., *Roman Britain: A Sourcebook*, 3rd edn, Abingdon, 2008.

Jones, M., *The End of Roman Britain*, Ithaca, 1996.

Kennedy, M., 'Ben Hur in Colchester? Race is on to save UK's only Roman chariot racetrack', *Guardian*, 7 February 2010.

—'Bronze helmet valued at £300,000 uncovered at farm near Crosby Garrett in Cumbria', ibid., 13 September 2010.

—'Campaign to keep Roman cavalry helmet in Cumbria given boost', ibid., 27 September 2010.

—'Roman helmet sold for £2m', ibid., 13 October 2010.

Keppie, L. J. F., *The Legacy of Rome: Scotland's Roman Remains*, 2nd edn, Edinburgh, 1998.

—*Roman Inscribed and Sculpted Stones in the Hunterian Museum, University of Glasgow*, Glasgow, 1998.

Kershaw, N. (ed. and trans.), *Anglo-Saxon and Norse Poems*, Cambridge, 1922.

Kipling, R., *Puck of Pook's Hill*, London, 1994.

Leach, S., Eckardt, H., Chenery, C., and Müldner, G. H., 'A Lady of York: migration, ethnicity and identity in Roman Britain', *Antiquity* 84 (323), 2010, pp. 131–45.

Leach, S., Lewis, M. E., Chenery, C., Müldner, G. H., and Eckardt, H., 'Migration and diversity in Roman Britain: a multidisciplinary approach to immigrants in Roman York, England', *American Journal of Physical Anthropology* 140 (3), 2009, pp. 546–61.

Linn, A., 'Charles Julius Bertram's Royal English–Danish Grammar: the linguistic work of an 18th-century fraud', in Cram, D., Linn, A., and Nowak, E., *History of Linguistics 1996, vol. 2, 1999: From Classical to Contemporary Linguistics*, pp. 183–93.

Lively, P., *Oleander, Jacaranda: A Childhood Perceived*, London, 1994.

Long, R., *Selected Statements & Interviews*, London, 2007.

Lukis, W. C. (ed.), *The Family Memoirs of the Rev. William Stukeley, MD, and the Antiquarian and Other Correspondence of William Stukeley*, Roger & Samuel Gale, Publications of the Surtees Society, vols. 73, 76, 80, 1882–7.

Lysons, S., *An Account of Roman Antiquities Discovered At Woodchester in the County of Gloucester*, London, 1797.

—*Reliquiae Britannico-Romanae, containing figures of Roman Antiquities discovered in England*, 3 vols., London, 1813–17.

—*An Account of the Remains of a Roman Villa at Bignor, in the County of Sussex, in the Year 1811 and Four Following Years*, London, 1815.

Macaulay, R., *The Pleasure of Ruins*, London, 1953.

Macdonald, G., *The Roman Wall in Scotland*, Glasgow, 1911.

Mackay, N. D., *Aberfeldy Past and Present*, Aberfeldy, 1954.

Mander, N., *Country Houses of the Cotswolds*, London, 2008.

Marshall, H. E. M., *Our Island Story, a History of England for Boys and Girls*, London, 1905.

Mattingley, D., *An Imperial Possession: Britain in the Roman Empire, 54 BC–AD 409*, London, 2006.

Mendelson, E. (ed.), *The Complete Works of W. H. Auden, Vol. 1, Plays and Other Dramatic Writings by W. H. Auden 1928–1938*, Princeton, 1988.

Merrifield, R., *The Roman City of London*, London, 1965.

Mikalachki, J., *The Legacy of Boadicea: Gender and Nation in Early Modern England*, London, 1998.

Millett, M., *The Romanisation of Britain*, Cambridge, 1990.

—*Roman Britain*, rev. edn, London, 2005.

Mitchell, D. (ed.), *Letters from a Life: the Selected Letters and Diaries of Benjamin Britten 1913–1976*, London, 1991.

Moore, Jerrold Northrop, *Edward Elgar: A Creative Life*, Oxford, 1984.

Morant, P., *The History and Antiquities of Colchester*, London, 1748.

Morris, J., 'Fantasy of Greatness: Bath, 1974', in *Among the Cities*, London, 1985.

Morton, H. V., *In Search of London*, London, 2001.

Mowl, T., and Earnshaw, B., *John Wood: Architect of Obsession*, Bath, 1988.

Neal, D. S., and Cosh, S. R., *Roman Mosaics of Britain*, 4 vols., London, 2002–10.

Nelson, J., *The History, Topography, and Antiquities of the Parish of St Mary Islington, in the County of Middlesex*, London, 1811.

Niblett, R., *Verulamium: The Roman City of St Albans*, Stroud, 2001.

Nicholson, E. W. B., *Vinisius to Nigra: a 4th-Century Christian Letter Written in South Britain and Discovered at Bath*, London, 1904.

Ottaway, P., *Roman York*, 2nd edn, 2004, Stroud.

Owen, H., and Bell, J. (eds.), *Wilfred Owen: Collected Letters*, London, 1967.

Pevsner, N., *London I: the Cities of London and Westminster*, Harmondsworth, 1957

Piggott, S., *William Stukeley, An Eighteenth-century Antiquary*, Oxford, 1950

—*Ancient Britons and the Antiquarian Imagination: Ideas from the Renaissance to the Regency*, London, 1989

Pitts, M., 'What the Romans Didn't Do for Us', *Guardian*, 16 March, 2011.

Plummer, J., and Godwin, G. N., *Silchester; or, the 'Pompeii of Hampshire': How To Get There, What To See*, Basingstoke, 1879.

Pooley, L., Crummy, P., Shimmin, D., et al., *Archaeological Investigations on the 'Alienated Land', Colchester Garrison, Colchester, Essex May 2004–October 2007*, http://cat.essex.ac.uk/reports/CAT-report-0412.pdf.

Port, M. H. (ed.), *The Houses of Parliament*, London, 1976.

Ransome, A., *The Autobiography of Arthur Ransome*, 2nd edn, London, 1985.

Reece, R., *My Roman Britain*, Cirencester, 1988.

Riding, C., and Riding, J. (eds.), *The Houses of Parliament: History, Art, Architecture*, London, 2000.

Robertson, D., *Sir Charles Eastlake and the Victorian Art World*, Princeton, 1978.

Roy, W., *A Very Large and Highly Finished Colored Military Survey of the Kingdom of Scotland, Exclusive of the Islands, Undertaken by Order of William Augustus, Duke of Cumberland*, London, 1747–55.

—, *The Military Antiquities of the Romans in Britain*, London, 1793.

Royal Commission on Historical Monuments (England), *An Inventory of the Historical Monuments in London, Vol. 3, Roman London*, London, 1928.

Salway, P., *'To Far-off Britain, a Whole World Away': Some Reflections on the Study of Roman Britain*, Milton Keynes, 1984.

—*A History of Roman Britain*, Oxford, 2001.

Scott, W., *The Antiquary*, London, 1816.

Sharples, N. M., *Maiden Castle*, London, 1991.

Sibbald R., *A Collection of Several Treatises in Folio, Concerning Scotland, As it was of Old, and also in Later Times*, Edinburgh, 1734.

Sitwell, E., *Bath*, London, 1932.

Skene, W. F. (ed.), *John of Fordun's Chronicle of the Scottish Nation, Translated from the Latin Text by Felix J. H. Skene*, Edinburgh, 1872.

Smith, C. Roach, *Illustrations of Roman London*, London, 1859.

Smith, D. J., *Roman Mosaics at Hull*, 3rd edn, Hull, 2005.

Steer, F. W. (ed.), *The Letters of John Hawkins and Samuel and Daniel Lysons, 1812–1830*, Chichester, 1966.

Stewart, P. C. N., 'Inventing Britain: the Roman Creation and Adaptation of an Image', *Britannia*, vol. 26 (1995), pp. 1–10.

Stukeley, W., *An Account of a Roman Temple, and Other Antiquities, Near Graham's Dike in Scotland*, London, 1720.

—*An Account of Richard of Cirencester, Monk of Westminster, and of his Works: with his Antient Map of Roman Brittain; and the Itinerary thereof*, London, 1757.

—*Itinerarium Curiosum*, 2nd edn, London, 1776.

Sutcliff, R., *The Eagle of the Ninth*, Harmondsworth, 1977.

—*The Silver Branch*, Oxford, 2007.

—*The Lantern Bearers*, Oxford, 2007.

Sweet, R., *Antiquaries: The Discovery of the Past in Eighteenth-Century Britain*, Oxford, 2004.

Terras, M., *Image to Interpretation: An Intelligent System to Aid Historians in Reading the Vindolanda Texts*, Oxford, 2006.

Thornbury, W., *Old and New London: Volume Two*, London, 1878.

Tomlin, R. S. O., 'Vinisius to Nigra: Evidence from Oxford of Christianity of Roman Britain', *Zeitschrift für Papyrologie und Epigraphik*, vol. 100, 1994, pp. 93–108.

—'The Girl in Question', *Britannia*, vol. 34, 2003, pp. 41–51.

Toulmin Smith, L. (ed.), *The Itinerary of John Leland In or About the Years 1535–1543, Parts 1 to 3*, London, 1907.

Wacher, J., *A Portrait of Roman Britain*, London, 2000.

Walpole, H., *The Letters of Horace Walpole, Earl of Orford: Including Numerous letters Now First Published From The Original Manuscripts. Vol 4, 1770–1797*, Philadelphia, 1842.

Warburton, J., *Vallum Romanaum: Or, The History and Antiquities of the Roman Wall, Commonly Called the Picts Wall*, London, 1753.

Warner, M., *Monuments and Maidens*, London, 1985.

Wheeler, R. E. M., *The Roman Fort Near Brecon*, London, 1926.

—and Wheeler, T. V., *Report on the Excavation of the Prehistoric, Roman and Post-Roman Site in Lydney Park, Gloucestershire*, Oxford, 1932.

—and Wheeler, T. V., *The Roman Amphitheatre at Caerleon*, London, 1935.

—and Wheeler, T. V., *Verulamium: A Belgic and two Roman Cities, Reports of the Research Committee of the Society of Antiquaries of London no. XI*, Oxford, 1936.

—, *Maiden Castle*, Oxford, 1943.

—, *Still Digging, Interleaves from an Antiquary's Notebook*, London, 1955.

White, R., *Wroxeter Roman City*, London, 1999 (English Heritage guidebook).

White, R., and Barker, P., *Wroxeter: Life and Death of a Roman City*, Stroud, 1998.

Williams, H. P. G., *Carausius: A Consideration of the Historical, Archaeological and Numismatic Aspects of His Reign*, Oxford, 2004.

Wilson, R. J. A., *A Guide to the Roman Remains in Britain*, 4th edn., London, 2002.

Wood, J., *The Origin of Building: or, the Plagiarism of the Heathens Detected*, Bath, 1741.

—*An Essay Towards the Description of Bath*, 2nd edn, Bath, 1749.

Woodward, B. B., 'A Literary Forgery: Richard of Cirencester's Tractate on Britain', *Gentleman's Magazine*, vol. 220, pp. 301–8; 617–24, 1866; vol. 221, pp. 458–66, 1866; vol. 223, pp. 443–51, 1867.

Woolf, G., 'The City of Letters', in Edwards, C., and Woolf, G. (eds.), *Rome the Cosmopolis*, Cambridge, 2003.

—'A Distant Mirror: Britain and Rome in the Representation of Empire', in Santos Yanguas, J., and Torregaray Pagola, E. (eds.), *Revisiones de Historia Antiqua V, Laudes Provinciarum, Rétorica y política en la representación del imperio romano*, Acts of the colloquium at Vitoria, vols. 17–18 (2007), pp. 135–47.

—*Tales of the Barbarians: Ethnography and Empire in the Roman West*, Oxford, 2011.

Worrell, S., Jackson, R., Mackay, A., Bland, B., and Pitts, M., 'The Crosby Garrett Roman Helmet', *British Archaeology*, January/February 2011.

Wren, C., *Life and Works of Sir Christopher Wren From the Parentalia; or Memoirs by his Son Christopher*, Camden, 1903.

Yassin-Kassab, R., 'On the Empire's Edge', the *National*, 22 November 2008, http://www.thenational.ae/lifestyle/travel/on-the-empires-edge

Acknowledgements

To Dan Franklin, Clare Bullock, Joe Burgis, Ruth Waldram, Jane Selley and all at Jonathan Cape. To Jane Randfield for the maps. To Peter Straus, my agent.

To the many scholars, archaeologists and curators who so generously shared their ideas, showed me sites, allowed themselves to be interviewed or helped in other ways: Richard Abdy, Mary Beard, Guy de la Bédoyère, Alan Bowman, Lydia Carr, Stephen Cosh, Michelle Cotton, Philip Crummy, Barry Cunliffe, Jane Draycott, Hella Eckardt, Michael Fulford, Jenny Hall, Richard Hingley, Richard Hobbs, Luke Houghton, Ralph Jackson, Lawrence Keppie, Thomas Leece, Andrew Morrison, Patrick Ottaway, Tim Padley, Mike Pitts, Jacqueline Riding, Darrell Rohl, Roy Stephenson, Roger Tomlin, Tim Whitmarsh, Jonathan Williams. My thanks also to Robert Clerk, Colin Matthews, and Matthew Paton and Georgina Aitken of Christie's.

To the many friends and family members who offered practical help or accommodation, were companions on the road, or listened patiently to talk of Roman Britain: Richard Baker; Andy Beckett and Sara Holloway; Isaac Bird; Sue Blundell and Nick Bailey; Fiona Bradley and Nick Barley; Neil Crombie; Phil Daoust; Jon Day; Susanna Eastburn; Damian Harland; Peter and Pamela Higgins; Rob Higgins and Pam Magee; Rupert Higgins and Dawn, Tilda and Eleanor Lawrence; Maev Kennedy; Clare and Andy Smith; Joshua St Johnston; Valerie and Colin St Johnston; Richard and Jane Wentworth.

To the staff of the Rare Books and Music reading room of the British Library; the Institute of Classical Studies Library; the Society of Antiquaries Library; and the National Archives of Scotland.

To Alan Rusbridger and colleagues at the *Guardian*, who tolerated several periods of absence – especially to Georgina Henry, whose passion and spirit are ever-inspiring.

To my first teacher of Latin and Greek, Cynthia Smart, and to the ones who came later.

To the council of the Classical Association, whose generous bestowal of the Classical Association prize for 2010 bought me valuable time.

Grateful thanks to those who kindly read portions of the manuscript: Alan Bowman, Lydia Carr, Stephen Cosh, Matthew Fox, Michael Fulford, Jenny Hall, Sara Holloway, Richard Hobbs, Roger Tomlin; and to those who with extraordinary generosity ploughed through the whole: Tom Holland, Sam Moorhead, Paul Myerscough and Greg Woolf. Their suggestions were invaluable; the errors are my own.

This book is, with love, dedicated to Matthew Fox, valiant driver of the camper van.

Index

Abaris 99–100
Abdy, Richard 195
Aberdeen 154
Aberfeldy 141–2
Achebe, Chinua 177–8
Actaeon 200–1
Actium, Battle of 32–3
Acworth, Harry Arbuthnot 36, 39
Adam, William 141
Adminius 11
Adraste 33
Aeneas 22, 39, 73, 83, 167, 174, 194, 197, 210–12, 249
Africa xviii, 21, 73, 163, 167–8
Agricola, Gnaeus Julius xxi, 15–16, 17, 62, 75, 137, 139, 140–1, 142, 156, 173
Aitken, Georgiana 189
Alaric 218
Albert, Prince 37, 227
Aldborough 78
Alfred the Great 23, 58, 217
Algerians 116
Allectus 192–3
All the Year Round 76
Ambleside 180
Ambrosius Aurelianus 219

Anchises 39
Ancient Monuments Act 57
Anderson, James: *The Constitutions of the Free-Masons* 101
Angles 216
Anglesey 27
Anglo-Saxons 58, 82, 87, 94, 122, 162, 181, 220, 226, 227, 228 *see also* Saxons
Antenociticus 116
Antiquity 168
Antonine Itineraries 153
Antonine Wall xx, 137, 143–8, 152, 164, 173, 206, 247, 248
Antoninus Pius, emperor 143
Aphrodisias 18
Apollo 46, 99, 180
Appendix Vergiliana 130
Aquae Sulis *see* Bath
Arbeia 116, 170–1, 248
Ardoch 141, 248
Argentocoxus 164
Arian heresy 105
Arles, Council of 105, 162
Armitage, Edward: *Caesar's First Invasion of Britain* 228
Armorica 218

Arnold, Thomas 226–7
Artemisia, Queen 32
art 185–7
Art Fund 242
Arthur, King 22, 56, 86, 88, 216, 219
Arthurian legends 219–20
Arthur's O'on (or Oven) 148–51, 248
Ascanius 210, 211
Ashmolean Museum 204
Aske, James: *Elizabetha Triumphans* 34
Asterix comics 27
Astures 116
Atargatis 118
Atrebates 12, 62
Attacotti 217
Aubrey, John 100
Auden, Revd John 122
Auden, W. H. xx, 122–7, 129, 185
    Hadrian's Wall 122–7
    'Roman Wall Blues' 122–7
Augustine, St 6, 14, 49, 105, 226, 228
Augustus, emperor 7, 8, 32, 171
Auld Kirk Museum, Kirkintilloch 247
Aurelius Victor 192
Avebury 100
Aves, Sophia 223
Avon, River 93, 94

Bacchus 221
Badon, Mount 219
Bagaudae 192
Balkans 217

Balkerne Gate, Colchester 19, 242
Baltic 8
Bank of England 51–2, 243
Bannavem Taberniae 219
Barates 170, 171
Barbarian Conspiracy 217
Bar Hill 143, 144, 147, 148, 247
Barnsley Park 199
Barry, Charles 227
Barton Farm mosaic 201, 202, 204
Batavians 128, 130
Bath (Aquae Sulis) 62, 93–107, 208
    the Circus 97, 102, 245
    Pump Room 95, 96, 97, 103, 105, 245
    Roman baths 93, 94, 96, 97, 102–3, 245
    Royal Crescent 97, 245
    temple of Sulis-Minerva 94, 97
    Thermae Baths spa 93, 100, 245
Bath to Bristol railway line 208
Bathurst family 86, 87
Battersea shield 44
Battle Bridge (now King's Cross) 45–6
Bearsden 143, 147–8, 247
Bede, Venerable 162
    Ecclesiastical History of the English People xxi, 216
Bédoyère, Guy de la 195–6, 197
Belerium 9
Belgians 116
Bellerophon 208

Bennachie, Mount 139
Berie 138
Berikos 12
Berlin: State Museums 165
Bertha, Queen 6
Bertram, Charles Julius xx, 152–3,
        154, 155, 156
    *Britannicarum Gentium
        Historiae Antiquae Scriptores
        Tres (Three Ancient Writers
        on the History of the British
        People)* 154
    *Essay on the Excellency and
        Style of the English Tongue*
        156
Bignor 208–10, 242, 249
Birdlip 11
Birdoswald 120, 246
Birley, Eric 127
Birley, Robin 127–8
Birnie 138
Bladud 98–100, 103
Blake, William 56
Blitz, the 45, 47–8, 50–1, 56
Board of Ordnance 142, 150
Boece, Hector 139
Bo'ness colliery 145
Bootham Bar, York 165, 166
Boudica 10, 23–4, 25, 27, 28, 30–6,
        38–9, 44, 45, 55, 62, 73, 84, 100,
        228, 243
Boulogne 192
Bowen, Elizabeth xxii
Bowman, Alan 128, 129, 130,
        132–3
Braco 141, 248
Bradbury, Darren 190
Brading 206

Brancaster 215
Brantwood 182, 249
Brasenose College, Oxford 130
Brecon: Brecknock Museum 84,
        244
Breeze, David
    The Antonine Wall 247
    Hadrian's Wall 247
Brenton, Howard 5
    The Romans in Britain xx,
        175
Brewer, Norris 61
Brigantes 10, 16, 25
Bristol City Museum 208
Britannia (female
    personification) 18
Britannia Flavia 153
Britannia Maxima 153
Britannia Prima 153, 199
Britannia Secunda 153
Britannicus 16
British Archaeology magazine
        190
British Library 45, 49, 142
British Museum 11, 30, 46, 56,
        132, 188, 189, 190, 195, 208, 211,
        216, 220, 221, 222, 223, 242, 243,
        248, 250
Britten, Benjamin xx, 124–7
    incidental music for *Hadrian's
        Wall* 122–7
    'Roman Wall Blues' 122–7
Brittium 218
Brocchus 129, 132
Brocolitia 121–2, 246
Brown, Gordon 188
Browning, Robert: 'Love Among
        the Ruins' 63

Bruce, Sir Michael 150

Brutus 22, 35, 45

Bucklersbury House, London
52–3

Bucklersbury mosaic 52

Burgh Castle 214–16, 220, 229,
250

Bury Free Press & Post 223

Bushe-Fox, J. P. 79

Busy-Gap 117

Butcher, Gordon 222, 223, 224,
225

Butterfield, William 22

Byker's Hill, Newcastle 119–20

Cadw 241, 244

Caerleon (Isca) 82, 84–6, 244
   amphitheatre 85–6
   National Roman Legion
      Museum 244

Caerwent (Venta Silurum) 153,
207, 244–5

Caesar, Julius xxi, 5–6, 7, 9, 10,
11, 12, 14, 15, 62, 100, 148–9,
153, 174, 226
   Commentaries on the Gallic War
     6, 10, 62

Caister-on-Sea 215

Caistor St Edmund 29–30, 207,
242

Caledonians 139, 140, 145, 149,
161, 164, 173, 176, 217

Calgacus 139–40, 141, 142, 173

Caligula, emperor 11–12

Callendar estate 146

Callendar House 146

Calleva Atrebatum *see* Silchester

Cambridge 64

Camden, William xx, 29–30, 43,
56, 63, 65, 77, 98, 117–18,
120, 154–5, 161, 172, 181, 185,
198
   Britannia xx, 29, 36, 155

Camelon 148

Camulodunum *see* Colchester

Candidus 129

Canterbury 14

Caracalla, emperor 161, 164, 165

Caratacus 12, 15, 25–7, 31, 35,
36–8, 227

Carausius 191–7

Cardiff, Museum of 81

Carlisle 116, 118, 245, 246, 247, 249
   Tullie House Museum 181,
     188, 190, 191, 193, 246, 249

Carlungie 138

Carriden House 145

Carron, River 148, 150

Carron Ironworks 150, 151

Carron Phoenix 151

Carter, Angela 93, 98

Cartimandua, Queen 10, 16, 25

Cartmel 182

Carvoran fort 116

Casley, Mr 154

Cassiterides 8

Castle Acre 28–9

Castlecary 206

Castle Douglas 170

Catena, Paul 'the Chain' 217

Catterick 166

Catullus xvii, 7

Catuvellauni 11, 170–1

Cawfields 112

Celtic art 186

Centurion (film) 176

Centurion Works 147

Chamberlin, Powell and Bon (architects) 47

Charles II, King 197

Charles Stuart (Bonnie Prince Charlie) 138, 139

Chedworth 198, 199, 249

Chester (Deva) 75, 82

Chesterholm 127 see also Vindolanda

Chesters Roman Fort and Museum 246

Chichester 16, 17–18, 62

Christ 208

Christianity 23, 103, 105, 161, 162, 172, 208, 228

Christie's 188, 189, 190

Cirencester (Corinium) 62, 199–201, 249
    Corinium Museum 199–201, 249

Classicianus, Gaius Julius Alpinus: tombstone of 55

Claudia Rufens 26

Claudius, emperor 11, 12, 14, 15, 16, 18, 19, 25, 26, 27, 36, 37, 44, 62, 100

Claudius Hieronymianus 166

Clayton, John xix, 246

Cleopatra 32, 33

Clerk, Sir James 151

Clerk, Sir John 150–1, 173, 174, 187, 226

Clerk, Sir Robert 151

Clodius Albinus 163, 164, 168

Clyde, River 148
    Firth of xx, 137

Clydebank Crematorium 148

Coel, King 22–3

Cogidubnus (or Togidubnus), Tiberius Claudius 17

Colchester (Camulodunum) 11, 15, 18–24, 27, 90, 194, 242
    Balkerne Gate 19, 242
    Colchester Castle Museum 11, 19, 20–1, 242
    map 2–3
    Roman wall 18–19
    St Helen's Chapel 22, 242

Collingwood, Arthur 184

Collingwood, Barbara 184

Collingwood, Dora 184

Collingwood, Dorrie 182

Collingwood, R. G. (Robin) 55, 84, 179, 181–7, 197, 219
    An Autobiography 181, 182
    The Idea of History 182
    The New Leviathan 183
    Roman Eskdale 185
    and Myres, J. N. L. The Oxford History of England, vol. I 181, 186–7

Collingwood, W. G. 182, 183, 184
    Thorstein of the Mere 183

Collingwood Bruce, John 111, 121–2
    Guide to Hadrian's Wall 176

Commius 62, 69, 73

Commodus, emperor 163

Coniston 182, 183, 184, 249
    Brantwood (home of John Ruskin) 182, 249
    Lanehead (home of Collingwood family) 182, 249

Coniston Water 184

Conrad, Joseph: *Heart of Darkness* xx, 177–8

Constans, emperor 217

Constantine the Great 22, 23, 161, 162, 163, 192, 194, 217

Constantine III, emperor 217–18

Constantius Chlorus, emperor 22, 23, 161, 192, 193–4

Constantius II, emperor 217

Conybeare, Daniel, and Phillips, William: *Outlines of the Geology of England and Wales* 154–5

Cook, Herbert 210

Copper Mines Beck 183

Corbridge 171

Corellia Optata 166–7

Corinium *see* Cirencester

Corinium Museum, Cirencester 199–201, 249

Cornovii tribe 76

Cornwall 8, 9

Corporation of London 49, 50, 54, 243

Cosh, Stephen 206, 207–8 and Neal, David, *Roman Mosaics of Britain* 206, 207

Cotswolds 11, 198–204, 205, 249

Cowper, William: 'Boadicea: An Ode' 37, 38–9

Cramond 137

Cramond Lion 137

Crete xvii

Crosby Garrett helmet 187–91

Croy Hill 143, 146–7, 247

Crummy, Philip 20, 21

Culloden 139

Cumberland, William Augustus ('Butcher'), Duke of 118, 142, 143

Cumberland and Westmorland Antiquarian Society 184

Cumbria 115, 179–97, 248–9

Cunliffe, Barry 17, 103

Cunobelinus 11, 12, 23, 25, 34

Cupid 211

Cymbeline 34

Dahl, Roald 223–4 *The Wonderful Story of Henry Sugar* 223–4

Daily Mail 85, 90, 168

Daily Telegraph 187–8

Dalmatians 116, 181

Davies, Hunter 114, 115 *A Walk on the Wall* 114

Deal 5–7, 241–2

Demetrius 172

Deva *see* Chester

Diana 200–1

Dickens, Charles 76, 119

Dido 73, 211, 212

Dio, Cassius 12, 14–15, 16, 33, 62, 72, 164, 165 *History of Rome* 12

Diocletian, emperor 192, 194, 196

Diodorus Siculus 9, 100 *Library*, 9

Dobbie's Garden Centre 147

Domitian, emperor 140

Donovan, Edward 206–7

Dorchester 10, 62, 88

Dorset County Museum 245

Douglas, Lord Alfred 184
Dover 215
Druids 101–3
'Duke of Cumberland's map' *see*
    Roy, William: maps
Dumbarton 154
Dundee 137
Duntocher 148
Durham, University of 128

Eagle (film) 176
Eboracum *see* York
Eckardt, Dr Hella 168
Eden Valley 122
Edinburgh 142
    National Museum of
        Scotland 137–8, 145, 188,
        247
    Scottish National Portrait
        Gallery 141
Edward the Elder 23
Edwyn, King of Northumbria
    162
Eldon, Lord 199
Elgar, Edward xx, 36–8
    Caractacus 36–8, 39, 40
    Enigma Variations 36, 37
Elizabeth I, Queen 34, 229
English Channel 7, 192
English Civil War 19
English Heritage xvii, xix, 75,
    241, 242, 244, 246, 247
Eppillus 62
Equites Romani (club within
    Society of Antiquaries) 173
Ermine Street 56
Erskine Bridge 148
Esk, River 179, 180

Eskdale 184–5
Essex and Kent 5–24, 241–2
Eudo Dapifer 20, 23
Eugenius 146
Eutropius 192
Evander 83
Evelyn, John 195, 196, 197
Exeter Book 94–5

Fairfax, Thomas 19
Falkirk 143, 144, 146, 148, 154
Falkirk Wheel 247
Farrer, James 199
Fawcett, Dr Hugh 222
Fine Arts Commission 227
First World War 14, 19, 77, 78,
    80, 91, 184
Fishbourne 16–18, 242, 250
Flavius Cerealis 128, 129, 132
Fletcher, John 25
    Bonduca 35–6
Ford, Sydney 222, 223, 224, 225
Forest of Dean 86–8
Forth, Firth of xx, 137
Forth-Clyde canal 139, 143, 144,
    247
Fortunata 51–2
Fosse Way 198, 199
Foster, Norman 53
Fowler, Gordon 224–5
Franks 217
Frederick, Prince of Denmark
    156
Freemasonry 101
Freind, Robert 141–2
Fulford, Michael 65, 67–8, 69, 70,
    73
Fullofaudes 217

Gale, Roger 98, 150, 173–4
Gandy, Joseph Michael 51
Ganymede 209–10
Gask Ridge 137
Gaul 5, 6, 7, 10, 11, 12, 14, 27,
    100, 140, 164, 192, 217, 218, 221,
    226
Genii Cucullati xviii
Gentleman's Magazine 155
Geoffrey of Monmouth 22, 29,
    34, 35, 44–5, 141, 219
    A History of the Kings of
    Britain 22, 98–9
George II, King 138, 141
Gerald of Wales: Itinerarium
    Kambriae, or Journey Around
    Wales 85
Germanic insurgents 217
Germans 140
Germany 72
Getty Museum, Malibu 204
Geta 161, 164, 165, 193
Gildas 218, 219
    On the Destruction of Britain
    105, 218
Glasgow 147–8, 247
    Bearsden 143, 147–8, 247
    Hunterian Museum 145, 247
    University 145, 174
Gloucester 168
    Museum 11
Gog 22
Gordon, Alexander 156, 173, 174
    Itinerarium Septentrionale
    146–7, 148, 149–50, 173
Goths 218
Gramm, Hans 156
Grampians 137, 139, 154

Grange 143
Grangemouth 143, 146
Grange Pans 143
Great Chesters 116, 246
Great North Museum,
    Newcastle 116, 246
Great Pavement see
    Woodchester Pavement
Great Western Railway 208
Great Witcombe 198, 249
Great Yarmouth 214, 215, 250
Greencarts Farm 114–15, 246
Grimes, W. F. 52
Gryme 146
Guardian 22
Guidott, Thomas: A Discourse of
    Bathe and the Hot Waters There
    95–6
Guildhall, London 47, 50, 243

Hadrian, emperor 50, 76, 112,
    119, 141, 181
Hadrian's Wall xvii, xviii–xix,
    108–32, 137, 143, 144, 153, 161,
    166, 170, 173, 181, 245–7
    map 108–9
Hadrumetum 168
Hall, Jenny 57, 58
Hambledon Hill 245
Hammia 116
Hardknott Castle 180–1, 185, 249
Hardy, Thomas xx, 75
    'A Tryst at an Ancient
    Earthwork' 89
Hargrove, W. M.: History and
    Description of the Ancient City
    of York 161
Harlow Hill 120

Harpocrates 69–70, 244

Hatcher, Henry 154

Haverfield, Francis 184, 214
  The Romanization of Roman
    Britain 175

Hawkes, Jacquetta 80, 81, 90

Hawkins, John 208–9

Hearne, Thomas 63–4, 65

Heddon-on-the-Wall 114, 117

Helen, St 22, 23, 24

Hengist 14, 219

Henry V, King 229

Hercules 221

Herefordshire Beacon 37

Hernstadt, Mr 14

Herodotus xvii, 8, 31, 32
  Histories 99

Hexham 121

Highlands 137, 138–42, 153

Hinton St Mary mosaic 208

Historia Augusta 168

Historic Scotland 241

History and Antiquities of
  Silchester in Hampshire, The 66

hoards 30–1, 220–5

Hobbs, Richard 220, 221–2, 223,
  224, 225

Hodges, C. Walter 70

Hod Hill 89, 245

Hole, William 141

Holinshed's Chronicles 33–4

Homer 7
  Iliad xv
  Odyssey xv

Honorius, emperor 218

Horace 32, 33

Horkstow Hall 205

Horsa 14, 219

Horsley, John: Britannia Romana
  174

Horus 70–1

'Hostess, The' 130

Houses of Parliament (Palace of
  Westminster) 227–8

Housesteads xvii, 111, 116, 121,
  122, 246

Housman, A. E. 78–9, 80
  A Shropshire Lad 78
  'On Wenlock Edge' 78–9

Howard, Philemon 29

Hoxne Treasure 220

Hull and East Riding Museum
  205, 249

Hutcheson's Hill 145, 148

Hunter, Dr Fraser 138

Hunterian Museum, Glasgow
  145, 247

Hutton, Catherine 119, 122

Hutton, William 111, 118–21, 122,
  125
  History of the Roman Wall
    118–21

Iceland 9

Iceni 16, 27, 28, 29, 30, 31

Iceni Village 28

Ictis 9

Illustrated London News 52

Illyricum 217

Institute of Archaeology,
  University of London 80

Inveresk 138

Inverness 153, 154

Iona 105

Iraqis 116

Ireland 10, 105, 139, 219

Iron Age 10–11 25, 30, 31, 44, 62, 68, 70, 77, 88, 89, 138, 245
Isca *see* Caerleon
Isle of Wight 62, 192–3, 206
ivory bangle lady 167–9

Jackson, Moses 78
Jackson, Dr Ralph 189, 190
Jacobite uprisings
    1715 and 1719 141
    1745 118, 138–9, 141, 142
Jaeger, A. J. 37, 38
James VI, King of Scotland (James I, King of England) 35
Jamrach (boat) 184
Januaria Martina 46
Jefferies, Richard: *After London* 58
Joan of Navarre 229
John of Fordun 137, 146, 148–9
John of Gaunt 229
Jones, Inigo 100
Joyce, Revd James 67, 70
Julia Domna 164, 165
Julian, emperor 217
Julia Pacata Indiana 55
Jull, Peter 6
Jupiter 200, 209–10, 211
Jutes 216

Kant, Immanuel: *Theory of Ethics* 182–3
Kelvin, River 147
Kent and Essex 5–24, 241–2
Keppie, Lawrence 145
    The Legacy of Rome: Scotland's Roman Remains 241, 247
Keswick 184

Keynsham railway station 208
King Arthur's Round Table (amphitheatre) 85–6
King's Cross (formerly Battle Bridge) 45–6
Kipling, Rudyard 229
Kinneil House 145, 247–8
Kirkintilloch 143, 145, 147
    Auld Kirk Museum 247
Kitchener camp 14
Knag Burn 112
Knossos xvii

Lake District 115, 121, 179–87, 248–9
Lanehead 182, 249
Laurieston 146
Lawrence, Thomas 201
Lear 22
Legions
    2nd 33, 84, 145
    6th 145, 166
    9th 27, 72, 74, 139, 166, 176
    10th 6
    14th 75
    20th 21, 75, 116, 145
Lehman Brothers 188
Leicester 199
Leland, John 97–8
Lepcis Magna 163
Lepidina, Sulpicia 128, 132
Lethbridge, Thomas 225
Lincoln 199
Lindisfarne 105
Listener 122
Lively, Penelope: *Jacaranda Oleander* 47–8

Livia (wife of emperor
    Augustus) 171
Loanhead 151
Loch Long 146
London (Londinium) 14, 23,
    27–8, 38, 42–61, 63, 188, 193,
    194, 216, 241, 243–4
    Bank of England 50–1, 243
    Barnsbury Square (formerly
        Reed Moat Field) 45
    Bastion Highwalk 47
    Blitz 47–8, 50, 53, 56
    British Library 49, 142
    British Museum 11, 30, 46, 54,
        132, 188, 189, 190, 195, 208,
        211, 216, 220, 221, 222, 223,
        241, 242, 243, 248, 250
    Bucklersbury House 52–3
    Guildhall (site of
        amphitheatre) 47, 50, 243
    King's Cross (formerly Battle
        Bridge) 45–6
    London Stone 55–6, 243
    map 40–1
    Mithraeum 52, 53, 55, 56, 243
    Museum of London 46, 47,
        49, 52, 53, 57, 58, 84, 243
    Nicholson & Griffin 56, 243
    Palace of Westminster
        (Houses of Parliament)
        227–8
    Roman baths 57–8
    Roman walls 43, 47, 48, 49, 54,
        243
    St Alphage Gardens 49, 243
    St Paul's 46, 47
    sculpture of Boadicea and Her
        Daughters 23, 37–8

    site of Roman forum 56
    Tower Hill 54–5
    see also University of London
Long, Richard 111
Longinus Sdapeze, memorial to
    21
Louise, Princess 156
Low Countries 140
Low Ham mosaic (Dido and
    Aeneas) 210–13, 249
Lucan: Pharsalia 174
Lucian xviii
Lydney Park 86–8, 245
Lympne 215
Lysons, Samuel 201–2, 204, 205,
    206, 207, 209
    Reliquiae Britannico-Romanae
    201–2

Macaulay, Rose 43
    The Pleasure of Ruins 48
Macdonald, Kevin: Eagle 176
Maclise, Daniel 228
Maeatae 161, 164
Maen y Morwynion (Maidens'
    Stone) 84, 244
Magnentius 217
Magnus Maximus, emperor 218
Magog 22
Maiden Castle 10, 88–92, 245
Maidens' Stone (Maen y
    Morwynion) 84, 244
Maldon 19
Malverns 36, 37
Manchester University 128
Maponus 179
Marcius Memor, Lucius 94, 103
Marcus Aurelius, emperor 163

Marcus Favonius Facilis, tombstone of 21
Marsh, Thomas 208
Marshall, Neil: *Centurion* 176
Martial xvii, 26
Martindale, Harry 166
Martinus, vicar of Britain 217
Maryport: Senhouse Museum 249
Massilia (modern Marseilles) 8
Matfen High House 246
Matres, the xvii, 200
Matthews, Colin 123
  piano accompaniment for 'Roman Wall Blues' 123–7
Maughan, Sandra 114–15
Maximian, emperor 192, 193, 194, 196
Maximus, Magnus *see* Magnus Maximus, emperor
Medway, River 15
Mendips 93
Mercury 206, 211
Merrifield, Ralph: *Roman London* 52
Messalina 15
Mildenhall Treasure 220–5, 250
  Great Dish 220, 221, 223, 224, 225
Millais, John Everett: *The Romans Leaving Britain* 225–6
Milvian Bridge, Battle of the 161
Minerva *see* Sulis-Minerva
Mithraeum
  Housesteads xviii, 116
  London 52, 53, 55, 56, 243
Mithras xviii, 52, 116
Monck, General 146
Monk Bar, York 166

Mons Graupius 139, 142, 154, 156, 173
Montanus 51–2
de Montford, Simon 229
Monthly Magazine 61
Morant, Philip 19
Moray Firth 137, 138
Morris, Jan 96–7
Morrison, Andrew 169
mosaics 200–13
Munday, Anthony: *The Triumphs of Re–united Britannia* 35
Museum of Cardiff 81
Museum of London 46, 47, 49, 52, 53, 57, 58, 84, 243
Museum of Somerset, Taunton 210, 249
Myres, J. N. L. (Nowell) 82, 86, 181
  and Collingwood, R. G. *Oxford History of England*, vol. I 181, 186–7

Naples 44
Nar, River 29
Narcissus 14
Nash, Beau 95
National Museum of Scotland, Edinburgh 137–8, 145, 188, 247
National Museum of Wales 244
National Roman Legion Museum, Caerleon 244
National Trust 199, 246, 249
Neal, David 206
  and Cosh, Stephen, *Roman Mosaics of Britain* 206, 207
Nelson, George, and Plummer, John: *Silchester: the Pompeii of Hampshire* 61, 67

Nelson, John 45
Nennius 219
Nero, emperor 16, 18, 25, 27, 33, 194
Newcastle 117, 118, 121, 122, 245, 246, 247
    Byker's Hill 119–20
    Great North Museum 116, 246
    Segedunum fort and museum 113–14, 115, 246
Newcastle Literary and Philosophical Society 121
New Kilpatrick cemetery 147
Newstead 138
Newstead helmet 188
Newton, Isaac 64
Newton St Loe 208
Nicaea, First Council of 105
Nicholson, Edward Williams Byron 104–5, 106, 107, 229
Nicomedes 171–2
Nodens 87
    temple of 86, 245
Norfolk 25–40, 214–16, 242–3, 250
Norfolk Archaeological Trust 242, 250
North Sea 192
Norway 9
Norwich
    Castle Museum 11, 30–1, 242
    cathedral 242
Notitia Dignitatum 215

Octavius (soldier at Vindolanda) 129
Old Kilpatrick 143–4, 148
Old Man of Coniston 182, 183

Old Polmont 146
Once Brewed 113, 116
Ordnance Survey 142
Orkneys 138
Orpheus 199, 201, 202, 204, 205, 208, 209–10
Ottaway, Patrick 163, 165–6, 248
Outer Hebrides 138
Ovid xviii
    Metamorphoses 200–1, 204, 209–10
Owen, Harold 75
Owen, Wilfred xviii, 75, 76, 77–8, 80, 81, 122, 184
    'Strange Meeting' 78
    'Uriconium: An Ode' 77, 78
Oxford Dictionary of Quotations 196
Oxford University 128, 181, 182, 226
    Brasenose College 130
    Wolfson College 130

Palermo 205
Palmyra 170, 171
Passchendaele 93, 94
Patrick, St: Confession 219
Peddars Way 29
Pelagius 105
Penicuik 150, 151, 248
Pennines 122, 155
Persian Wars 32
Pertinax, emperor 163
Petergate, York 166
Peterill, River 191
Petilius Cerealis 27
Petrie, Flinders 82
Pevensey Castle 215, 229, 230, 250

Pevsner, Nikolaus 46–7, 49, 50

Phillips, William, and
    Conybeare, Daniel: *Outlines
    of the Geology of England and
    Wales* 154–5

Piazza Armerina 205

Picts 217, 219

Pillerton Priors 207

Pindar: *Olympian Ode* 95

Pitt-Rivers, Augustus 44

Placida 76

Plautius, Aulus 13, 14, 62

Pliny the Elder 8

Plummer, John, and Nelson,
    George: *Silchester: the Pompeii
    of Hampshire* 61, 67

Polmont Woods 146

Pompeii 200

Poundbury 10, 88

Praetorian Guard 12

Prasutagus 16, 27

Prinknash Abbey 203

Propertius 60

Ptolemy 29

Pugin, Augustus 227

Pump Room, Bath 95, 96, 97,
    103, 105, 245

Pytheas: *On the Ocean* 8–9

Quintus Corellis Fortis 167

Raetians 116

Ransome, Arthur 183–4
    Oscar Wilde: A Critical Study
    184

Rape of Pevensey 229

Ravenglass 180, 185, 248–9

Reading Museum 67, 70, 73, 244

Reculver 215

Regina, tombstone of 170–1,
    248

Remus 195

Reynolds, Joshua 201

Rhine, the 217

Ribchester 179, 248

Ribchester helmet 188, 248

Richard I, King 229

Richard of Cirencester (Richard
    of Westminster) 152–5
    *De Situ Britanniae (On the
    Situation in Britain)* 153, 154,
    156

Richardson, Steve 113–14

Richborough (Rutupiae) 12–14,
    242

Roach Smith, Charles 53–5
    Illustrations of Roman London
    54

Robert (brother of William the
    Conqueror) 229

Roebuck, John 145

Rogers, Richard 49, 56

Rolfe, Fred 222

Roman Army Museum,
    Vindolanda 246

Roman Inscriptions of Britain, The
    181

Rome xviii, xxii, 15, 16, 22, 26,
    36–7, 38–9, 83, 139, 163, 164,
    195, 196, 211, 218

Romulus 83, 195

Rough Castle 146, 247

Roy, William 142, 143, 152, 154
    maps (*Military Survey of
    Scotland*) 142–3, 143–4, 148,
    150

Military Antiquities of Britain
143, 152
Royal Academy of Arts 191
Royal Commission on the
Ancient and Historical
Monuments of Scotland 145,
247
Rudston Venus 205–6
'Ruin, The' 220
Ruskin, John 182, 184, 249

Sachsenhausen 14
St Albans 11, 28, 89–90
St Helen's Chapel, Colchester
22, 242
St Michael's Mount 9
St Oswald's 120
St Paul's, London 46, 47
Salamis, Battle of 32
Sandwich 13–14
Sappho xvii
Sarmatia 179
Saxons 14, 58, 59, 60, 192,
215, 216, 217, 219, 226–7,
228, 229
Saxon shore forts 215, 229
Scafell 185
Scotland 75, 134–56, 173–4, 206,
241, 247–8
Scots 217, 219
Scotsman 106
Scott, Sir Walter: *The Antiquary*
155–6
Scottish National Portrait
Gallery, Edinburgh 141
Seabegs 144
Seaber, 'Black Jack' 225
Sebasteion, Aphrodisias 18

Second World War 229
Segedunum fort and museum
113–14, 115, 246
Selous, H. C.: *Boadicea
Haranguing the Iceni* 228
Senhouse Museum, Maryport
249
Septimius Severus, emperor 120,
137, 161, 163–5, 168, 248
Septimius stone 200
Serapis 166, 167
Seton-Williams, Veronica 90–1
Severa, Claudia 132
Severus *see* Septimius Severus,
emperor
Sewingshields Crags 111, 112
Sextus Valerius Genialis,
tombstone of 200
Shakespeare, William 5, 7, 33
Cymbeline 11, 34–5, 36
Henry V 36
King Lear 35
Richard II 36
Shetlands 9
Shrewsbury Museum 76, 244
Sibbald, Robert 100
Sicily 205
Silchester (Calleva Atrebatum)
60–74, 198, 244
Silenus 221
Skye 139
Snettisham hoard 11, 30–1, 242
Soane, Sir John 50, 51, 227
Society of Antiquaries 86, 143,
150, 153, 173, 204, 206
Solinus, Gaius Julius 5, 153
*Collectanea rerum mirabilium, A
Collection of Marvels* 98

Solway Firth xvii, 112

South Shields: Arbeia fort 116, 170–1, 248

South Wales News 84

Southwark 43

Spain xviii, 82, 218

Stainton Fell 179

Stair, John 67

Stallworthy, Jon 77

Stane Street 208

Stanton Drew 100–1, 102

Stanwix 120

State Museums of Berlin 165

Stenhousemuir 150

Stephenson, Roy 53

Step to the Bath, A 96

Stirling, James 51

Stonehenge 100

Stour, River 13, 14

Strabo 8, 10, 100

Stratfield Saye 67

Strawberry Hill 187

Stroud 201

Stuart, Charles (Bonnie Prince Charlie) 138, 139

Stukeley, William xix, xx, 6, 64–5, 96, 98, 100, 101, 149–50, 151, 152–4, 156, 173, 187, 194, 226

    An Account of Richard of Cirencester, Monk of Westminster, and of his Works 153–4

    Itinerarium Curiosum 64

Suetonius 11–12, 14, 15, 88, 100

    Twelve Caesars 11

Suetonius Paulinus 27–8, 31, 32, 45, 100

Sulis-Minerva 93–4, 98, 103

    temple of 94, 97, 98

Sussex 17–18, 229–30, 242, 250

Sutcliff, Rosemary 70–1, 72, 244

    The Eagle of the Ninth xviii, 70–2, 176, 197

    The Silver Branch 197

Swaffham 28

Swaledale 122

Swallow (boat) 184

Swan Hunter 115–16

Sycamore Gap 112

Syria xviii, 200

Syrians 170

Tacitus xvii, xxi, 7, 9, 10, 17, 19, 25, 26, 27, 28, 31, 32–3, 34, 35, 44, 45, 62, 100, 137, 139–41, 142, 153, 155, 173, 176, 177, 192, 228

    Agricola 17, 62, 137

    Annals 25, 55

    Histories 140

Tas, River 30

Taunton: Museum of Somerset 210, 249

Tennyson, Alfred, Lord 8

Terence xviii

Thames, River 11, 15, 27, 43, 44, 47, 57, 177

Thanet 13, 14, 219

Theodosius (father of Theodosius the Great) 217

Thermae Baths Spa, Bath 93, 99, 245

Thomas, Professor David 128, 129, 130

Thomas, John 84
Thornbury, Walter: *Old and New London* 46
Thornycroft, Thomas: *Boadicea and Her Daughters* 23, 37–8, 39
Thule 9
Tiberius, emperor 8, 17, 18
Tilbury 34
Times, The 90, 223
Tineius Longus 116
Togodumnus 12, 15, 25
Toland, John 100
Tolkien, J. R. R. 87
Tomlin, Dr Roger 51, 104, 106, 107, 129, 130–1
Trajan, emperor 112, 166–7
Trapain Law 138
Trinovantes 11, 99
Trinovantum 45, 99
Tulip, Henry 120
Tullie House Museum, Carlisle 181, 188, 190, 191, 193, 246, 249
Tungrians 116
Tupper, George 208–9
Tupper, Thomas 209
Turkey 18
Turner, J. M. W. 187, 227
Tutankhamun, tomb of 85
Tuttiett, Linda 115
Twechar 147
Twice Brewed pub 120
Tyne, River xvii, xix, 112, 116, 246

Ulpha Fell 179
University of London
    Institute of Archaeology 80
    University College 80, 81

Valentia 153, 217
Vaughan Williams, Ralph 78–9
Vegetus 51–2
Venta Icenorum 29, 30
Venta Silurum *see* Caerwent
Venus 205–6, 211
Vercingetorix 27
Verica 12
Verney, Tessa *see* Wheeler, Tessa Verney
Verulamium 28, 89–90
Vespasian 15, 62, 88, 91
Vespasiana 153
Victoria, Queen 36, 38, 122
Vikings 58
Vindolanda 116, 127–32, 246
Virgil vii, xvii, 8, 130, 195–6
    Aeneid vii, 12, 37, 39, 73, 83, 167, 174, 194, 197, 211, 213
    Eclogues 8, 196, 197
    Georgics 130
Viroconium Cornoviorum *see* Wroxeter
Vivius Marcianus, tombstone of 46, 53
Vortigern 219

Wade, General 141, 142
Wade, John 202
Walbrook Stream 44, 51
Wales 25, 81–6, 207, 244–5
Walmer 5, 6
Walpole, Horace 187
Wantsum channel 14
Warburton, John 118, 119
Waterloo, Battle of 67
Watling Lodge 146
Watling Street 14, 75

Watt, James 145
Watts, George Frederick 26–7, 227, 228
Waveney, River 215
Webb, Stanley 75, 78
Wedlake, William 90
Wellington, Duke of 67
Westminster, Palace of 227–8
Westray 138
West Row 220
Wheeler, Michael 81
Wheeler, Mortimer 19, 79–81, 82–3, 84–6, 87, 88, 89–91, 92, 184
    Still Digging 80, 82, 91
Wheeler, Tessa Verney 81, 82–3, 86, 88, 89–91, 92, 181
Whin Sill 111
Whitfell 179
Wilderness Plantation 147
William the Conqueror 20, 229
Wilson, Roger: A Guide to the Roman Remains in Britain xix, 60–1, 81, 241, 244
Winchester 62, 168
Wisdom, Norman 7
Wolfson College, Oxford 130
Wood, John 97, 98–102, 245
    Essay Towards a Description of Bath 98–100
    The Origin of Building 101

Woodchester Pavement (Great Pavement) 201–4, 207, 249
Woodward, Bernard Bolingbroke 155
Woodward, Bob and John 202–4, 249
Wotton-under-Edge 202–3
Wrekin, the 77
Wren, Christopher 46, 47, 49, 50, 55–6
Wright, Thomas 76
Wroxeter (Viroconium Cornoviorum) 14, 75–80, 122, 244

Xerxes 32

Yassin-Kassab, Robin 170
Y Gaer 81–4, 244
York (Eboracum) 23, 72, 158–97, 207–8, 217, 248
    Bootham Bar 165, 166
    map 158–9
    Minster 162–3, 248
    Monk Bar 166
    multiangular tower 163, 248
    Petergate 166
    walls 163, 165, 166
Yorkshire Museum 162, 166–7, 169–70, 171, 248

Zosimus 218